IBM Lotus Domino: Classic Web Application Development Techniques

A step-by-step guide for web application development and quick tips to enhance applications using IBM Lotus Domino

Richard G. Ellis

[PACKT] enterprise 88
PUBLISHING
professional expertise distilled

BIRMINGHAM - MUMBAI

IBM Lotus Domino: Classic Web Application Development Techniques

First published: March 2011

Production Reference: 1180311

Published by Packt Publishing Ltd.
32 Lincoln Road
Olton
Birmingham, B27 6PA, UK.

ISBN 978-1-849682-40-4

www.packtpub.com

Cover Image by Artie Ng (artherng@yahoo.com.au)

Credits

Author
Richard G. Ellis

Reviewers
Karen Hobert

Mark Vincenzes

Development Editor
Rukhsana Khambatta

Technical Editors
Sakina Kaydawala

Pallavi Kachare

Manasi Poonthottam

Indexer
Rekha Nair

Editorial Team Leader
Mithun Sehgal

Project Team Leader
Lata Basantani

Project Coordinator
Leena Purkait

Proofreader
Stephen Swaney

Production Coordinator
Arvindkumar Gupta

Cover Work
Arvindkumar Gupta

About the Author

Richard G. Ellis currently works as a Domino developer supporting several hundred classically crafted, web-enabled applications. He has held positions as a programmer, systems administrator, technical manager, and IT director in major commercial and university settings. He has taught undergraduate and graduate level courses as well as numerous workshops on programming languages and other computer-related subjects. He also provides quality assurance testing and technical writing services for major commercial and educational institutions. Mr. Ellis is certified both as a Domino developer and administrator.

I very much appreciate the people at Packt Publishing for their support and guidance, and the folks at IBM for building Lotus Notes and Domino. I would also like to thank Anne Agee, Kevin Chick, Jeff Clark, Adrienne Connolly, Al Cote, Eric Forte, Corey Kimball, Debbie Magoon, Fred Sollars, and Kevin Suares for their support, insight, and encouragement. Most of all I would like to thank my long-time friend and mentor Mac Toedt for the many opportunities and solid guidance he has given me over the years.

About the Reviewers

Karen Hobert is an IT market research analyst and strategy consultant with deep practical and market expertise in collaboration, communications, content management, and social software technologies. Karen has over twenty years of communication, collaboration, and social software platform expertise that she uses to help organizations design and deploy shared information systems. She has an extensive working knowledge of communication, collaboration, and social technologies including technologies from Microsoft, IBM, Google, and other best-of-breed vendors. Additional areas of expertise include collaborative application design and web development platforms. Karen is a contributor on numerous technical articles and is the author of courses and workshops on programming and deploying web-based business process applications.

Karen is a technical reviewer for the *IBM Lotus Notes 8.5 User Guide* published by Packt.

Mark Vincenzes is a software engineer at IBM, where he works on web application servers. Over the past 30 years, Mark has contributed to projects such as custom I/O and networking subsystems, database management systems, object request brokers, and source control systems. Mark's past employers include Burroughs, Xerox, Apollo, and Hewlett-Packard.

www.PacktPub.com

Support files, eBooks, discount offers and more

You might want to visit www.PacktPub.com for support files and downloads related to your book.

Did you know that Packt offers eBook versions of every book published, with PDF and ePub files available? You can upgrade to the eBook version at www.PacktPub.com and as a print book customer, you are entitled to a discount on the eBook copy. Get in touch with us at service@packtpub.com for more details.

At www.PacktPub.com, you can also read a collection of free technical articles, sign up for a range of free newsletters, and receive exclusive discounts and offers on Packt books and eBooks.

PACKTLIB®

http://PacktLib.PacktPub.com

Do you need instant solutions to your IT questions? PacktLib is Packt's online digital book library. Here, you can access, read and search across Packt's entire library of books.

Why Subscribe?

- Fully searchable across every book published by Packt
- Copy and paste, print and bookmark content
- On demand and accessible via web browser

Free Access for Packt account holders

If you have an account with Packt at www.PacktPub.com, you can use this to access PacktLib today and view nine entirely free books. Simply use your login credentials for immediate access.

Instant Updates on New Packt Books

Get notified! Find out when new books are published by following @PacktEnterprise on Twitter, or the Packt Enterprise Facebook page.

Dedication

I dedicate this book to Doreen, my wife and dearest friend for several decades now, and to my children and grandchildren: Jeffrey, Derrick, Caroline, Carrie, Owen, Eileen, and the new grandson on the way.

Table of Contents

Preface

Boss: I need some web pages up as soon as you can.

Developer: No problem. I'll get you something before lunch.

Creating web pages was fairly straight-forward — in the early 1990's. Today, there are many, often competing technologies available for creating a web experience. Remarkably, all these differing technologies and strategies interoperate in a relatively seamless way to serve the billions of people who use the World Wide Web and the Internet.

IBM's Lotus Notes and Domino product set — the subject of this book — is a feature-rich, application development technology that has been used to create web-enabled applications since the late 1990's. Since then, it has evolved substantially through several major software versions, and it will continue to advance into the foreseeable future, adapting to the changing web landscape and incorporating new technologies and methods as appropriate.

One of the delightful aspects of Domino is its backwards compatibility. With few or no changes, applications written with previous versions of the software, untouched for a decade or more, will run as expected on the newest Domino server.

It is also important to understand that useful applications can be crafted and deployed on a wide range of platforms with relatively little work. A simple application can be cobbled together and rolled out in less than an hour. It would not be a complex application, of course, but it might suffice for basic data collection or an informational website. After that first version rolls to production, providing immediate benefit to users, features and improvements could be added incrementally with little or no downtime.

Quickly-crafted applications are probably not polished applications in terms of look-and-feel or function. This author has worked with a number of these earlier, rapidly-developed applications; they are still functional, but by contemporary web standards, they are not pretty.

Improving an existing, web-enabled application comes with a number of challenges. How can the design be upgraded without impacting users or disturbing the data?

It was in facing the challenge of working with some of these older applications that I first began making notes which led to this publication.

Getting started

If you are a developer new to Lotus Notes and Domino, you face a substantial learning curve. If you are already a Domino developer, but are new to working with Domino applications on the Web, then the learning curve is not so steep.

As a Domino developer, you must master the Notes and Designer clients, and you must achieve some level of coding competence with Formula Language, LotusScript, HTML, CSS, JavaScript, and possibly Java. In addition, you must embrace the Domino way of doing things. You must understand its security features, design templates, replication, workflow, and so on. In a web application, all of these elements work together to achieve some desirable business purpose.

What this book covers

Topics in these chapters offer tips, suggestions, and code snippets to help you understand and resolve specific problems you may encounter when working with Domino applications for the Web. You will likely encounter problems not covered within these pages, but the tips provided here should save you some puzzlement, aggravation, and research time.

Many techniques covered in these pages are now referred to by the Domino community as "classic" or "traditional" web development techniques. Not covered here are XPages and other development strategies that were introduced in Domino 8.5 and later. If you need such information, you must seek it elsewhere.

My overarching intent was to bring together in one place some useful tips and techniques that are otherwise scattered across the Web. Ideas offered here derive from experience, mine and others. Code samples are for illustration only and should not be interpreted as a guarantee of performance or suitability for a specific situation. Everything covered should be useful for versions of Domino 6.5 and later. Domino Designer 8.0 was used to develop and verify all the sample code.

Keep in mind that there are often several ways to create a feature or to solve a problem. While classic techniques work with current and older versions of Domino, the preferred way to create new applications is to use the latest techniques such as XPages. However, even in an up-to-date Domino environment, it may not be practical to redesign an existing application to take advantage of them. If you cannot take advantage of those newer techniques for whatever reason, then certainly use techniques catalogued in this volume. Use what makes sense to you and what works for you. Test thoroughly.

Chapter 1, Preparation and Habits, provides suggestions for developers seeking to improve their knowledge, skill, and productivity. Issues related to executing development projects are discussed.

Chapter 2, Design and Development Strategies, provides recommendations for planning development projects and for developing applications.

Chapter 3, Form and Pages, illustrates selected design choices related to forms and pages, including properties, composing and saving documents, improving layout, using view templates, incorporating HTML tags, and using hidden fields and computed text.

Chapter 4, Navigation, illustrates selected navigational strategies, including application launch options, custom login forms, menus, default error pages, and providing direction and help.

Chapter 5, Cascading Style Sheets, illustrates how CSS rules can be incorporated into applications to style forms and pages for the Web.

Chapter 6, JavaScript, illustrates how client-side JavaScript can be incorporated into applications for such purposes as validating fields, changing element style, enabling a date picker, providing a warning before leaving a form if changed data has not been saved, and retrieving data with Ajax.

Chapter 7, Views, illustrates design choices for displaying views on the Web.

Chapter 8, Agents, illustrates how to incorporate agents in web applications, including setting properties and security, adding error traps, accessing documents, processing selected documents in a view, sending e-mail notifications, and extracting data to a spreadsheet.

Chapter 9, Security and Performance, discusses security planning, implementing security features, tracking document changes, and designing for good performance.

Chapter 10, Testing and Debugging, discusses testing strategies, test plans, tracking issues, and selected debugging techniques.

What you need for this book

To explore the techniques discussed and illustrated in this book, readers should have access to Lotus Notes, Domino Designer, and a web browser. Ideally, readers are able to save sandbox applications to a Domino server for experimentation and testing.

Who this book is for

This book is for novice to moderately experienced Domino developers who are new to the task of web-enabling traditional Domino applications. Readers should be familiar with using Domino Designer to develop applications for the Lotus Notes client. It is also assumed that readers have, or can acquire, at least rudimentary knowledge of HTML, CSS, and JavaScript.

Conventions

In this book, you will find a number of styles of text that distinguish different kinds of information. Here are some examples of these styles, and an explanation of their meaning.

Code within text is shown as follows: "The `styleActionBar` JavaScript function in the `ActionBar.js` JavaScript library contains just a few lines."

A block of code is set as follows:

```
function styleActionBar() {
  var form = document.forms[0] ;
  var tables = form.getElementsByTagName("TABLE") ;
  var actionbar = tables[0] ;
  actionbar.className += " actionbar" ;
  return true ;
  }
```

When we wish to draw your attention to a particular part of a code block, the relevant lines or items are set in bold:

```
Dim session As New NotesSession
Dim db As NotesDatabase
Dim doc As NotesDocument
```

New terms and important words are shown in bold. Words that you see on the screen, in menus or dialog boxes for example, appear in the text like this: "On the **Basic Notes Client Configuration** tab, in the **Additional options** list, check the **Use Web palette** option."

> Warnings or important notes appear in a box like this.

> Tips and tricks appear like this.

Reader feedback

Feedback from our readers is always welcome. Let us know what you think about this book—what you liked or may have disliked. Reader feedback is important for us to develop titles that you really get the most out of.

To send us general feedback, simply send an e-mail to feedback@packtpub.com, and mention the book title via the subject of your message.

If there is a book that you need and would like to see us publish, please send us a note in the **SUGGEST A TITLE** form on www.packtpub.com or e-mail suggest@packtpub.com.

If there is a topic that you have expertise in and you are interested in either writing or contributing to a book, see our author guide on www.packtpub.com/authors.

Customer support

Now that you are the proud owner of a Packt book, we have a number of things to help you to get the most from your purchase.

Downloading the example code

You can download the example code files for all Packt books you have purchased from your account at http://www.PacktPub.com. If you purchased this book elsewhere, you can visit http://www.PacktPub.com/support and register to have the files e-mailed directly to you.

Errata

Although we have taken every care to ensure the accuracy of our content, mistakes do happen. If you find a mistake in one of our books—maybe a mistake in the text or the code—we would be grateful if you would report this to us. By doing so, you can save other readers from frustration and help us improve subsequent versions of this book. If you find any errata, please report them by visiting http://www.packtpub.com/support, selecting your book, clicking on the **errata submission form** link, and entering the details of your errata. Once your errata are verified, your submission will be accepted and the errata will be uploaded on our website, or added to any list of existing errata, under the Errata section of that title. Any existing errata can be viewed by selecting your title from http://www.packtpub.com/support.

Piracy

Piracy of copyright material on the Internet is an ongoing problem across all media. At Packt, we take the protection of our copyright and licenses very seriously. If you come across any illegal copies of our works, in any form, on the Internet, please provide us with the location address or website name immediately so that we can pursue a remedy.

Please contact us at copyright@packtpub.com with a link to the suspected pirated material.

We appreciate your help in protecting our authors, and our ability to bring you valuable content.

Questions

You can contact us at questions@packtpub.com if you are having a problem with any aspect of the book, and we will do our best to address it.

1
Preparation and Habits

A fresh start is invigorating, a chance to look forward with high expectations and new resolve. It's a time to put into practice all the lessons you have learned and to put behind you the issues and problems which previously bogged you down. Take advantage of every fresh start. Look forward to and accept every new challenge and opportunity.

Especially when starting a new job, it is important to take stock of your skills, both technical and non-technical. If you succeeded wildly at your last job or project, then hooray for you! Do it again! But if you fell short in some ways, resolve to do better.

The topics in this chapter address the human and organizational context within which you will develop your Domino applications. Most of these suggestions are relatively non-technical, as they deal with how you might organize yourself and your time and how you might work more effectively with your customers. Topics focus on these key issues:

- Preparing yourself as a Domino developer
- The importance of using standards and guidelines
- Planning your work
- Handling a development project
- Documenting your design

Preparing yourself as a developer

A craftsman is only as good as his tools, and in a very real sense, you are your tools. To remain capable and versatile, you should commit to the life-long task of continually acquiring knowledge and skills—people-skills as well as technical skills.

As you begin your work on a new project, keep in mind the larger picture. This new project will be followed by others. One polished application will lead to another. One happy and satisfied customer will spread the word about how good you are.

Gather a list of public websites that use Domino

While you browse the Web, gather ideas about what makes web pages look good. Great websites should inspire you. Inspect the layout, the use of images and color, and the navigational strategies. If you see an interesting control, peek under the covers and take notes about how it was coded. But be sensitive to intellectual property and copyright laws—not everything published on the Web is free.

In particular, collect links to public websites that use Domino and show it to good advantage. Relatively speaking, only a smaller number of public-facing websites are served by Domino. But browse around; you will find hundreds of them in short order. This collection of websites can become a marketing and public relations tool for you as you sell your ideas to your customers.

Too often Domino web applications crafted in the past were functional, but not pretty. That might have been okay ten years ago, but no longer. Today's customers expect the same kind of functionality from your applications that they see elsewhere on the Web. And there really is no reason why you can't provide it to them.

Take some time and build yourself a small application to hold the links. Eventually, roll this application to the Web so that the links can be shared readily with customers and others who are interested.

In this sample **Domino Websites** application, details about each website are stored in a separate document. The blue hotspots link to views which display lists of **Commercial**, **Consultants**, **Government**, and **Other Sites**. With sufficient privileges to the database, a user can add, edit, and delete these documents with the Notes client or with a browser.

Domino Websites

Refresh

Commercial   Consultants   Government   Other Sites   About

Consultant Domino Websites

Prev   Next

Title (click to open record)	URL (click to open Website)
ABC Systems	www.abcsys.cz
Advanced Systems for Intelligence and Communication	www.asic.ca
Alan Lepofsky	www.alanlepofsky.net
Blue Sky Hosting	www.bluesky.co.uk
Breaking Par Consulting, Inc	www.breakingpar.com
Brefere	Link to site is disabled locally.
Caliton Innovations	www.caliton.com
Captain Oblivious	www.captainoblivious.com
Clickbook	www.clickbook.net
CodeStore	www.codestore.net

Get certified in Lotus Notes / Domino application development

Honing your skills by doing is essential. The more applications you build and the more time you spend on this work, the better you should become at it. Experience is a great teacher.

But you do not have time to figure everything out yourself. So you must read and study what others have done, which is especially easy today with a fast connection to the Internet. Set aside some time every week (or each day if you can swing it) and graze the web landscape.

Commit yourself to preparing for, taking, and passing certification exams in Lotus Notes / Domino application development. If possible work through the Administrator exams as well. Effortful and extensive preparation should make it easier to pass the exams the first time. More importantly, preparation for the exams will broaden your understanding of Domino and teach you about features and techniques that you might not otherwise stumble upon by yourself.

And, of course, holding this certificate looks good on the resume.

Use Domino Help

Experienced developers rely on Domino Help. Be aware that there are separate help databases for each of the clients: Notes, Administrator, and Designer.

Lotus. Notes and Domino Help   IBM.

Lotus Domino Designer 8 Help

Welcome to Help, the documentation for IBM® Lotus® Notes® and Domino® 8. To find topics in this Help database, use the Contents on the left, or click the Index or Search icon. To expand a section of the Contents outline, click a triangle to the left of a topic. To expand the entire outline, choose View - Expand All.

The **Lotus Domino Designer 8 Help** database contains over 9,000 documents. In it, you will find extensive information about features, language syntax, classes, limits, errors, tips, and code examples.

The code examples can be particularly useful. If you find some code that looks just like what you need, simply copy it into your application, and then modify it as necessary.

Especially if you are new to Domino, spend enough time with **Help** to be comfortable with where things are and how to find information on specific topics. The **Contents** view organizes the information like a book, by general subject area. Use the **Index** if you know what you are looking for — the syntax of a specific @ function, for example. Use the **Search** feature when you are not quite sure for what you are looking. Beware of searching too broadly. Search for the term "web" and you will find over a thousand documents!

Once you are comfortable with **Designer Help**, try Designer's context sensitive help, which is invoked by opening or highlighting a design element and then pressing *F1*. Display forms in the **Work pane** and press *F1* — help on designing forms displays. Select a tab in a **Properties** box and press *F1* — help on that tab displays, and so on.

Consider using external editors and development tools

Designer provides basic editing for text, so for the most part, you can develop applications without using external editors. However, dedicated editors for HTML, JavaScript, Java, and CSS will provide you with conveniences such as syntax checking, color coding, validation, and ready-made functions which may appeal to you. If you develop code in an external editor, you will have to import the files as resources into your application or copy/paste the text into appropriate locations in your design.

You can reasonably get on without external text editors, but learning to use an image editor may be well worth the time it takes, especially if you do not have access to a graphic designer or a library of images. Almost any image editor will do as long as it saves images as JPEG or GIF files. (Designer can accommodate other graphic types, but JPEG and GIF files are natively compatible with the Web.) Although it may take some effort to learn, the open source program **GIMP** is a no-cost, feature-rich image editor. Find more information at the GIMP website: `http://www.gimp.org`.

In this book, except where noted, examples rely on only the native capabilities of Designer.

Create sandbox applications

New ideas for solving problems constantly present themselves. But introducing a new, untried technique into an existing application may result in many more problems than it solves due to unintended consequences and side-effects.

Create one or more sandbox applications in which to try out new ideas. Constraining new development this way facilitates isolating and resolving problems specifically related to the new technique. And if, at the end of the day, the technique does not live up to its promise, then nothing needs to be removed from the real application design on which you are working.

Create a personal cookbook

Solutions discovered or invented for one application inevitably find their way into other applications. Code snippets, strategies, and even entire agents are often reused to save development time and effort.

Keeping track of such ideas may be difficult over a period of years, especially if you work on dozens of applications or move from job to job. It might be inappropriate (ethically or legally) to keep personal copies of designs created for previous employers without permission, but it is certainly reasonable to keep detailed personal notes in one form or another. The tools are readily available: paper notebook, flash drive, optical disk.

Keep your notes organized and periodically review items in your cookbook. Revise and annotate. Include variations and caveats. As it is impossible to remember in detail all the code you will ever write, you will find your notes to be an invaluable resource.

Create a personal document library

As a Notes developer, you should always have access to the Notes and Designer clients, so creating a personal document library or a simple Notes application is certainly an option. You can use the standard Lotus Document Library template or you can simply create your own application with whatever features work for you.

One database might contain notes and descriptions. A second database might contain working examples of many techniques — a private code library if you will.

Create a website

The Web is a wonderful repository of ideas. Consider keeping a website (blog or Wiki) on which you can post code and ideas that may be helpful to others. Of course this approach may entail some expense and extra effort, but it is also a great way to contribute to the development community. And if you are a freelance consultant, it is also a way to market your skills.

Alternatively, consider contributing ideas to existing websites with blog entries or even entire development projects.

Adopt new language and terms

Over time, the language of Notes and Domino changes, as do the tools. At one time, the *Domino Directory* was called the *Name and Address Book* or NAB. The file that contains design elements and documents was called a *database* and is now referred to as an *application*. In Designer, the *Design Pane* became the *Application Navigator*. Of course, you will come across references that use the older language and some developers who continue to use deprecated terms out of habit or stubbornness.

Be alert for these changes of terms and the definitions which go with them. Be mindful of the old names, but use contemporary and correct vocabulary, just as you should use contemporary development techniques.

Pay attention to web programming developments and practices

Domino applications intended to be accessed with a web browser can take advantage of many contemporary web technologies like Ajax, CSS, and XML. In fact, support for these standards has been included in Domino for many years. As web technologies evolve, so does Domino.

So pay attention to non-Domino web technologies and strategies. Web-enabled Domino applications should be crafted using the best web programming practices.

Standardizing applications

Application development is part engineering and part art. Building some pieces of an application is fairly routine, while other aspects call for inventiveness and creativity.

Domino caters to developers to some extent by enabling applications to be built with any of the several programming languages. It also supports many web technologies which can be pieced together in an unlimited number of ways. This flexibility enables programmers to work the way they want to work. But this same flexibility makes it all too easy to ignore organizational standards.

Standardizing applications makes it easier to develop new ones since reusable components may already exist. And if applications look and operate in a similar manner, then users of new applications will need less training and will be more willing to use them.

Abide by your organization's web development guidelines

If your organization has written web development guidelines, find out what they are and try to embrace them in your own applications. The set of web applications deployed by your organization is probably much larger than just the Domino applications. If they exist, these development guidelines and standards define stylistic and functional commonality that your organization determined to be beneficial. Someone above your pay grade approved those standards, so abide by them!

Web application development guidelines can provide several benefits. They promote an organizational identity or brand through a common look and feel. They improve the effectiveness and the usability of web applications as a whole by standardizing how features and functions operate. And from a developer's point of view, they speed the deployment of new applications and simplify the maintenance and enhancement of existing ones.

If your organization has no written standards, consider discussing this issue with management. Consider taking on the task yourself.

The number of specific development standards can easily number in the hundreds, depending upon how detailed they are. Whoever determines these standards must understand to some extent the entire universe of options, and then must select those guidelines which make sense and which can be implemented within the existing development environment. Many guidelines turn out to be "nice to have" suggestions that are not practical to implement within the confines of budget and project deadlines.

Development guidelines can be classified roughly into three kinds:

- Usability guidelines
- Stylistic guidelines
- Mechanical or process guidelines

Usability

Guidelines that address the usability of an application or website concern themselves with issues of effectiveness, efficiency, learnability, and overall user satisfaction. How well does this application achieve its goals? How easy is it to learn to use? How well do users like it? Usability influences how willing people are to use an application, which can have a dramatic impact on whether they choose your solution or go somewhere else for assistance.

Usability guidelines focus on what things make a website easy to use from the end user's point of view. Examples of usability considerations include the following:

- Content organization
- Headings and labels
- Page and form layout
- Features and functions
- Accessibility
- Navigation
- Images

Explore this topic in greater detail. One online reference which you might consider reviewing is the `http://usability.gov` website maintained by the U.S. Department of Health and Human Services.

The Guidelines documents at this site were written based on the extensive research. They can serve as a good starting point for understanding usability issues.

Style

Guidelines which address style concern themselves with issues of look and feel, and sometimes function. An organization's font preferences and color palette can be identified. Layouts and menu styles can be defined. Acceptable logos and images can be specified, as can boilerplate text for Copyright, Privacy, and other notices. Very specific guidelines might address issues such as whether or not to underline links or how wide margins should be.

Beyond simply specifying preferences, an organization might codify style requirements into common style sheets. The guidelines would then provide information about how to link to and incorporate those style sheets into applications. Details such as style class names for headings and labels would be included.

Mechanics and process

Guidelines which address issues of coding and application deployment can be extensive and no small task to gather together.

Because Domino web applications can include so many different technologies, coding guidelines could address various options, including the use of these design tools:

- HTML
- CSS
- JavaScript and JavaScript frameworks
- LotusScript
- Java
- Images

Other guidelines might specify requirements for the following design aspects:

- The About and Using documents
- Element naming conventions
- Form and page layout
- Navigation
- E-mail notifications
- Data import and extract
- Context sensitive help
- Agent error handling
- Security and access control

Still other guidelines might concern themselves with the general way in which applications are designed, tested, and rolled into production:

- How development work is requested and prioritized
- How applications are named and sponsored
- The use of templates
- The use of shared code and resource libraries
- The use of roles
- The use and management of Domino groups
- Application signing
- Replication
- Testing and approval
- Migration to production
- Documentation and user training

Some developers might find coding and process guidelines to be onerous and overly constraining. Inevitably, there will be requests for exceptions to the rules, so organizations must be prepared to deal with the issues of exceptions and non-compliance.

Clearly, an extensive effort is required to compile standards and guidelines that are appropriate to application development within the context of a specific organization. Additional effort will be required periodically to review, update, and reapprove those guidelines.

Create libraries of common resources

Organizations should consider creating common repositories of reusable objects. The most obvious kinds of libraries (not surprisingly supported natively by Designer) would contain standard design elements such as:

- Images
- Java code
- JavaScript code
- LotusScript code
- Style sheets

Images can be organized into common types as follows:

- Arrows and lines
- Banners and logos
- Buttons
- Patterns
- Photos
- Squares and other common shapes
- Watermarks

Other repositories might include standard or approved "boilerplate" text:

- Copyright notice
- Disclaimers and caveats
- Error messages
- Privacy notice

Common repositories enable developers to work more rapidly and to create products which conform to organizational standards. Organizational management must address the following issues:

- Who will create and maintain the repositories?
- What process will be used to approve, add, and deprecate repository objects?
- Will applications be reviewed to assure the use of the approved objects?
- How will developers (especially new developers) be informed about the repositories and how to use them?

Common repositories, like development standards in general, can seriously boost productivity, but they also require ongoing maintenance and commitment. If your organization has such repositories, learn to use them. If no such collections yet exist, speak to management about instituting common repositories for approved design resources.

Planning your work

Volumes have been written about planning, and even more volumes have been written about how to become and stay organized. Here are just a few simple ideas that can be enormously powerful in keeping you personally on task.

Take notes

When you are young and brilliant, your mind might be as sharp as a tack and your memory as long as the Great Wall of China. But as your responsibilities increase, as your projects become larger, as you attend more meetings and deal with more customers — as you get older — your infallible memory will become fallible.

Take notes. Write things down. Some people prefer to use a laptop or PDA. Personally, after many years of trying several methods, I've come to appreciate the simple notebook. I jot notes all day long at my desk, in the car, at a meeting, in bed at night. It contains my list of tasks, my key contacts, notes from meetings, to-do lists, and timestamps. It is my work-life in a compact, lightweight, versatile package — and it works without electricity.

Use to-do lists

It is a simple fact that people who make lists of things they must do, tend to get more things done. This is true on a personal level as well as on the job.

Start each day by making a list of tasks you will work on, meetings you will attend, and phone calls you must make. Keep that list nearby and refer to it often. If things come up during the day, add them to your to-do list. As you finish an item, check it off or scratch it out.

At the end of the day, review what you achieved and what is still undone. Create a new to-do list for the next day. Prioritize each item either in terms of how important it is to do or in terms of when you will do it. This simple activity will help you focus, and when you focus, you accomplish more.

If you are not used to working with to-do lists, it will take some self-discipline. You might also consider creating weekly, monthly, quarterly, or annual to-do lists as well. As you plan each day, consult the lists which deal with the longer timeframes and incorporate all relevant items on the daily to-do. The adage "Plan the work and work the plan" can be fulfilled easily with the simple to-do list.

Keep a list of all active projects and tasks

You should maintain a current list of all your active and pending projects, tasks, and commitments. Each item should include a rough estimate of how long it takes or will take, when you might start and finish it, and who the key contacts are for each item.

Inevitably, you will be asked to undertake new tasks, join committees, attend meetings, and perform services which take time. People easily become overbooked because, with an eagerness to please or to start something new, they simply do not estimate well how much time tasks take to do. Keeping a list of projects and tasks to which you can refer will help you and your boss allocate your time more effectively.

Report your progress

Developers and other technicians are often loath to spend time documenting, especially writing progress reports to managers. Managers, on the other hand, really do need to understand what their employees are doing. Well-informed managers can make better decisions when authorizing new work, prioritizing current tasks, handling contrary customers, reporting accomplishments to *their* managers, and requesting budget for the coming year.

As a developer, you should submit a summary of your work on a regular basis. Your organization may have a prescribed format for this activity. If not, here is a simple outline for weekly e-mail which can work satisfactorily:

- Highlights from this week
- Tasks for next week
- Issues and other items
- Pending projects

Add bulleted items in each section. Be concise, clear, and plain-spoken. Your goal is to convey a sense of your activities and progress to your (possibly non-technical) manager. Send this summary to him or to a project leader at the end of each work week when the information is fresh. Do not embellish, don't minimize. Use this report also to help plan the week ahead.

Working the project

The right way to begin any project is to plan it. That means taking a decent amount of time to think about what needs to be done, to make lists of requirements and notes about issues, to talk over the effort with customers, to create a project plan, to estimate the time it may take to do the work, and to get all of this approved. Many youthful developers fail to see much value in all that paperwork. They jump right in to begin crafting the prototype. Occasionally, this approach might work, but more often a lack of planning will lead to a lot of rework, missed requirements, and less than happy customers.

Prototyping is of course a great way to prove or present an idea, but do not make the mistake of deploying a prototype. Consider how long it might take to create the production version of your application, and get management's buy-in. Otherwise, you may get stuck supporting a lot of incomplete applications and handling many user complaints.

Work with users, not against them

Some users will tell you exactly what to do and how to do it; others are reluctant to ask for any changes whatsoever. Some developers would rather not speak with customers at all, believing they "know" what the customer needs.

The best circumstance is that in which the developer and the customer work together to advance a project. They share ideas and come to a common understanding of what needs to be done.

Lotus Notes and the Web are very visual environments. As a developer, you need all the help you can get to craft a good-looking and functional application which helps and pleases the customer. Engage with the customer early and often.

It may be difficult to convey in words what a screen will look like or how a workflow will progress. Early in the project, develop a prototype which includes approximations of the forms, pages, views, and other visual elements of the design. Take screenshots and paste those images into an e-mail or a document, and send them along to the customer. Ask for feedback.

If possible, sit with the customer in front of a computer and show him what you want to do. A picture can convey meaning clearly and efficiently, and workflow can be demonstrated really only by trying it out. Do this several times. The customer will share ownership of the project and will offer suggestions to improve the final product. Take notes and take heed. Be a hero.

Identify the champion and other players

With most projects there is one person who will really drive the effort. Identify this champion. He will know the requirements deeply or he will know who knows. He will address resource issues, especially the issue of finding time for customer testing.

Often the most important people are the line staff who will use your application. Find time to discuss with them how they see the new application helping them.

During the planning phase, identify as many people as possible who are interested in the project or who will use the fruits of your labor. Find time to talk with all of them. Your product will be richer and more on-target for the effort.

Don't start without clear requirements

Once in a while you might be required to begin a project without clear, well-written requirements. Resist!

Some customers are notoriously unable to think clearly through and write down what it is they want you to do. They may be willing, but they just do not work that way. Your customer may have an excellent plan in his head, but he just can't get it down on paper.

You may end up writing the specifications yourself and then seeking your customer's approval. So be it. Sit with him, watch what he does on the screen, take notes, and make diagrams. When everything is finally written down, have him sign off on this *requirements document*. This is the working agreement for the project, and it becomes the arbiter if what you deliver is not what he is expecting.

Understand the budget and timeline; provide an estimate

Requirements identify what the customer wants. You are the resource with the talent who will do whatever needs to be done to satisfy the requirements. But you also must operate within budget and time constraints. How much time, hours or days or weeks, are you authorized to work on this project? Are there any hard deadlines which must be met?

Most likely, before work begins, you will be asked to provide a time estimate for your work on the project. Study the requirements in detail and make notes. Estimate how long each task is likely to take. Be as realistic as possible with each estimate.

If you are familiar with the application, then the project will move along more rapidly. If you must *discover* the application — learn about it from scratch — then time must be allotted to that effort as well.

Include time in your overall estimate for the following work:

- Planning and setup (time to create development and test databases)
- Discovery (familiarization with the current design, if there is one)
- Development (all the fun stuff)
- Developer testing (once the coding is done)
- Working with customers to test the changes (including code corrections)
- End-user training
- Rollover to production
- Documentation (including suggestions for the next release)

Estimate the work in as detailed a manner as possible, and then roll-up the details into a grand total. Some people suggest adding a contingency factor, perhaps 10-20%, for unknowns. Remember, this is the actual time on the task that you anticipate will be required. It does not take into account non-project commitments, vacations, sick time, and so on.

Avoid scope creep

As the project moves forward, the customer will likely ask for additional features or changes that were not included in the original requirements document. It is tempting to agree to make changes, but such scope creep can be costly in terms of time and money. On the other hand, if the changes are sensible, consider including them. Discuss all such changes with the formal project coordinator or with your manager.

Assume that all Notes applications will be web-enabled in the future

Many times the Web is the first target for a new deployment, but sometimes a customer does not request web-enablement for an application. All well and good, but barring some unexpected international catastrophe, the trend towards moving applications to the Web should continue into the foreseeable future. So assume that a request will come along eventually to make that new "Notes only" application accessible from the Web. And assume also that older Notes applications, if they are not replaced, will in time be web-enabled as well.

With this in mind, it makes sense to focus on using only techniques that are directly transferable to the Web or that have highly comparable correlates. So as you develop, don't rely on techniques (like Environment variables and @Picklist) that have no direct counterpart for web applications. Check the Designer Help files for the lists of features that do and do not work on the Web. Keep this list handy.

Familiarize yourself with an unknown design

If the task at hand involves enhancing or web-enabling an existing application, then one of your first tasks is to familiarize yourself with the application as it exists already. If there is any existing documentation, read it. If not, you will have to undertake the discovery process on your own.

Start by taking a copy of the design. If there is an archived authoritative design, request a copy of it. If there is no authoritative design, don't trust any copies you may find on the development or staging servers. Previous developers may have left pre-production changes lying around that never made it to production before they moved onto something else. Ask for Editor access to the production database and take the design from there.

Examine the agents in the current design. If any of them are enabled and scheduled, make notes about which ones are enabled and then disable them. It may well be that some of these agents send e-mail notifications to people as part of a workflow. Other agents may automatically download or upload data to other databases. Until you know what the agents do, disable them.

Determine if there is a version or release designation for the production design. If not, assign it one. Then set the designation for the new version you are about to craft (for example, "Version 1.3").

Create a development database from the production design on your development server. You will be accessing this database with a web browser, so placing it on a server provides you with a more realistic view of how the application is accessed (or will be accessed) by your customers.

If you can copy documents from production without compromising security, then do so. Otherwise, copy some documents from another non-production database or simply create your own documents with the current design.

Examine the Access Control List (ACL) of the production database. Take note of which groups are listed and what privileges and roles each is assigned. Adjust the ACL of your development database if necessary to assure you have Manager access to it. This level of access enables you to modify the ACL if your design changes require it.

Open the application with Notes and look around. Read the About and Using documents. Look to see if there is any other internal documentation which may be helpful in understanding the design. Open the views and a document or two. Look over the agents.

Open your web browser and create a bookmark to the development database. Try to open it. If the database fails to open properly, re-open it with Notes and look for a "configuration" view and document of some sort. A configuration document or application profile may require changes before the database will open properly on the Web—perhaps the configuration document lists the wrong server name or database file path. Make changes and try again. Once you have the application open in a browser, explore it. Begin to think about what you must change in order to implement the requested changes.

Assess an existing application for web enablement

A customer may inquire about web-enabling an existing Notes application. As a first step you may be called upon to assess the condition of the application as it currently exists and to provide a work estimate for the uplift.

The first task, assessing the application as it currently exists, might best be undertaken by a quality assurance tester or by a power user who will "think like a user" rather than like a developer. On the other hand, if someone like that is not available, you may be tasked to perform the assessment.

Think like a user

Understanding an application from a user's perspective is an important part of designing a good application. Take off your developer's hat for a time, and do not think about how this or that feature might be coded. Experience the application. Is the navigation intuitive? Do the forms look good? Is it clear what needs to be done?

Make at least two passes through the application before drafting a proposal. During the first pass access the application with Notes to understand what the application is supposed to do. Reviewing the application with Notes provides a baseline of expectations and may also uncover anomalies which warrant fixing.

Then access the application from the Web to see how it already compares (favorably or unfavorably) to the Notes version. Start at the beginning—when the application first launches—and proceed in an orderly fashion through all the features. Make notes. Take screenshots.

Think like a developer

Once the initial functional and UI assessment takes shape, go back through the application with Designer to get some ideas about what needs to be done to correct the application and to get it ready for the Web.

Especially if the application is several years old, there may be many opportunities to spruce it up by making relatively modest changes that won't break the bank and that may greatly improve customer satisfaction. After all, older "out of the box" Domino applications can look dated compared to contemporary websites and well-crafted web applications. Here are some cosmetic, "low hanging fruits" to consider. Some of these issues are covered in more depth in later chapters:

- Change to web-oriented fonts like Verdana or Tahoma, rather than fonts which are more suitable to the printed page
- Add accent color
- Adjust field alignment and layout
- Convert styling to CSS (Cascading Style Sheets) for maximum flexibility and styling options
- Standardize the size and color of buttons
- Try using tabbed tables
- Style **Action Bar** buttons or remove the **Action Bar** altogether
- Use some visually interesting HTML, like the `<fieldset>` and `<legend>` tags

Write a report

The end product of the assessment should be a report with plenty of screenshots which demonstrate the current state of the design. Here is a simple outline which can be used for such an assessment report:

Title Page

> Business owner name and contact information
>
> Developer name and contact information

Table of Contents

Summary

> Purpose of the application
>
> Summary table (information about the application: name, owner, location, size, replication, indexing)
>
> General recommendations

Notes

> Screenshot upon opening the application
>
> Testing notes
>
> Errors encountered
>
> Deficiencies noted
>
> Other observations

Web Browser

> Screenshot upon opening the application
>
> Testing notes
>
> Errors encountered
>
> Deficiencies noted
>
> Other observations

Developer Recommendations

> Each observation and recommendation can be assigned a specific number and title using the form in this example.
>
> APP-01: There is no obvious way to create a new document

The assessment report can be used in discussions with the customer to illustrate how features currently work (or do not work) on the Web. Screenshots can help to set customer expectations about how much work is required.

The outcome of the general assessment would be a decision whether or not to allocate resources for refreshing and upgrading the Domino application.

Keep an issues log

Issues arise during the course of development, and even during routine maintenance tasks. There are decisions to make, problems to investigate, code to fix, tests to run, and documents to write. Typically, there are too many items to keep in your head, and jotting notes on scraps of paper, frankly, does not work well when there are many issues or when several people are involved in a project.

Keep an active log of items in a spreadsheet, in Team Room documents, or even in outline form with a word processor. Read and prioritize this list regularly. Review items with your project team, manager, and customer as appropriate. The issues log will help to keep you focused and moving forward. Fewer issues will fall through the cracks.

Track information about each issue in a consistent way. Keep enough information about each item to answer questions that arise, but do not overdo it. Create the issues log which *you* need for *your* project. Here are a few key items which might be tracked. Add to or subtract from this list as appropriate to your needs:

- Item number
- Title or subject
- Status
- Short description
- Date reported
- Who reported
- Dependencies
- Assigned developer
- Assigned tester
- Comments

Improve the application under the covers

Customers are concerned with look and feel and with functionality. These are aspects of an application which they can see and about which they may have opinions or demands. They assume that applications will perform well and flawlessly, and therefore considerations like good response time and effective error trapping are unlikely to make it to their requirements list.

However, these are things which developers should care about in great detail. A good looking, feature-rich application which is slow or which hangs, or displays many error messages, such an application is a failure.

Here are some things to consider. Each of these topics is elaborated in later chapters.

Enhance performance wherever possible

Web applications require significantly more server and network resources than do comparable Notes applications. Reduce this performance hit by using strategies known to help. For example, use Ajax calls to refresh a pick list rather than re-compute the entire form with a round-trip to the server. Compile a list of performance techniques and implement them.

Add error trapping

Nothing is more annoying than seeing an HTTP 500 error displayed in a browser. This and related error messages are generic; they provide little value in determining what went wrong. Aggravated, the user calls the Help Desk to complain, a ticket is issued, the developer interrupts his current task to attend to the user's problem.

Thorough testing will uncover the majority of error conditions, but never all of them. Again, compile a list of error handling techniques and implement them in your applications.

Add diagnostic and repair aids

Views that display data in ways that simplify troubleshooting can be invaluable when tracking down obscure data issues. Small agents that repair various problems within documents can also be added. It might be best to allow these tools to be seen and used only by the application administrators and developers.

Provide the customer with a summary of changes

Prior to or coincident with rolling a new application or a design upgrade to production, prepare a somewhat detailed *Summary of Changes* for the new version or release. In this document, identify for each change the following things:

- An identifier and a title
- A statement of the customer requirement fulfilled by the change
- The design elements that were added or modified
- Screenshots before and after if appropriate
- Other notes
- Test that were run to verify the change

The *Summary of Changes* is the final report of the project, a clear statement of what was done. You may wish to include a list of suggestions for the next design upgrade.

Documenting your applications

Application documentation provides a more detailed record of what was done and why. Months or years later, you will appreciate such notes when you revisit the code to make modifications. And it is certainly a professional courtesy to other developers to provide insight about why some aspect of an application works the way it does.

There may be an organizational requirement to document applications in a certain way, and if so, do so. Consider going beyond the minimum requirements. In any case, leave tracks.

Add comments to the code

If you took a programming class somewhere along the way, you were told to add comments to your code. This admonition is still valid today. Comment complex or obscure code in a plain way so that future developers can more readily grasp the associated technical implementation.

Every agent should include a summary of what it does, how it is called, what calls it makes, and how and when it was revised. A complex @ formula or JavaScript function should likewise include statements describing what it does. Sometimes hidden text placed on forms also can be helpful.

Create internal developer notes

Developers generally write too little documentation, and what is written is often found in documents external to the Notes application itself. Months or years later, no one can find the external documentation. A new developer begins discovery of the application all over again.

Instead of writing external documents, use the Page design element to record developer documentation. Maintain a consistent naming scheme, and identify them as 'Developer Notes' in the **Comment** field on the **Page Info** tab of **Page Properties**. Keep these pages within the design template. They will take little space, and they will always be there for the next developer.

Add release notes to the About document

In addition to the application owner and developer contact information, an application's About document often includes release notes. Details about a specific release can be included in a separate collapsible section that lists changed elements.

Consider organizing release notes in an outline form. Here is a sample:

- Summary of Changes
- Developer(s)
- Database as a whole
- Framesets
- Pages
- Forms, and so on

Add numbered or bulleted items in each section with specific information about the changed design elements.

Include external documentation in the design as file resources

Word processing documents, spreadsheets, presentations, and so on created during the course of a project can be imported into the design template as file resources. In this way, relevant external documents are never lost and remain with the design for future reference.

Create user-oriented help pages

Application discovery is a great time to make notes about how an application works. If little or no useful user-oriented documentation exists, consider saving notes and screenshots on pages in a separate user help database. Work out a simple, common navigational menu for each page. Once the collection of pages is complete, deploy it for customer use as well as your own.

Summary

Application development is about more than mastering a set of technical skills. It is also about you, the developer, and your customers. It involves strategies for staying organized, gathering information and requirements, estimating how long work will take, and reporting progress. It also involves going the extra mile to enhance performance, harden applications against unexpected failures, and documenting what you did and why. This chapter has provided general suggestions which may be applied to any development project.

2
Design and Development Strategies

An application enhancement or development task can be daunting depending upon your experience and the size of the task. In practice Domino developers can play several project roles: analyst, architect, programmer, coder, tester, technical writer, and often database administrator, trainer, and help desk as well. New developers may be assigned modest enhancement assignments while the more experienced tackle the more challenging projects. But you may not have a choice in the matter; you may be the only Domino developer in your organization and a part-time one at that.

Your goal is to align the application design with the business, to make users more productive — more effective, accurate, and timely. The more you know about the business jargon, processes, priorities, and problems, the better positioned you are to interpret user requirements, and to offer suggestions for enhancing an application.

Your application should satisfy user requirements and launch as defect-free as possible, as defects and errors impact productivity and create rework for users, developers, administrators, and managers. Good planning, design, development, and testing will ferret out most issues before the code reaches production.

Topics in this chapter focus upon general design and development considerations which apply to most projects:

- Planning the design
- Applying standard practices
- Attending to human factors
- Using appropriate design elements and techniques
- Testing and promoting the design to production

Planning the design

Time spent planning means less time spent debugging and reworking the application later on. Resist the "newbie" tendency to jump right to the programming. Take some time to think, to write, to plan.

Identify your key user contacts and strike up relationships. Your customers will clarify their requirements, offer suggestions, and weigh in on decisions about the design. They will approach and test the application from different perspectives, which will highlight issues you had not considered.

Understand the scope of the project

From the requirements that you have, determine what kind of project this is. Are you changing the design of an existing application? Web-enabling an application? Or crafting an entirely new design? The answer to this question will in part tell you how much planning effort is required; the larger the task, the more planning that should be done.

Classify the project and its requirements. Here is a straight-forward taxonomy:

- Bug fixes
- Modifications to existing features
- Feature addition or removal
- Web-enablement
- New design

Decompose each requirement into one or more units of work. A unit of work may be quite limited, such as adding a field to a form, or more complex such as revising the way an application's search process works. It helps to think about each unit of work as a feature or change involving one or more design elements. Subdividing requirements this way helps to focus on one issue at a time.

How many changes are there? While you are assessing the requirements, set about discovering the application. For each requirement, investigate which major design elements are likely to be involved and what needs to be changed. Think about the order in which you might handle each item; are there any dependencies? Think about how you might test each change to assure that it does what it is supposed to do. Take notes.

Annotate the requirements document

It can be very helpful to restate and clarify each user requirement in a new working document, your *developer notes* or the *changes document*. This annotated requirements document should include the set of tasks you have identified, the design elements that should be reviewed and modified, and the test plan.

If a requirement is extensive, or if the assignment involves designing a new application, your planning must be much more extensive. The following list is intended to illustrate the kinds of questions you should ask:

- How many new forms will there be? Containing what information?
- What new views are required with what columns?
- Upon launch, what will be displayed first?
- How will users navigate between views?
- How will documents be created, edited, or deleted?
- What workflow is required?
- What roles are needed? With what privileges and responsibilities?
- Should security features be modified in some way?
- How will required changes impact other parts of the application?
- Will data in existing documents need updating to support the changes?
- Will users require additional training?
- What types of documentation are required?

Sketch or mock up forms and pages, draw workflow diagrams, make lists of issues, jot down any related notions or concerns. Of course all this writing takes time! But this is the essence of planning, and planning *will* save you time over the life of the project.

Understand the workflow

The concept of *workflow* can be difficult to understand, even though all of us routinely participate in workflow whenever we fill out a form or request a service. Volumes have been written about process analysis and modeling, and it is not my intent to do those subjects justice here.

In essence, workflow in a Domino context consists of a set of actions performed on documents by people over a period of time. Documents themselves are often the end product of a workflow process. But a document can also be a record of work that is done external to the application; the state (or status) of a document mirrors the state of the external work.

Work is initiated, assigned, performed, reviewed, and approved or rejected. A workflow application that tracks tasks from initiation to completion will offer some means of identifying the state of the work. It may also generate automated notifications through e-mail and provide reports of one sort or another. How all of this is instantiated in an application is up to the developer.

Here are some questions the answers to which will provide a general understanding of the workflow in (or required of) an application:

- What is the business process which this application's workflow will support?
- Who uses the application? Are there classes of users or actors? What do they do?
- Who originates or composes a document, and why?
- What is the life cycle of a document or task tracked by the application? In what states can a document or task exist (for example, New, Assigned, In Process, Approved, Complete)?
- What are the allowable sequence of states? What states can precede and follow other states? What sequence of states is not allowed?
- What must happen for a document or task to move from one state to another? What triggers a state change? What information must be recorded or who must do what?
- What conditions must exist for a document or task to be considered as complete?

Once you understand the gist of the workflow, drill down for additional information:

- What defined Domino groups are used or required? With what privileges? What roles are assigned? Is anonymous access required?
- What actions do each role and group perform?
- How is the state of a document known? (for example, what status values are used?)
- What agents are involved? Are they scheduled or triggered? What do they do to which documents?
- Are users notified that work has been assigned to them? Is anyone notified when a task is completed? How is this done?

Document your understanding of the application's workflow. Use the language that your customers use; do not use unfamiliar terms or jargon, even if your words are more "correct". Share your notes with your key contacts and ask for verification that the workflow processes work the way you think they do.

Determine the need to access external databases

Find out if the existing application or the new requirements rely upon an external data source to feed data into the Domino application or to receive data from the application. You may need to look into technologies like DECS, LEI, Notrix, Web Services, and so on. You may also need to engage an expert in Oracle, DB2, or some other database technology with which you are unfamiliar. These kinds of issues must be factored into the overall plan.

Decide on one database or several

Probably a large majority of Domino applications consist of one **NSF** file. But applications exist that consist of more than one NSF file, perhaps a few, perhaps dozens of interoperating and interdependent components. If you are dealing with an existing design, become familiar with the collection of components and how they interoperate. If you are creating a design from scratch, consider how best to organize the features. For example, you might architect an application with these NSF files:

- Main application
- Configuration and keywords database
- Log file
- Archive database

Consider the pros and cons of splitting an application into separate files. For example, an application consisting of several NSF databases may be a bit harder to manage, but it does facilitate multiple developers working in concert on different pieces, and it may actually be simpler to introduce incremental changes since each component is less complicated.

Review existing designs

IBM provides a few ready-made database templates which are usually installed along with Notes and Domino. If you are new to working with templates, this is a good way to practice creating databases with templates. And it is a good way to review the capabilities of some basic out-of-the-box applications.

For the most part, the IBM templates are used to create containers for documents; some, like Team Room, include a bit of workflow. Look at these templates in particular:

- Document Library
- Domino Blog (may be located on a server)
- Personal Journal
- Team Room (may be located on a server)

Which templates are available to you and where they are located depends of course upon your installation.

To create a new instance of an application from a template with the Notes client, open the following dialog through the menu **File | Application | New**:

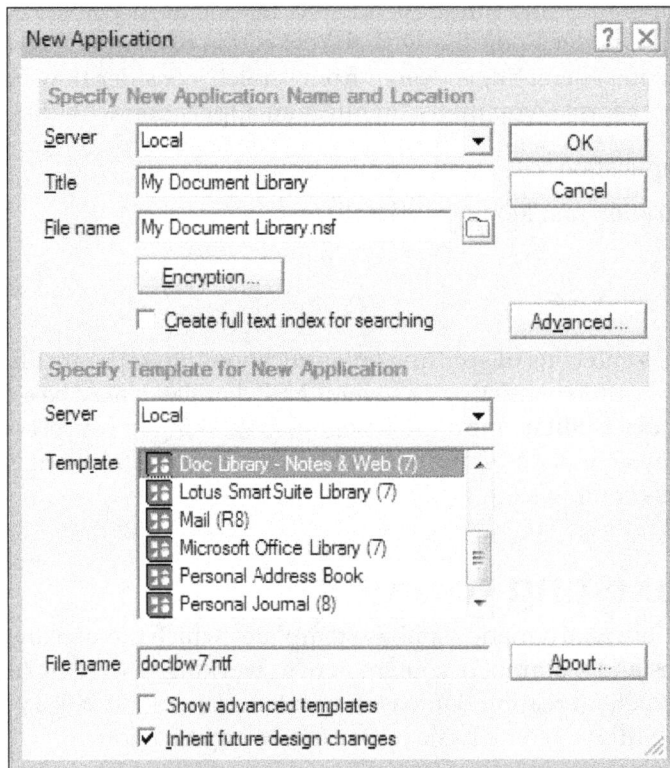

To identify the new application, perform the following steps:

1. Select the host computer that will house the application (your local workstation or a server).

2. Enter a title for the new application.

3. Enter a filename (the filename extension has to be .nsf).

4. Select a target directory or folder.

To identify the source template, perform the following:

1. Select a template server.

2. Select a template name.

3. Click on the **OK** button.

The new application is created.

You might find suitable or inspiring templates on the Web. One popular site for projects is http://www.openntf.org.

Copy the design of an existing application

Applications already deployed in your organization also can provide you with a design which fits—or nearly fits—the requirements. Using an existing application design as a starting point for building a similar application can save considerable time and effort. If an existing application might satisfy the majority of customer requirements, consider copying and reviewing that design with an eye towards repurposing it.

Copying a design is relatively straightforward. You must have Editor or higher access rights to the source application. Locate the application and bookmark it. Select the bookmark and open the following dialog using the menu **File** | **Application** | **New Copy...**:

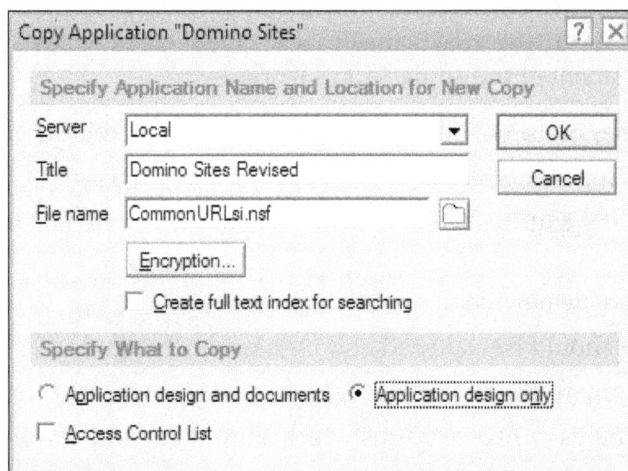

Perform the following steps:

1. Select a target server.

2. Enter a title for the new application or template.

3. Enter a filename (the file extension should be .nsf for an application or .ntf for a template).

4. Select a target directory or folder.

5. Select **Application design only**.

6. Uncheck **Access Control List**.

7. Click on the **OK** button.

The design of the existing application is extracted and copied into the new "template" file.

There is a downside to repurposing existing designs. Too often unused design elements, features, and code remain in the new template, cluttering it up, and consuming resources. This "developer debris" can linger for years and migrate from design to design, serving no purpose. Future developers will puzzle over these abandoned elements until someone takes the time to delete them. Take some time towards the end of the development cycle to clear out unused elements.

Evaluate the security needs of the application

Domino security is multi-layered. Many options exist to protect the database, the documents, and the design elements within the application. Discuss security concerns and requirements with your customers early in the design phase of the project. In a new design, or a major redesign, building in the necessary controls early in development will save considerable rework later on. Here are some questions that can help to clarify security needs. Some of these questions may have been answered during your assessment of the application's workflow:

- What classes of users will there be? Administrators, editors, authors, readers?

- What privileges and restrictions will apply to each class?

- Are there any features which should be restricted or denied to classes of users?

- Who can create new documents in the database?

- What data should be captured and then never changed?

- Are there any restrictions about who can edit certain fields on forms?

- Are there fields or text on forms which should be hidden from certain users?

- What restrictions are there on who can perform the workflow actions?
- Are there any buttons, menu items, views, reports, or help pages that should be restricted in some way?

These kinds of issues should be discussed early in the project and then reconfirmed during development and testing. Getting security right is very important.

Using consistent naming conventions

If you have only a few things to keep track of—your children, for example—then it probably makes little sense to worry about a consistent naming strategy. But as a developer, you will create or modify hundreds or even thousands of objects (fields, forms, views, roles, databases) over a period of years. Consistent naming conventions will help you to reduce errors and to be more productive.

The name of a file or design element should convey some human meaning about its purpose. Elements which belong together should be named in some common manner. If a design element provides a space for comments, use it to further clarify the purpose of the element.

Name databases so that URLs are easy to remember

Meaningful and non-cryptic URLs are easier to remember and less likely to be mistyped by users. When you create an application, use simple and meaningful titles and filenames. Filenames like the following are easier to remember:

- `Resumes.nsf`
- `ProcessingErrors.nsf`
- `TechNotes.nsf`
- `YearEnd2012.nsf`

Using a consistent directory structure will also make URLs easier to use:

- `http://prod01.mycompany.com/ENG/TechNotes.nsf`
- `http://prod01.mycompany.com/HR/Resumes.nsf`
- `http://prod01.mycompany.com/IT/ProcessingErrors.nsf`
- `http://prod01.mycompany.com/FIN/YearEnd2012.nsf`

Use standard versioning for design templates

It is good practice to archive a copy of the current production design template before beginning to modify that design. If code management tools are installed in your organization, use them and adhere to local development standards. However, if you are on your own to handle your design templates, then use a consistent procedure for managing them. For example, archive templates in an organized fashion in a restricted location on a server that is routinely backed up to an offsite location.

Keep copies of the previous design(s). There will be times when you will want to review how something was done before you changed it. And in the case of a major problem with the new design, it may be required to reapply the old design to the staging or production databases.

A simple naming strategy adds a version number to the title and to the filename of a new template and a new development database. This *version identifier* should be recorded with the design's *release notes,* perhaps in the application's About document.

In this example, the application is entitled "ABC Change Management". Using a specific versioning scheme, the following titles and files might exist. (Files with the ntf extension are templates; files with the nsf extension are applications).

The current and some previous design templates may be stored on the development server. By way of illustration, here is a set of templates; the application titles are followed by the filenames (title / file name):

```
ABC Change Management 2.3 Template / ABCChangeManagement23.ntf

ABC Change Management 2.4 Template / ABCChangeManagement24.ntf

ABC Change Management 2.5 Template / ABCChangeManagement25.ntf

ABC Change Management 2.6 Template / ABCChangeManagement26.ntf
```

 Also on the development server, one or two test databases might exist; the database filenames are matched easily with the associated templates. Consistency in naming is important:

```
ABC Change Management 2.5 / ABCChangeManagement25.nsf

ABC Change Management 2.6 / ABCChangeManagement26.nsf
```

When a design moves from a development server to a staging server where the users will test the application, the version identifier should be removed. This enables a user to establish a single URL bookmark that will still work even as the design is upgraded.

```
ABC Change Management / ABCChangeManagement.nsf
```

On the production server, the title, directory, and filename mirror those on the staging server. Again, this scheme simplifies a user's transition from testing to production.

```
ABC Change Management / ABCChangeManagement.nsf
```

The template from the development server is applied to the existing database on the staging server. After user acceptance testing is complete, the template is then applied to the production server. If for any reason the application's design must be rolled back, the previous design template is still available on the development server.

This example is intended to illustrate how templates can be easily versioned. Other factors should be taken into account when setting up your code management practice.

Keep in mind that design elements on the development server are signed by the developer who last updates them. Designs migrated to staging and production servers are generally signed with a specific organizational signing ID by the Domino administrator. It is not a good practice for users to run code signed by developers.

Use standard versioning for major design elements

Enhancing an existing application generally means changing one or more major design elements, perhaps a form or view or an agent. In addition to versioning the design template, developers should consider versioning design elements within a template.

A simple versioning strategy for major design elements would include the following steps:

1. Make a copy of the design element from the **Work Pane** or **Design List**.
2. Open the copied element and then open **Properties**.
3. Rename the copy to include the date the copy was last changed.
4. Rename the **Alias**, if one exists.
5. Add a **Comment** indicating that the element can be deleted in the future.
6. Uncheck all **Display** options.
7. Save and close the element.
8. Hide the design element from all clients from the **Work Pane** or **Design List**.

Set most of these attributes on the **Info** tab of **Properties**. For a form, here's what it might look like:

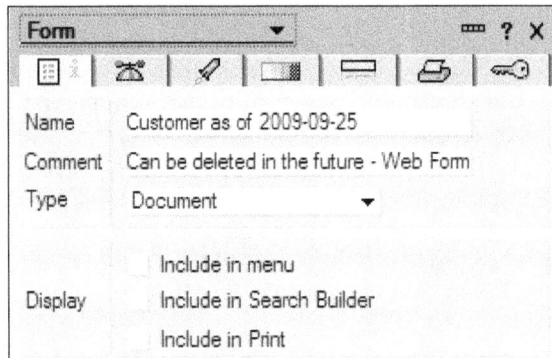

To hide a design element, follow these steps:

1. Select the element in the **Work Pane** or **Design List**.
2. Open **Design Properties** from the context menu.
3. Hide the element from the all clients on the **Design** tab.

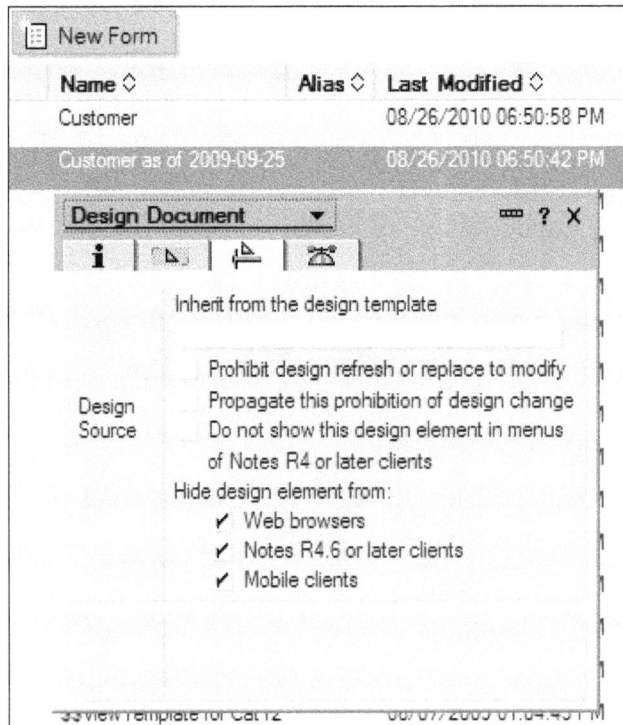

In this example, the Customer form was versioned. It was last changed on September 25, 2009. The old form is hidden from all clients, while the new form is available on the Web. A comment indicates that the old form can be deleted in the future:

New Form										
Name ◇	Alias ◇	Last Modified ◇	La: ◇	✕	⊞	⊕	⊛	▯	Comment ◇
Customer		08/26/2010 06:50:58 PM	Admin./				✓		Web Form
Customer as of 2009-09-25		08/26/2010 06:50:42 PM	Admin./						Can be deleted in the future - Web Form

Use unique names for all major design elements

If two major design elements share a common name, Domino may select the wrong element, leading to incorrect and confusing results.

In the following example, a view and a form are each named *XML1*. The intent of the URL is to link to an attachment stored in a document.

Opening the document from the *XML1* view was successful, but then opening the attachment in that document was unsuccessful:

`http://server/path/database.nsf/XML1/document-unid/$file/filename.ext.`

The browser displayed an error message: **HTTP 500**.

The Domino log entry contained an error message:
HTTP Web Server: Lotus Notes Exception – Note Item not Found.

Changing the name of the view to *XML1vw* solved the problem:
`http://server/path/database.nsf/XML1vw/document-unid/$file/filename.ext.`

Uniquely naming all major design elements will avoid some rather obscure problems.

Name design elements sensibly

Design element names should reflect their purpose. These element names convey meaning:

- `AttendanceRecord` (a form)
- `Resumes by Skill` (a view)
- `ReportOverdueTasks` (an agent)

These element names are less meaningful:

- `HRATT1` (a form)
- `Skills` (a view)
- `agent007` (an agent)

Using Title Case (capitalizing each word within a name) is a good way to make design elements easier to read. Compare these two names:

- `CreatedOnDate`
- `createdondate`

Another convention recommends including a prefix or suffix which identifies the element type in the element's alias. Consider these aliases for a form, page, and view:

- `foAttendanceRecord`
- `pgIntroduction`
- `vwResumesBySkill`

Name form fields consistently and appropriately

Admittedly, it is difficult to plan for all the fields that may be required on a form. As designs evolve, the number of fields seems to expand. Be kind to the next developer and try to name fields in an orderly manner and with common sense.

If an application contains several forms or subforms, and those elements collect the same information, then name the fields the same. Views which include documents from multiple forms will be easier to create and will generally perform better. But if there is no commonality, consider naming the fields on a specific form or subform in a way that identifies those fields as belonging together. An "Action Item" form might contain fields named such as the following:

- `AISubject`
- `AIProblemText`
- `AIAssignee`

Sometimes it is desirable to allow one class of users to edit a field while another class of users can only view the information. One solution to this problem is to provide the same information in two fields, one editable and one computed. Name these fields in a manner that clearly indicates their relationship:

- `DueDate`
- `DueDateREAD or DueDateDISPLAY`

As with design element names in general, Title Case enhances the readability of the field names.

Create different versions of design elements for Notes and the Web

At one time it was estimated that 70-80% of Notes functionality translated well to the Web. Personally, I think that estimate is a bit high, especially for earlier versions of Domino. Design elements (forms, pages, views) can be crafted to look reasonably good both in the Notes client and in web browsers, but at some point, particularly with regard to styling, you simply cannot achieve what you want to achieve with a single dual-purpose design element. When HTML, CSS, and JavaScript are fully supported by the Notes client, this issue may become moot. Until then you may want to develop two versions of a design element, one for Notes and one for the Web, to achieve the results you desire.

Beyond styling, other issues should be considered, such as:

- Certain UI features and techniques are available only in one environment or the other, but not both.

- Navigation between views and forms in Notes is relatively simple, while on the Web, somewhat more complex techniques are required.

- The WYSIWYG styling techniques used in the Designer to style for Notes often take precedence over CSS rules attached to those same elements when they are viewed on the Web.

- Techniques used in agents vary somewhat depending upon whether the document context is Notes or a browser.

Simply create two forms (or views, and so on) with the same name. Use **Design Properties** to hide one form from Notes and the other from web browsers. In this example, two forms share the same name. Comments remind us which form is for the Web and which is for Notes:

New Form									
Name ◇	**Alias** ◇	**Last Modified** ◇	**La:** ◇						**Comment** ◇
Customer		08/26/2010 06:50:58 PM	Admin./					✔	Web Form
Customer		08/26/2010 08:29:11 PM	Admin./			✔			Notes Form

You may be tempted to complete a development task for Notes, which is often the simpler environment to develop within, and then to see how the design works on the Web. I would recommend working both sets of enhancements more or less at the same time.

For example, if you have several forms and views to update, start with one form and make sure that it works well in both environments. You may find that some of your basic assumptions about how a feature will translate to the Web just don't work out. Lessons learned earlier in a project can shorten the development effort for similar design elements later on.

Name Domino groups and roles appropriately

Domino groups are defined in the Domino directory. Each group contains a list of Notes IDs. When a group name is added to an application's ACL, individuals included in the group are permitted access to the application; privileges group members receive are also defined in the ACL. Creating a group is a task for the Domino administrator. Naming that group may be a task for you, the developer.

Consider defining unique Domino groups for each application or suite of related applications. Use names that can be readily identified with the application they support. Use a consistent naming convention. For a "Help Desk" application, the following names might be appropriate:

- HelpDeskAdmins
- HelpDeskConsultants
- HelpDeskUsers
- HelpDeskManagers

Use the **Comments** field in a Domino Directory group document to provide more information about the use of the group, especially which applications use it:

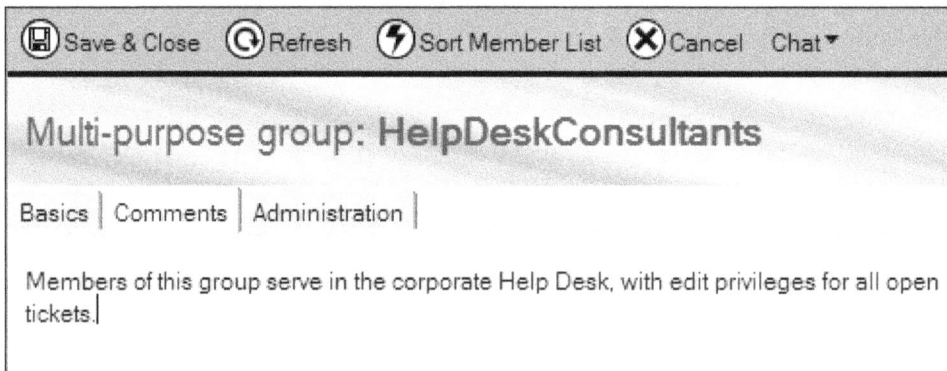

Document the groups associated with an application in the application's About or Using documents. Down the road there will be fewer questions about which groups belong to which applications.

Use Domino groups and roles appropriately

In general, groups should be added to the ACL of an application to specify who can access it and with what privileges and roles. Rarely should a group name be hardwired into a design. Use roles instead, which are considerably more flexible. Define roles in the ACL and assign one or more roles to the groups. In your design formulas and elsewhere, reference the roles.

Name roles consistent with other applications

If at all possible, define roles within an application in a manner which is consistent with the way roles are named and used in other applications. It simply makes the application harder to understand if the same kinds of privileges and authorities are assigned to the "Administrator" role in one application and to the "Chief" or "Lead", or "Director" roles in other applications. Be consistent.

Attending to human factor issues

Application usability considerations were noted in *Chapter 1*, *Preparation and Habits*. Consideration should be given also to other aspects of your applications that will make them easier to use or to change later on.

Create clean and flexible designs

Keep in mind that your application will likely be enhanced or modified in some way in the future. If your design is convoluted and uses clever but difficult to understand algorithms or techniques, you do a disservice to future developers. Cleaner, more straight-forward designs are easy enough to create and certainly easier to rework.

As you learned in your first programming class, comment your code and otherwise document it.

Use shared elements like subforms, image resources, and script libraries to minimize the number of design elements that may have to be modified in the future.

Limit the scope of the JavaScript functions, and LotusScript functions and subroutines. Simpler functions and subroutines are easier to understand and repair or change. On the other hand, creating dozens and dozens of simple functions as primitives may not be a good choice either. Achieving a balance here is important.

Remove developer debris: unused design elements and sections of code that are commented-out.

Design for specific display characteristics

It can be challenging to craft applications that work optimally for all users because computer monitors differ, personal computer operating systems differ, and network speeds differ. With Web applications, screen resolution is certainly an important issue.

When this is being written, the most common screen resolution seen on the Web is 1024 x 768 pixels, with 1280 x 800 and 1280 x 1024 in second and third place, both with respectable percentages of Web traffic. One website that tracks these and other Web trends is the NetmarketShare website at `http://marketshare.hitslink.com`.

If the application is intended for specific devices — handheld devices or specific screen sizes — then use those specifications. But if the target screen is unknown, adopt organizational standards or develop towards the most currently used screen resolution.

You might experiment a bit with **liquid designs** (using Cascading Style Sheets) that can work well as screen resolutions change, but sometimes Notes elements do not flow or scale the way you might want them to regardless of what you do.

In previous years, developers were more concerned about color palettes, since many personal systems displayed only 256 colors, and the quality of displayed images was impacted both by how they were created and how they rendered on the screen. Of course, perceived color is also determined by the quality of the computer monitor, something over which the developer has no control.

Although color may not be of as much concern as it once was, two color palettes are available to you, the default Notes palette and the "Web-safe" Web palette which is intended to display colors that should work well in Web pages. If you are having trouble finding the exact color that a previous developer applied to an element, check the Web palette.

Enable the Web color palette with User Preferences. In Notes 8, the **Preferences** dialog is opened from the menu **File | Preferences**.

On the **Basic Notes Client Configuration** tab, in the **Additional options** list, check the **Use Web palette** option:

Additional options

	Enable MS Office 97 SendTo to Notes
✓	Use Web palette
✓	Show extended accelerators
✓	Enable MIME save warning
✓	Enable Unicode display
	Launch the CORBA (DIIOP) server on Preview in web browser
	Standard dialog boxes

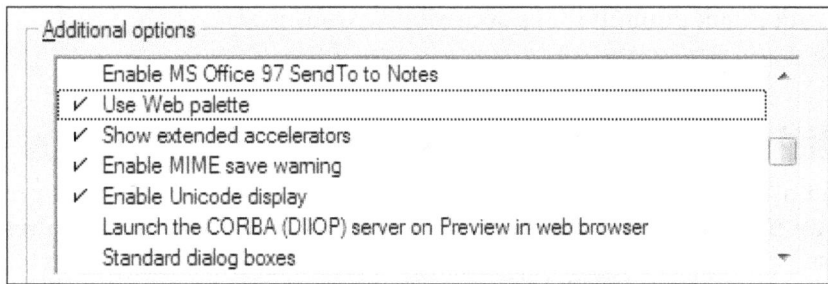

The Web palette then displays whenever you use the color picker:

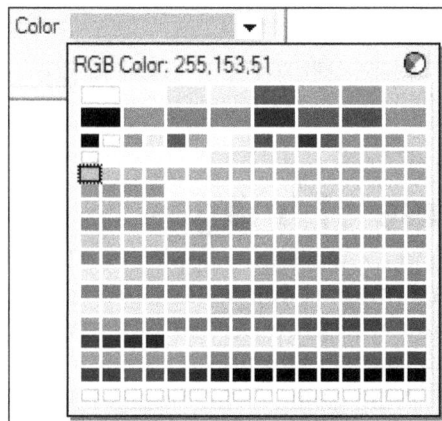

Color

RGB Color: 255,153,51

Design for accessibility

In reviewing the application requirements or in discussions with the intended users, you may become aware of individuals who might have difficulty using a typical web application. Such individuals may not see well or may be color-blind; they may have difficulty reading or making sense of text; they may not easily understand the local language. These and other challenging personal circumstances can influence the design choices you make. For example, you might decide to use icons as well as text for certain features, to use larger fonts for onscreen text, or to utilize special HTML tags and attributes.

Whether due to knowledge of your users or due to laws and regulations in your service area, if you find yourself faced with the need to make a design more accessible, delve more deeply into the subject during the design phase of the project. As a starting point, take a look at the W3C Recommendation, *Web Content Accessibility Guidelines 2.0* at
`http://www.w3.org/TR/WCAG20/`.

You might also look through IBM's accessibility website at
`http://www-03.ibm.com/able/`.

Add titles to pages, forms, and framesets

A frameset title overrides the titles of embedded elements, but it is a good practice to provide a title for every major design element that supports one. Titles dress up the browser title bar. The first following title bar shows the default, a basic URL. The second title bar displays a more pleasing title:

> http://192.168.1.210/ellisits/notesviews.nsf/Hello2?open - Powered by Charter Communications

> Owen and Eileen - Powered by Charter Communications

Optimize the use of images

Logos and graphics are good for website or application branding, and sometimes for location awareness within a complex application. Used correctly, images dress up a page pleasantly and facilitate user productivity. But images are costly in terms of the resources required to create, store, manipulate, and download them. On the Web, especially with a slower Internet connection, image-heavy pages can be very slow to load.

Use images sparingly. Unless there is a good reason to do otherwise, use smaller, well thought out graphics that serve a meaningful and obvious purpose. Use organizationally approved images if they exist. Rarely use large graphics.

Do not downsize images within Designer. Doing so does not really reduce the size of images within the application, and transmitting forms or pages containing those images to a browser will take longer than it has to. With GIMP or another image manipulation tool, optimize photos and graphics by cropping and rescaling them before importing them into a template.

Some numbers might be interesting here. Compare the results of manipulating a 1600 x 1199 JPG photograph both inside and outside Designer. The images were inserted into a page.

```
Page with full-sized photo                        214,177 bytes
Page with photo resized by Designer to 25%        214,179 bytes
Page with photo resized by GIMP to 25%            103,353 bytes
```

The second and third pages rendered identically in the browser, but as you can see, fewer than half the bytes were transmitted to the browser in the third case to achieve the exact same result.

Use image resources instead of pasted images

When Domino serves out pages with pasted or embedded images, those images must be converted to GIF or JPG images by the server before transmission to a browser; this takes time and resources. Import an image into a template as an **image resource** and then insert that resource into pages or forms that require it. Pasting the same image directly onto a number of pages or forms simply inflates the size of the template and slows down the overall responsiveness of the application.

Load optimized images into your design as image resources:

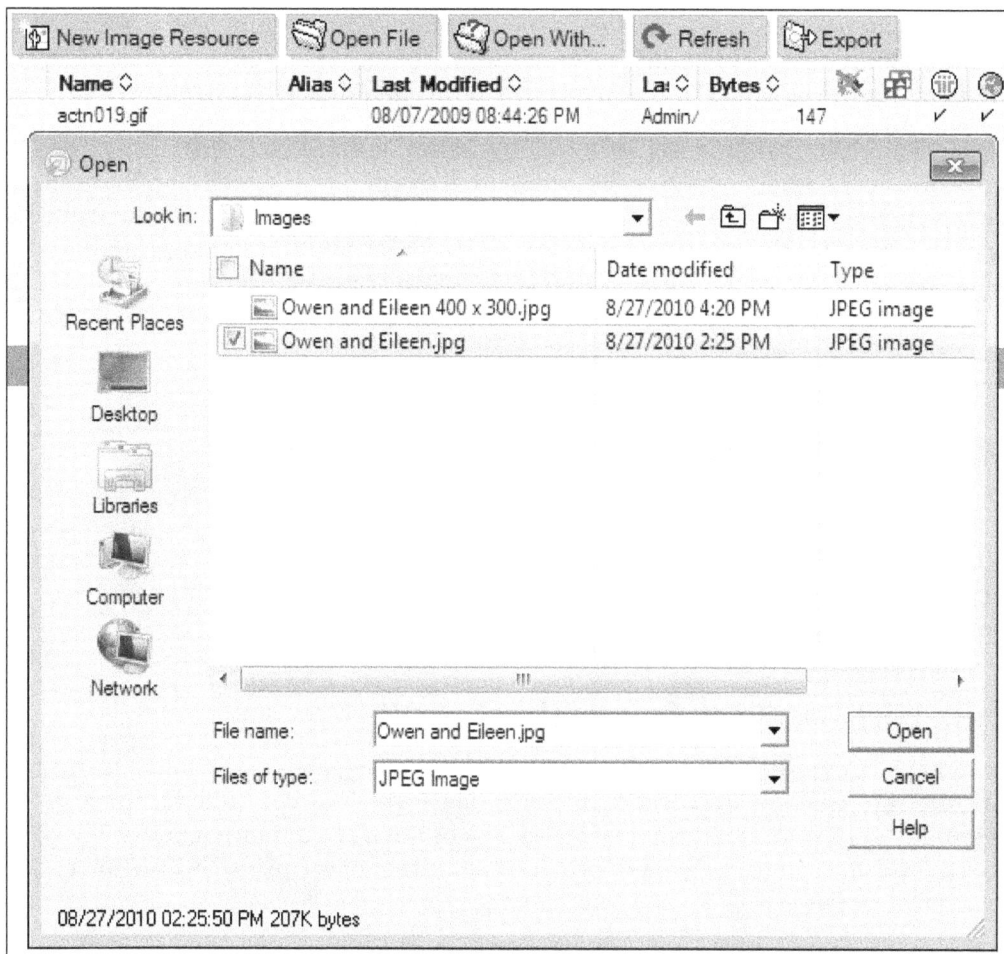

Using appropriate design elements and techniques

Understand that not all design elements work on the Web. Native `@Prompt` or `@PickList` functions, for example, do not translate to the Web. Refer to Designer Help for a list of @Functions and @Commands that do not translate to the Web.

On the other hand, some Web techniques do not work within Notes. For example, if you build a process which relies on CGI variables, that process will not work in the Notes client.

Consider alternate design strategies

After your first project or two, you will begin to see that there are usually several ways to build a feature. Designer enables you to use several coding and mark up languages, several kinds of images, several ways to control layout, several strategies for validating input, and so on. You are free to mix and match techniques within an application.

Topics in later chapters often suggest alternate ways of doing something. Typically every technique offers benefits and limitations. As you dive into development, consider alternate strategies; experiment with different solutions in your sandbox applications. Do not code something a certain way just to be clever. Keep in mind each idea's impact on the performance, usability, and maintainability of the application over time.

Learn the Properties dialog box

Only if you are a fresh newbie in the world of Domino development should you have to be told to learn to use the **Properties** dialog box, also sometimes called the **Infobox**. A complicated control, whose style and contents change with each version of Domino, this is the first place you should look to set properties and otherwise manipulate design elements.

Use hide-when formulas

If you have not worked much with hide-when formulas, take some time to learn what they are and how they work. Such formulas, which can be quite complex, determine whether or not design elements like buttons or guidance text display on the screen. Topics in later chapters provide examples of how using this feature can solve many problems.

Avoid using the Java applets

Java applets are a convenience, but they can be slow to initialize and problematic to work with. The performance of the View applet, for example, can degrade with large views. And any of the applets may not initialize properly depending upon a user's JVM, network proxy settings, and so on. Troubleshooting such issues can be difficult.

Designs that incorporate the Java applets require extensive testing in the users' environment. If a design works well without them, great! If you really do need their functionality on the Web, then test and test often.

Avoid server refresh round trips

Some application elements that work well and quickly in the Notes environment are annoying and problematic on the Web. For example, if a field on a form is set to refresh the form whenever the field's value is changed, then the form is refreshed *from the server*. The changed value is transmitted to the server; the server re-computes the form, translates the form to HTML, and sends the result back to the browser; the browser receives and renders the page.

There is a noticeable delay during the server round trip, and then, to make matters worse, the form is repositioned on the screen, usually with the changed field at the top of the browser window, and text recently entered into some fields may be lost. Behavior like this gives Domino applications a bad reputation.

In applications designed with XPages, this server refresh behavior should be a thing of the past. Existing applications that are not being rewritten to take advantage of the newer functionality can be modified to use Ajax and other JavaScript-based techniques with dramatic, customer-pleasing results. Topics in later chapters discuss some of these strategies.

Conform to HTML standards

Best practices recommend that well-formed pages be coded properly. Web browsers are often forgiving of HTML coding errors, such as missing end tags. The version of Domino serving out your application may not produce standards-compliant HTML, but you should assure that any HTML *you* code is written correctly.

Abide by the XHTML standards to minimize problems that may be encountered with current and future browsers. Attend to the following guidelines:

- Element names should be written in lower case.
- Element attributes should be quoted.
- Element end tags should be used if they exist.

Avoid using non-standard, deprecated, and invalid HTML tags

Non-standard HTML tags like `<blink>` and `<marquee>` provided interesting behavior in the early days of Web designing, but they are now obsolete and may not be supported by all browsers.

Deprecated HTML tags like `<center>`, `<font>`, and `<u>` are those tags that were at one time part of the standards but are now out-of-favor and should not be used. Although browsers do render these elements today, in the long term they may become *invalid* and dropped from support altogether. If you find these tags in the older applications—and you will—take steps to remove them.

Avoid using HTML formatting tags

Still seen on forms and pages in older templates are HTML formatting tags, especially `<p>`, `<br>`, and ` `. At one time these tags were used to achieve certain effects like blank lines, blank columns, and indenting.

These older techniques clutter up pages and forms in the Designer and can actually limit the styling available with CSS. So remove all of these formatting tags or at least as many as possible. Remove blank table rows and columns. Use CSS classes and other styling techniques instead. Topics in the later chapters illustrate how to use CSS within a design.

Use configuration documents

Not uncommonly, it is desirable to change certain global aspects of an application without changing the design. This is true, for example, when the same template is used to create several instances of an application for different departments or groups. Instance-specific information might include items such as the following:

- Displayable title for forms
- Enabled and disabled features
- Options for dialog lists
- Application messages
- URLs of related applications (for example, an archive or agent log)
- URLs of a departmental website or external support sites
- Contact information

Designing an application with hard-coded, instance-specific information would result in a new template for each instance of an application. Another (bad) alternative is to apply design changes directly to an application instance with Designer. Both of these options require a developer to make changes, and neither option enables an application administrator to handle routine configuration tasks.

A common technique implemented to address this issue is to create an application *configuration document* or *application profile* which contains key instance-specific information. Formulas on pages and forms then look up values on this document as needed.

To create a configuration document, first create the configuration form. Follow these general steps:

1. Create a form containing a table with two or three columns; one column contains the fields and the other column(s) contain explanations and examples of required information.

2. Secure the form with a Readers field, enabling all users to access the values, and an Authors field that allows only the application administrators (for example, those assigned the [Admin] role) to edit fields on the form.

3. Alternatively, allow only the [Admin] role to edit the fields; display read-only fields to non-privileged users.

Create a configuration view that selects the configuration document by form name:

- While not strictly necessary, column one should contain a key value, such as the word 'Configuration'. This key value is referenced by lookup formulas.

- Sort column one in ascending order. Even though there may only ever be one application configuration document, the column must be sorted for @DbLookup formulas.

- Optionally, add columns to the view to display values from the configuration document. This enables configuration values to be selected according to column number, which is a bit faster than retrieving those values from the configuration document itself. On the other hand, once the configuration view columns are set, it becomes problematic to rearrange the columns if @DbLookup formulas retrieve data by column number.

Pages and forms access configuration document field values with @DbLookup formulas.

LotusScript agents access configuration document field values with code such as the following. In this example, the view is named `ConfigurationView`:

```
Dim session As New NotesSession
Dim db As NotesDatabase
Dim configView as NotesView
Dim configDoc as NotesDocument
Dim stringVariable as String 'depends on field type
Set db = session.CurrentDatabase
Set configView = db.GetView("ConfigurationView")
Set configDoc = configView.GetFirstDocument
stringVariable = configDoc.fieldname(0) 'use actual field name
```

If there is no configuration view, use code similar to the following:

```
Dim session As New NoteSession
Dim db As NotesDatabase
Dim dc As NotesDocumentCollection
Dim configDoc as NotesDocument
Dim formula As String
Dim stringVariable as String 'depends on field type
Set db = session.CurrentDatabase
formula = "Form=""Configuration"""
Set dc = db.Search(formula,Nothing,0)
Set configDoc = dc.GetFirstDocument
stringVariable = configDoc.fieldname(0) 'use actual field name
```

In addition to a single application configuration document, there also may be a need for multiple configuration-like documents or profiles that describe keywords, processes, organizations, or workflow rules. These "behind the scenes" documents are typically editable only by the application's administrator or the developer.

Developer testing

As you develop, you will continually test the design as you implement features and make other changes in accordance with the requirements. At the end of the development phase, and before you turn the application over for user acceptance testing, spend some time seriously challenging the revised application. See if you can break it.

Add diagnostic and repair tools

Especially for existing applications with which you are unfamiliar, create some diagnostic and repair tools that do not interfere with or depend upon any functional components. For example, views that display documents in ways that help you to understand the data can be extremely helpful during development and testing, and also afterward when the design is in production. If test cases fail to produce expected results, diagnostic views can help you locate incorrect documents and provide insight into what went wrong.

If you are aware of data errors which exist in some of the documents, code some agents to repair those documents. You may want to restrict these views and repair tools to users with the [Admin] or [Developer] roles. Topics in later chapters provide additional suggestions and examples.

Set up test IDs

It is important to set up two or more Tester IDs with which you can challenge the application. As the developer, you have Manager or Designer access to the application on the development server. These higher privileges enable to you to do things in the application that someone with Author access, for example, is not able to do. If you only test the application only with elevated privileges, you will likely miss errors.

Use the Tester IDs to simulate the end users. Make one Tester an application administrator, and assign to that ID the [Admin] or other privileged roles. Make another Tester a regular user who will create documents and participate in the workflow. If other real users are authorized only Reader access in the application, then set up a Tester ID as a reader. Your goal is to work with the application in exactly the same ways as would all your classes of users.

Test with browsers used by your users

You may work in an organization which restricts the browsers that employees can use. This is good, as it limits the amount of testing you should do. But if the organization allows many different browsers, and several versions of each browser, then the testing phase is that much more complicated.

While the situation is getting better, all browsers do not render pages identically, nor do they always support JavaScript or CSS consistently. The only way to determine if your application will work satisfactorily for all end users is to test it with a number of browsers.

Find out which browsers and which versions of those browsers are installed in the organization. Then set up virtual machines or individual workstations such that each testing station provides a different browser. Ideally, you should test each role with each browser.

Clear the browser cache

It may seem a bit odd to include a comment here about clearing the browser cache, but I have found, both in development and in QA testing, that clearing the browser cache solves a lot of puzzles. Clear the cache frequently, especially if you are recoding CSS or JavaScript functions. Nothing is more frustrating than puzzling over why an obvious CSS rule change does not work, only to find that clearing the cache removed the old rule so that the new rule can do its magic.

Promoting the design from testing to production

An experienced QA Tester can be invaluable to your project. Engage one if possible to challenge your application before you turn it over for customer testing.

Once the application is turned over for customer testing, engage your users early and often to discuss progress and findings. Several customers are better than one. They will discover things you don't find because they will challenge the application in ways you did not consider.

Provide your testers with test scripts and suggestions appropriate to specific design changes or features. Remind them that only after they sign off can the new design move to production.

Use a staging server for user acceptance testing

A staging server should be configured as if it were a full production server. You and your customers should have the same privileges on the staging server as you do on the production server, no more, no less. Identical privileges and conditions will tend to root out many residual problems.

Take care of scheduled agents. Understand what they do and what will happen when they fire off. If e-mail notifications are automatically sent out, make sure recipients are alerted to the possibility of test messages to which they need not respond.

Segregate administrative and developer duties

It is a considered a best practice to segregate Domino administrator and Domino developer duties. Developers build applications and work with data issues. Administrators control the servers and the introduction of design changes into production. Segregation of duties pleases the auditors and the security professionals.

At the same time, it is very helpful if developers understand what administrators do, and vice versa. Developers with the chance to administer a development server should take that opportunity to learn as much as they can about what the other half of the Domino team does for a living.

Request that templates be signed by an authorized signing ID

A new or revised template should be signed by an authorized signing ID set up for that purpose. During development, every design element saved by the developer is signed with the developer's ID. Those signatures should be changed when the application design rolls over to the staging server, and "signing the design" is one of those tasks generally delegated to the Domino administrators.

When using the Notes client, the signing ID is allowed, through the client's Execution Control List or the ECL, to perform various actions on behalf of the applications. On a Domino server, the signing ID is often allowed to run scheduled agents, so when an application fires off an agent in the middle of the night, it runs with the authority of the signing ID.

Depending upon how the developer defines them in a web application, agents may run as the signing ID or as the currently active web user. If agents run with the authority of the signing ID, then that ID should be authorized to the application through its ACL.

Understand how templates are applied to production applications

The Designer task runs at night and updates all applications on the server that are associated with specific master templates. In this way, applying a new design to several databases can be accomplished with a minimum of human intervention.

Some organizations, however, prefer to apply designs manually. A Domino administrator creates a template from the application on the staging server and then applies that template to the target production database.

It is useful to understand clearly how your organization applies updated templates to the production files. Strategies vary. Ask the administrator.

Reviewing other sources of help

Some of your development time will be spent browsing the Web and reading articles that address specific issues with which you are dealing. In addition, find some off-task time to read more generally in order to pick up ideas for your projects. There are many sources of information on the Web. Here are some places to start:

```
http://www-01.ibm.com/software/lotus/notesanddomino/library.html
```

```
http://www.ibm.com/developerworks/lotus/products/notesdomino/
```

> URLs are subject to change over time, so these and other referenced links may not work in the future.

Read the Notes and Domino release notes

Release notes are prepared for each version and numbered release of the product. Up through Version 8, release notes were generally available as NSF, PDF, or possibly HTML files. After Version 8, these documents may be available only as Web or Wiki pages.

Browse through the release notes for your current and the new versions of the software. Pay special attention to those sections that deal with the Designer client. You will find information about known errors and problems, new features, features that are fixed, and features that are deprecated.

Summary

A development project begins with a set of requirements, proceeds through design, development, and testing phases, and then fulfills when the new or revised design is rolled into production. Good planning and sensible execution of the plan are essential to every successful deployment, although the effort required should be commensurate with size of the project. This chapter has provided tips and recommendations applicable to all phases of a project, but especially to the design phase.

3

Forms and Pages

A web-enablement or application modernization project should probably start by considering what can be done to update forms and pages. As you familiarize yourself with an application assigned to you, you may identify any number of aspects that could be done better. Some of those aspects have to do with look of the application, the fonts used, the color schemes, how fields are placed on the forms, and so on. You may notice other issues, such as lack of validation for a field, poorly stated error messages, or a less-than-contemporary navigational strategy.

Domino Designer provides many techniques for creating and styling forms and pages within an application. Unfortunately, there are times when design strategies that work well in Notes work less-well on the Web. And the reverse is also true; some techniques are very suitable for the Web, but fall short (or are unsupported) in the Notes client.

This chapter addresses selected issues and problems you may encounter while crafting forms and pages for the Web. In some cases, several ways to do the same thing are presented, not necessarily because all techniques are equally good, but because you may run into these strategies as you root around in older applications. Older applications naturally would use older techniques, and which techniques were used was generally due to the preferences and knowledge of previous developers. If you come across an unfamiliar way of doing something, ask yourself whether you know something those previous developers did not know, or did they know something you don't know.

Topics in this chapter focus upon design and development considerations for forms and pages. Keep in mind the primary difference between a form and a page—forms can contain fields into which information can be entered, and pages do not. The following topics are covered in this chapter:

- Setting appropriate properties
- Using the rendered source

- Editing and saving documents (forms only)
- Improving layout
- Using computed text
- Using hidden fields
- Adding HTML tags
- Creating pseudo action bars

Setting properties appropriately

A few key properties affect the way Domino generates forms and pages. Setting these properties correctly for your application is important, since setting them incorrectly can result in wasted time spent tracking down seemingly obscure problems.

Set the content type (MIME) property

Forms and pages should be identified regarding the kind of content contained in them because Domino generates different HTML code (in a browser, the "source") depending upon how the content type is set. Specifying the content type is most important when creating pages that contain CSS, JavaScript, or something even more exotic.

Set the **Content type** on the form **Defaults** tab or the page **Info** tab of the appropriate **Properties**.

For most forms, the default **Notes** should be fine.

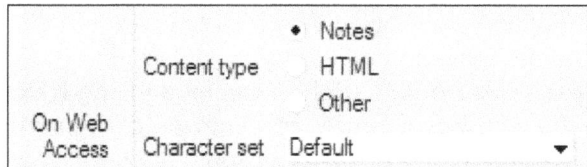

For a form or page containing only HTML, set the **Content type** to **HTML**. Forms set to HTML that include Designer-inserted fields generate an HTTP 500 error when opened for edit. You may need to code your own `<input>` tags (to represent the fields) or convert the fields to HTML.

The following screenshot shows the setting for a page containing just CSS rules:

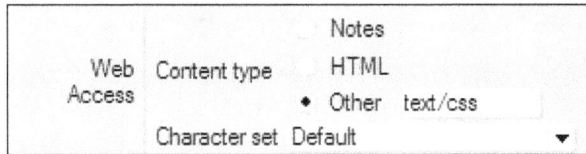

		Notes	
Web Access	Content type	HTML	
		• Other	text/css
	Character set	Default	▼

The following screenshot shows the setting for a page containing just JavaScript:

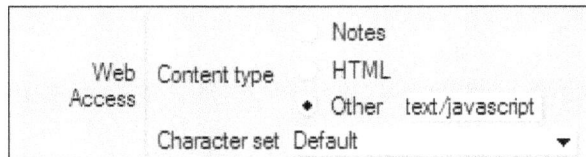

		Notes	
Web Access	Content type	HTML	
		• Other	text/javascript
	Character set	Default	▼

Take full control with content type HTML

Sometimes the HTML for a page already exists external to your Domino application; you can copy that HTML onto a page element as is. And of course, you can write your own page completely in HTML.

For pages that contain just HTML (and perhaps some computed text), you can use either the **Notes** or **HTML** content types. However, these settings generate different HTML code. For example, here is a simple page as seen in Designer, with the HTML tags marked as Pass-Thru HTML.

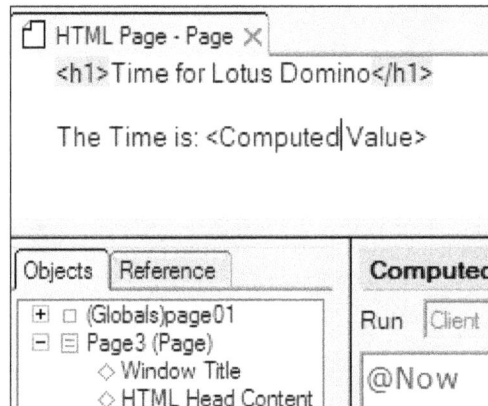

```
HTML Page - Page ×

<h1>Time for Lotus Domino</h1>

The Time is: <Computed|Value>

Objects | Reference              Computed

⊞ □ (Globals)page01           Run | Client
⊟ ⊟ Page3 (Page)
     ◇ Window Title            @Now
     ◇ HTML Head Content
```

With the content type of the page set to **Notes,** Domino generates the following HTML source code, including header tags, JavaScript, and some HTML formatting tags, which you can see by opening the page in a browser and viewing the page source:

```
<!DOCTYPE HTML PUBLIC "-//W3C//DTD HTML 4.01 Transitional//EN">
<html>
<head>
<script language="JavaScript" type="text/javascript">
<!--
document._domino_target = "_self";
function _doClick(v, o, t) {
  var returnValue = false;
  var url="/ellisits/websandbox03.nsf/page01?OpenPage&Click=" + v;
  if (o.href != null) {
    o.href = url;
    returnValue = true;
  } else {
    if (t == null)
      t = document._domino_target;
    window.open(url, t);
  }
  return returnValue;
}
// -->
</script>
</head>
<body text="#000000" bgcolor="#FFFFFF">
<form action=""><h1>Time for Lotus Domino</h1><br>
The Time is: 01/15/2011 12:46:15 PM</form>
</body>
</html>
```

With content type of the same page set to **HTML,** Domino generates the following HTML source code:

```
<h1>Time for Lotus Domino</h1>
The Time is: 01/15/2011 12:49:41 PM
```

This HTML is neither well-formed nor valid; it lacks a DOCTYPE declaration and the structural HTML tags (<html>, <head>, <body>). Only onscreen text and the result of the computed text are provided.

With the content type set to **HTML**, you take full control of the contents of the page. If the DOCTYPE declaration and other HTML tags are desired or required, they can be added to the page in Designer.

```
HTML Page - Page ×
<!DOCTYPE HTML PUBLIC "-//W3C//DTD HTML 4.01 Transitional//EN">
<html>
<head>
<h1>Time for Lotus Domino</h1>

The Time is: <Computed Value>

</body>
</html>
```

Note that if **HTML** is selected as the content type for a page, there is no need to mark HTML tags as Pass-Thru HTML.

Leave the "Use JavaScript when generating pages" option enabled

Today client-side JavaScript is ubiquitous on the Web, and we code with it to implement form and page behavior. Unless your requirements include designing for browsers that do not support JavaScript or for environments where JavaScript support is disabled due to security concerns, code your application to use JavaScript.

By default, Domino generates JavaScript for some design elements (for example, Action Bar buttons) in order to provide web functionality. The **Use JavaScript when generating pages** property can be disabled (not a good idea) on the **Database Basics** tab of **Database Properties**.

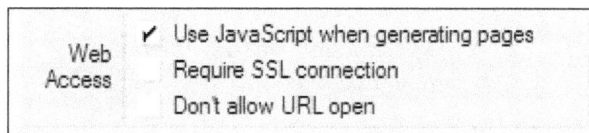

```
             ✔  Use JavaScript when generating pages
   Web          Require SSL connection
   Access       Don't allow URL open
```

With this property disabled, certain active elements of a form are not available on the Web. For example, Action Bar buttons that are coded only with @Formulas may not display. In addition, a form may load more slowly, certain @Commands do not work, and Domino either inserts a **Submit** button at the bottom of the form or converts the last button on a form to a **Submit** button.

This property does *not* disallow your use of JavaScript with design elements in the application. Even with this property unchecked, if you code a button to run some JavaScript, then clicking that button will run the JavaScript. If you code JavaScript to run in the JS Header, it will run when the page loads.

In general, if you are building web applications, you should leave this application property enabled. Domino then provides the JavaScript required by your buttons, collapsible sections, and other elements.

Generate HTML for all fields

The option **Generate HTML for all fields** on the **Defaults** tab of **Form Properties** determines whether hidden fields are passed to the browser. Please note that this does not work if the content type is set to HTML.

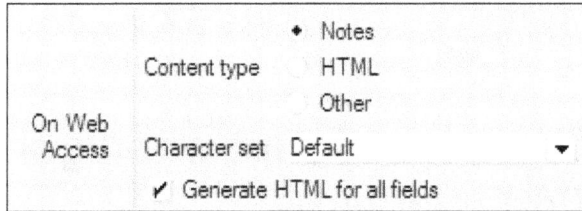

With this property enabled, hidden fields on the form are passed as "hidden" fields to the browser; the page source contains appropriate tags and values. These hidden fields then can be accessed by JavaScript. Here is what the page source might look like with a document in Edit mode.

```
<input name="Field1" value="Dexter">
<input name="Hidden1" type="hidden" value="John">
```

Both hidden and viewable fields are passed to the browser as hidden fields when a document is in Read mode.

```
<input name="Field1" type="hidden" value="Dexter">
<input name="Hidden1" type="hidden" value="John">
```

If this property is disabled, then hidden fields are not passed to the browser. JavaScript that relies on values in these fields will fail. If formulas and scripts are not working as they should, it may be because referenced hidden fields are not available.

Be aware of the security exposure here. If all hidden fields are transmitted to the browser, then a user may be able to see the values of those fields by viewing the form's source. Hidden fields are extremely useful in Domino web applications, but hiding fields is not a security measure to be relied upon.

Opening forms and pages directly

You can save some development time by bookmarking and linking directly to the form or page on which you are currently working. Browse directly to a design element with the following syntax:

```
http://server-name/directory/database.nsf/formname?openform
```

```
http://server-name/directory/database.nsf/pagename?openpage
```

If major design elements are uniquely named, the shorter forms should work as well.

```
http://server-name/directory/database.nsf/formname
```

```
http://server-name/directory/database.nsf/pagename
```

Opening design elements directly like this is referred to as **URL open**, and by default it is enabled in applications. This capability can be disabled (for security reasons), but doing so prevents an application from being opened on the Web. If URL open is disallowed for an application, trying to open that application or to link directly to a form or page results in an HTTP 500 error (not authorized).

To disable URL open, check **Don't allow URL open** on the **Basics** tab of **Database Properties**.

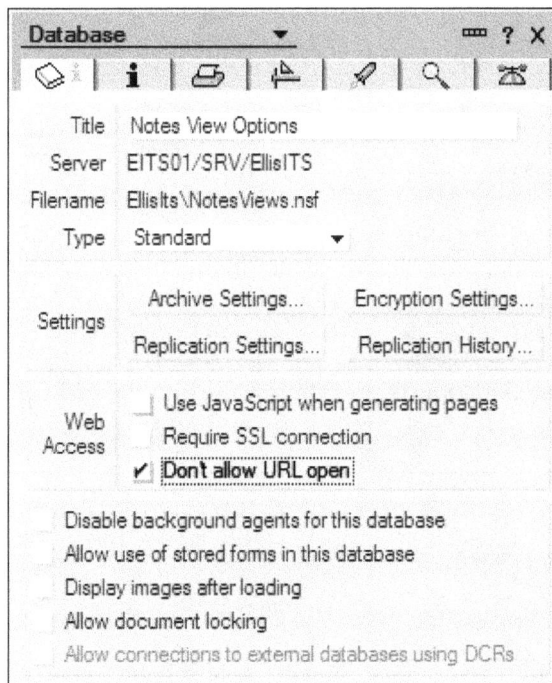

Viewing the source in a browser to investigate anomalies

This suggestion rightfully belongs in the troubleshooting chapter, but it is inserted at this point because of how useful it can be when debugging forms and pages.

On occasion, a form or page looks fine in Designer, but the rendered results are not correct. This can happen because Domino sometimes generates HTML code that you may not expect. Or perhaps an error message displays indicating that some field or variable is undefined.

If rendered results are anomalous or if the behavior of a form is not what you expect, it can be helpful to look at the web page source for clues, either with a simple editor or with a browser's developer tools. For example, here is a simple page consisting of a heading and an image. The HTML is marked as Pass-Thru HTML:

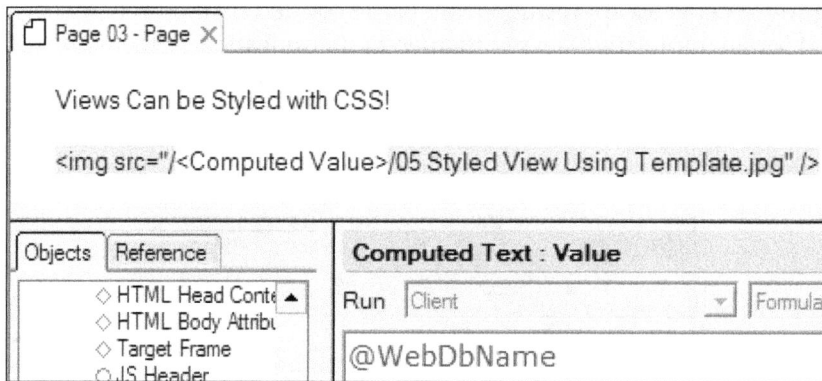

Here the computed text @formula supplies part of the source value for the image that displays on the page. There are other ways to include images on pages, of course. This construction is intended primarily to illustrate what can happen if Domino inserts erroneous HTML when composing a page for the Web.

Initially the page renders properly, but then we decide to add some color to the text. In Designer, we select all the text on the page and apply red and bold formats.

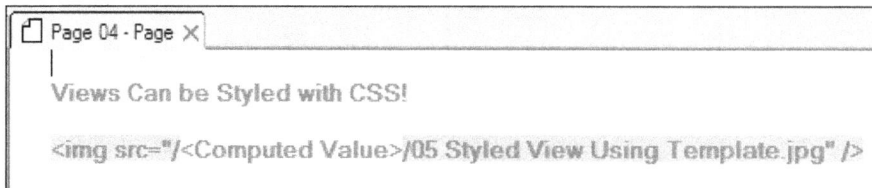

Now, part of the page fails to render as expected.

Here is the HTML source that displays the heading and the image. Note the malformed <img> tag. Domino inserts bold and font tags around the computed text, which results in clearly invalid HTML.

```
<b><font color="#FF0000">Views Can be Styled with CSS!</font></b><br>
<img src="/<b><font color="#FF0000">ellisits/websandbox03.nsf</font>
</b>/05 Styled View Using Template.jpg" /></form>
```

Removing bold and color formats from the computed text in Designer results in cleaner source and a properly rendered page.

```
<b><font color="#FF0000">Views Can be Styled with CSS!</font></b><br>
<img src="/ellisits/websandbox03.nsf/05 Styled View Using Template.
jpg"/>
```

Composing and saving documents

As you start to look at older applications that were not intentionally enabled for the Web, you may find some that provide no way to create a new document or to toggle an existing document into Edit mode. In such cases, you will have to create buttons or hotspots to provide these features.

Please note that the @Command alternatives illustrated in this section work on the Web only if the application property **Use JavaScript when generating pages** is enabled, as discussed in a previous topic.

Create documents

In a web application, a new document can be created when a user clicks a button or hotspot whose formula includes an appropriate @Command. Here "Customer" is the name of the form.

```
@Command([Compose];"Customer")
```

Alternatively, a blank form can be opened with a URL attached to a button or hotspot.

```
http://192.168.1.210/ellisits/websandbox03.nsf/customer?openform
```

The URL can be computed using an @Command, JavaScript, or even LotusScript (running in an agent). This example uses an @Command to compute a URL.

```
@URLOpen("/" + @WebDbName + "/customer?openform")
```

Assuming that an open document contains a field named webdbname whose value is the file path of the application, then this JavaScript formula opens a new form named **customer2**.

```
var f = document.forms[0];
location.href="/" + f.webdbname.value + "/customer2?openform";
```

A LotusScript agent running on a server can also open a new form in the browser.

```
Dim session As New NotesSession
Dim db As NotesDatabase
Set db = session.CurrentDatabase
Print "[/" & db.FilePath & "/customer2?openform]"
```

Edit documents

Existing documents opened from views typically open in Read mode. To toggle an existing document from Read mode to Edit mode, create a button on the form and attach this familiar command to it.

```
@Command([EditDocument])
```

You can toggle a document into Edit mode also with JavaScript, but more coding is involved. Here is one way to do this. First, add three hidden Computed for display fields to the form with these values.

- **docID:** @Text(@DocumentUniqueID)

- **viewname** (assumes the view alias contains only alphanumerics):@Subset(@ViewTitle; -1)

- **webdbname:** @WebDbName

Then add the following or similar JavaScript to the onClick event of a button on the form:

```
var f = document.forms[0] ;
var a = f.webdbname.value ;
var v = f.viewname.value ;
var d = f.docID.value ;
location.href="/" + a + "/" + v + "/" + d + "?editdocument" ;
```

Save documents

Data collected in fields on a form is usually saved into the database for later processing. Entered data is usually validated in some way, either at the field level or at the form level, before the document is saved. This topic is taken up in a later chapter.

After a document is saved, a new page is presented to the user. Post-save navigation is treated here briefly in the context of saving documents; additional options are considered in more detail in a later chapter.

Several techniques can be used to save a document and display the next page; here are three variations.

A simple way to save a document is to rely on @Formulas. Designer Help recommends adding these commands to a button on a form.

```
@Command([FileSave]) ;
@Command([CloseWindow]) ;
```

In the Notes client, clicking a button coded with this @formula saves and closes the document; UI focus returns to the previous view (or other design element). But clicking this same button on the Web results in a different user experience. The @Commands do indeed submit the document to the database, but then the following default page displays:

Form processed

The default **Form processed** page contains no buttons or other indicators about what to do next. A user must click on the browser's **Back** button to return through the previously edited document to find a useful page. But relying on the browser's **Back** button for any purpose is not recommended. Here is a clear and simple case that illustrates how important it is to design good user navigation into a web application.

If the requirement is to save a document and then to return to it in Read mode, create a button on the form with this formula to achieve that result. The last line of the formula assures that the screen is refreshed with the newly saved information.

```
@Command([FileSave]) ;
@Command([EditDocument]) ;
@If(!@IsDocBeingEdited;@Command([RefreshWindow]);"") ;
```

If the requirement is to save a document and then to return to a specific view or another page, create a button with this formula to achieve that result. The last line of the formula fetches and displays the view whose name or alias is `allcustomers`.

```
@Command([FileSave]) ;
@Command([FileCloseWindow]) ;
@URLOpen("/"+@WebDbName+"/allcustomers") ;
```

Save documents using $$Return to specify the next page

In many cases, separating the logic for saving a document and specifying the next page makes sense. One way to specify the next page is to use a special field named `$$Return` on the form, whose value is the URL of the next page. When a document is saved, Domino redirects the browser to the location specified in `$$Return`.

Think of `$$Return` not as a data input field, but rather as container for information that Domino uses to determine what to do after a document is saved. To implement this simple technique, create a hidden Computed for display field named `$$Return`. In this example, the value of `$$Return` is the URL of the next page to be displayed:

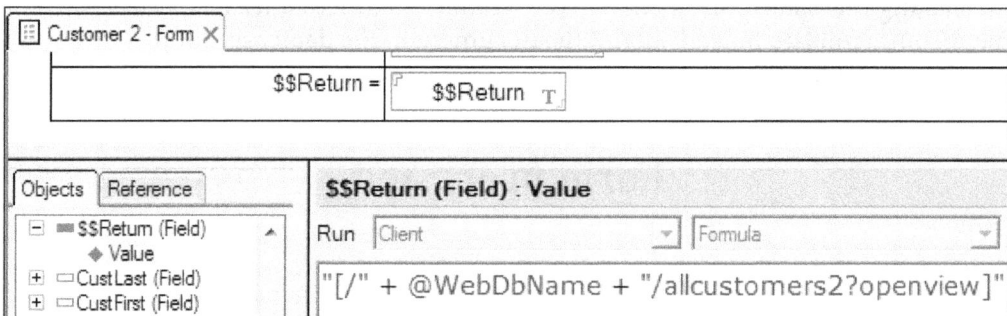

After a document is saved, Domino redirects the browser to the `allcustomers2` view within the application. The square brackets are required to identify the string as a URL. If they are omitted, then the URL is simply printed to the browser window.

`$$Return` is often used in other ways, some of which can be problematic. Cautions about using `$$Return` for other purposes are included in a later chapter.

Save documents using a WebQuerySave agent to specify the next page

The **WebQuerySave** form event provides a place to specify an agent that should run before a document is saved. Considerable processing can be included in the agent, depending upon the needs of the application. An agent intercepts documents and then can manipulate fields, kick off email notifications, prevent documents from being saved, and so on. The agent can also direct the browser to display a specific page after the document is saved. Here is the skeleton of how this works.

First, enter the name of the agent into the `ToolsRunMacro` @Command in the form's `WebQuerySave` event. Here, the name of the LotusScript agent is `SaveAgent`:

Next, code the agent. Here is the bare-bones code for the `SaveAgent` agent. This agent does no processing except to redirect the browser to the next page. Note that `SaveAgent` requires the view name and the file path information to be computed in the `viewname` and `webdbname` fields on the form, as in the illustration. Also, note that the agent tests for the existence of a view name. For new documents, the `viewname` field is blank because a new document is not yet associated with a view.

```
Sub Initialize
  Dim session As New NotesSession
  Dim doc As NotesDocument
  Set doc = session.DocumentContext
  If doc.viewname(0) = "" Then
    Print "[/" & doc.webdbname(0) & "]"
  Else
    Print "[/" & doc.webdbname(0) & "/" & _
    doc.viewname(0) & "?openview]"
  End If
End Sub
```

Finally, set the agent's **Runtime** properties on the **Basics** tab of **Agent Properties**.

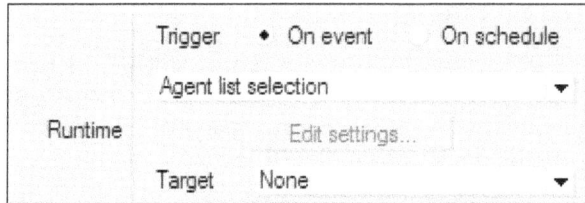

	Trigger	◆ On event	On schedule
	Agent list selection		▼
Runtime	Edit settings...		
	Target	None	▼

When a document is saved, the agent runs and redirects the browser to display a specific view within the database.

This example shows the basic components required to use a `WebQuerySave` agent. Such an agent would typically do more than simply redirect the browser to a new page, but the example here is sufficient to demonstrate how these features work together and can be used as a starting point in building your own agent.

Improving the layout of design elements

Layout refers to the arrangement of design elements on forms and pages, and also to the positioning of those major design elements within other design elements—pages within framesets, for example. In many web applications, Designer options and raw HTML coding are used synergistically to create a final result.

The layout of a form or page has to do with the arrangement of text, fields, images, buttons, and other elements. The layout affects not only the look of the form, but also contributes to its usability. Here are some issues which should be taken into account.

- The grouping of related fields
- The alignment of fields
- The position of buttons and navigational hotspots
- The location of onscreen guidance text
- Margins and whitespace

Layout provides an overall structure to the application as displayed by a browser, as well as to individual forms and pages. But layout and style are interdependent, so the final look and feel results from considering both. Styling with Cascading Style Sheets(CSS) is discussed here when relevant; the subject is taken up in more detail in a later chapter.

Topics in this section focus on key issues related to application design element layout.

Identify all HTML tags

HTML offers some interesting layout options that can be included on a form or page by coding specific HTML tags. Illustrations of some of these layout options are presented a bit later in this chapter.

HTML tags provide information to a browser concerning how a page is to be rendered. In order for Domino to construct a page properly, you have to identify your HTML tags as such, so that Domino knows what is and what is not HTML. There are two ways to do this.

- Surround the HTML with square brackets
- Select and mark the HTML tags as Pass-Thru HTML

Here is an example showing a form that uses both techniques. Heading 1 is surrounded by HTML tags that are not identified as such. The tags for Heading 2 are surrounded with left and right square brackets. The tags for Heading 3 have been selected and marked as Pass-Thru HTML.

```
Form4 - Form ✕

    <h2>Heading 1</h2>

    [<h2>]Heading 2[</h2>]

    <h2>Heading 3</h2>
```

Here is the resulting rendered form. The tags for Heading 1 are not interpreted as HTML because they have not been identified as tags. Heading 2 and Heading 3 render identically.

```
<h2>Heading 1</h2>

Heading 2

Heading 3
```

Identify HTML tags with left and right square brackets or by marking them as Pass-Thru HTML. Square brackets add a bit of clutter to a form, but they provide a precise delineation of what is and what is not included with a tag. Tags marked as Pass-Thru HTML are highlighted in gray and are easier to identify, but care must be taken not to mark as Pass-Thru HTML any fields or nearby text; unexpected results can occur if a field or other text is marked as Pass-Thru HTML when it should not be.

Select and mark HTML tags as Pass-Thru HTML using the Text menu option **Pass-Thru HTML**. To remove the attribute, select the HTML tags and unselect the option using the **Text** menu.

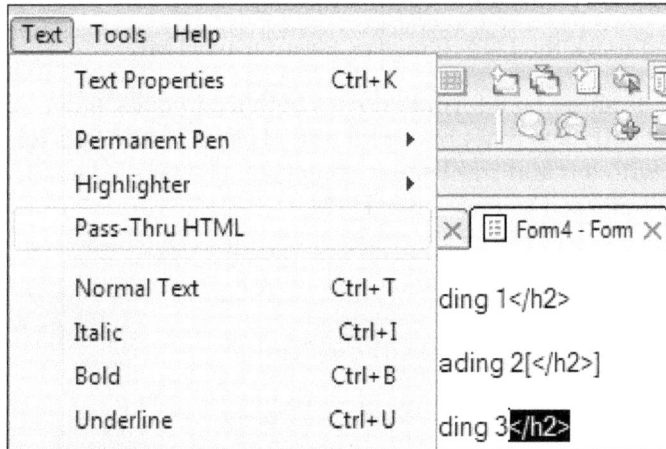

Also, check **Render pass through HTML in Notes** on the **Info** tab of **Form Properties**.

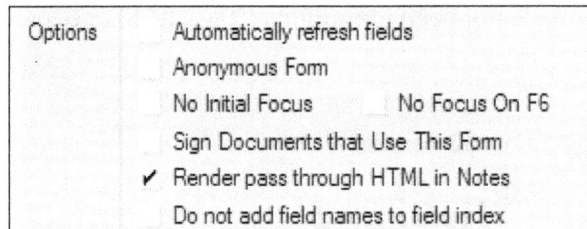

Note that not all layout HTML tags are interpreted by Notes.

Use view template forms to display views

Here is an unadorned basic web view as provided by Domino. This view displays some hotspots above and below the list of documents, the view title, and the documents themselves. Many older applications displayed views similar to this one whenever they were launched on the Web.

⇦Previous ⇨Next ⬦Expand ⇁Collapse 🔍Search

All Customers 1

Last Name	First Name	Age	City
Tarzan	ApeMan	48	JungleVille
Pluto	Dog	24	Paris
Duck	Huey	5	Ducktown
Duck	Dewey	5	Ducktown
Duck	Louie	5	Ducktown

⇦Previous ⇨Next ⬦Expand ⇁Collapse 🔍Search

The default view is functional but not very inspiring, and it certainly does not present Domino in a good light. The layout is the default layout for views. If you see this kind of view in one of your older applications, you have found an excellent candidate for rehabilitation. Several additional classic techniques for improving these basic views are presented in a later chapter. Here we focus on using a special kind of form called a **view template**.

A view template is a form that serves as a container for a view. Because the view template is a form, additional buttons, text, and fields can be added to it. When Domino prepares a view for display on the Web, it looks for an appropriate view template, and if it finds one, it inserts the view in the template and then transmits the template+view source to the browser for rendering.

If a single generic layout is suitable for all views, then create a single form with the following name:

```
$$ViewTemplateDefault
```

To provide a layout for a specific view, create a view template form and name it in this manner, which includes the name of the view for which the template is defined. In this case, allcustomers2 is the alias for the view.

```
$$ViewTemplate for allcustomers2
```

Somewhere on the view template form, define a container for the view. There are two ways to do this:

- Create a field named $$ViewBody
- Create an Embedded Element / View

In Designer, a view template with a $$ViewBody field might look similar to the following example:

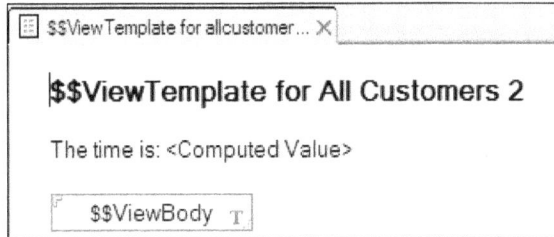

Rendered in a browser, the template+view includes all elements of each. The view template's action buttons are included at the top of the form. If the view also contains action buttons, they also display at the top of the form in the same row.

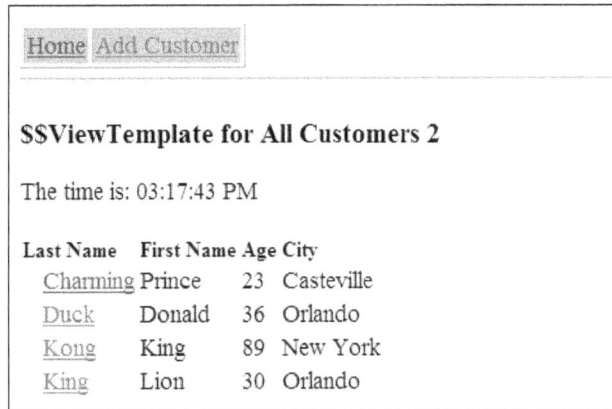

If an embedded view is placed in a view template as the container for the view, enable the property **Choose a View based on a formula**. Leave the formula blank or null.

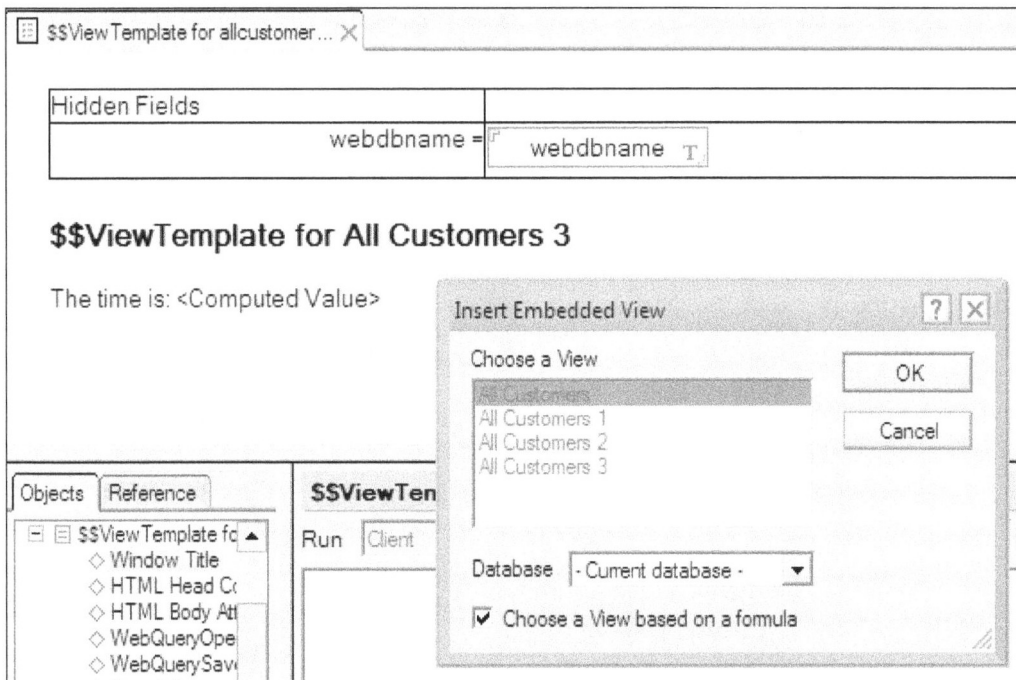

An embedded view control can use either HTML or the **Java View applet** to display the view in the browser. Each of these options offers some advantages and disadvantages, discussed at greater length in a later chapter. View templates can be styled either with CSS or with Properties.

Use framesets for layout

Framesets were at one time a common technique used to display multiple panes in a browser window. A top frame might contain a banner and some hotspots. The left-hand frame might contain a menu of links. The rest of the screen might contain the view or another page.

The use of framesets lost favor due to the way earlier browsers handled frame printing and navigation, and also because of difficulties presented to screen reader technologies. Contemporary browsers handle these issues more satisfactorily, so framesets are not as problematic as once they were. If your existing application already uses a frameset, then you may have no choice but to stick with it. But if you are crafting a new application, and if the application can be done without a frameset, then you might consider designing without one.

If you use a frameset, be sure to provide a frameset title.

To designate the frameset as the initial element to be displayed when the application opens, select the **Open designated Frameset** option on the **Launch** tab of **Database Properties**.

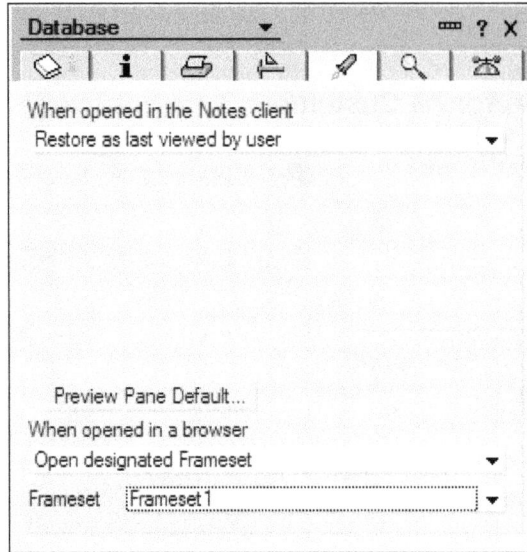

In this example, a basic three-frame frameset forms the basis for the application. A banner page is attached to the top frame. A page with a menu of links is attached to the left-hand frame. A view is attached to the main frame. Since a view template is defined for this view, the main frame contains the template+view. Note that a **Customer** form was previously defined and several test documents were created to better understand how this layout might look with data in it. Prototypes like this can be built very quickly in Designer.

Further work is needed, of course, to create other required forms, to style the design elements, and to extend the navigational features; but the basic layout for the application is now defined.

Use <div> tags to replace framesets

It is possible to achieve a good layout without framesets by using HTML `<div>` tags and some CSS positional styling. This example is intended to demonstrate how `<div>` tags and CSS can be used to create a sectioned page without a frameset.

First, create a new page with some Pass-Thru HTML and some hotspot links to other design elements. Note the use of three HTML divisions. Each division simulates a frame in a frameset. Hotspot links to views and to the About and Using documents are included.

```
Main Page - Page  X
    <div id="banner">
    Toontown Motors
    </div>
    <div id="leftmenu">

    Left Hand Menu

    All Customers

    All Customers 1

    All Customers 2

    All Customers 3

    About

    Using

    </div>
    <div id="main">
    Welcome to Toontown Motors!

    Click on a link to open that view or document.
    </div>
```

To establish the window position for each division (and some other styling), CSS rules are written as a page element named `CSS Rules | websandbox03.css` saved in the application template. In the rules, note the position, top and left declarations in particular. These are the attributes that fix the divisions on the page in specific locations. Please keep in mind that CSS is a rich language in its own right, and there are other ways to achieve interesting layout results with it.

```
/* CSS Rules for ViewTemplate */
#banner {
  position: absolute;
  top: 25px;
  left: 0;
  width: 100%;
  border-bottom: solid 1px black;
  padding-left: 50px;
  padding-bottom: 20px;
  color: #7F0000;
  font-size: 20pt;
  }
#leftmenu {
  position: absolute;
  top:76px;
  left: 10px;
  height: 100%;
  border-right: solid 1px black;
  padding: 10px;
  color: #FF0000;
  }
#main {
  position: absolute;
  top:80px;
  left: 160px;
  padding: 20px;
  color: #0000FF;
  }
```

The linkage between the CSS page element and the main page is contained in the @formula coded in the page's **HTML Head Content** area.

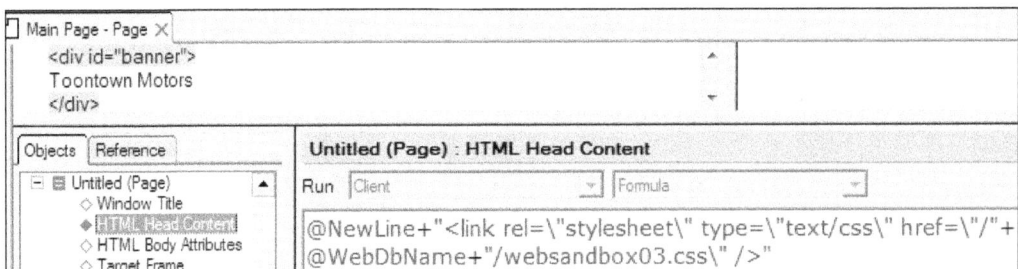

Here is the result, rendered in a browser.

Alternatively, a view template with HTML divisions can be embedded in a single-frame frameset, and the database launch property could be configured to launch that frameset, although this somewhat defeats our ambition of doing away with framesets.

Align fields

Left alone, fields on forms generally do not line up the way you might like them to. Here are three techniques which can be used to create a more orderly appearance.

Use tables to align fields

Add one or more tables to a form. For a single column of fields, place labels in the left-hand column and fields in the right-hand column. Use Designer or CSS styling as desired to remove cell and table borders, and to adjust cell width, padding, and other characteristics. Using tables to align fields is easy to do, and tables are easy to style. On the downside, the result is just rows and columns. More interesting layouts can be achieved by nesting tables within tables and by merging cells.

Use <div> and <label> tags to align fields

A table-like arrangement of fields can be created with HTML tags and CSS styling. The `<label>` tags enhance a form for users of screen readers. Each label / field combination is coded into its own division.

```
<div><label for="CustLast">Last Name</label>    CustLast  T </div>

<div><label for="CustFirst">First Name</label>    CustFirst  T </div>

<div><label for="CustAge">Age</label>    CustAge  T </div>

<div><label for="CustCity">City</label>    CustCity  T </div>
```

CSS rules can be written to style the labels and input fields.

```
div label {
   background-color: #DFE7F2;
   color: Black;
   float: left;
   font-family: Verdana;
   font-size: 10pt;
   padding-right: .25em;
   text-align: right;
   width: 10em;
   }
div input.txt {
   display: inline;
   float: left;
   width: 10em;
   }
```

Note that an ID equal to the name of the field is entered on the **HTML tab** of **Field Properties**. Likewise, the CSS class **txt** is entered for the **Class** attribute.

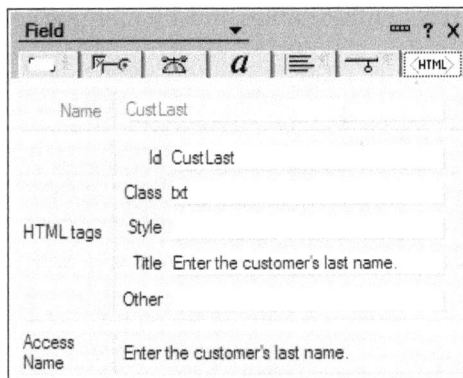

Field		▼	▦ ? X
	📑	🔒	a ≡ 🖉 HTML
Name	CustLast		
	Id	CustLast	
	Class	txt	
HTML tags	Style		
	Title	Enter the customer's last name.	
	Other		
Access Name	Enter the customer's last name.		

Here is the result as rendered by a browser:

Last Name	
First Name	
Age	
City	

Adjust the size of any specific field by entering an HTML attribute for that field: **size=50**.

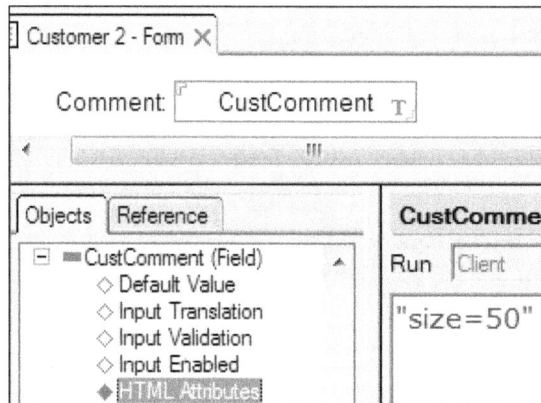

Customer 2 - Form ×

Comment: CustComment T

Objects | Reference   **CustComme**

⊟ ▬CustComment (Field)   Run | Client
  ◇ Default Value
  ◇ Input Translation   "size=50"
  ◇ Input Validation
  ◇ Input Enabled
  ◆ HTML Attributes

Or enter a CSS declaration into the **Style** attribute on the **Field Extra HTML** tab of **Field Properties**: **width: 30em**.

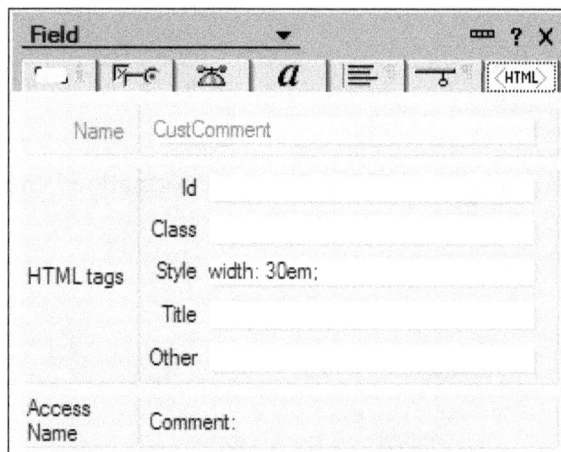

Field ▼   ▭ ? X

Name   CustComment

  Id
  Class
HTML tags   Style   width: 30em;
  Title
  Other

Access Name   Comment:

Use <fieldset> and <legend> tags to group related fields

Onscreen elements which naturally belong together should be co-located and identified in some way as belonging together. On the Web, try using `<fieldset>` and `<legend>` tags for a sharp, professional look.

```
<fieldset>
<legend>Personal Information</legend>
<div><label for="CustLast">Last Name</label>    CustLast  T </div>

<div><label for="CustFirst">First Name</label>    CustFirst  T </div>

<div><label for="CustAge">Age</label>    CustAge  T </div>

<div><label for="CustCity">City</label>    CustCity  T </div>
</fieldset>
```

Define CSS rules for the `<fieldset>` and `<legend>` tags.

```
fieldset {
  border-right: solid 2px #000;
  border-bottom: solid 2px #000;
  float: left;
  margin: 0;
  padding: 1em;
  width: 30em;
  }
legend {
  color: #7F0000;
  font-family: Arial;
  font-size: 110%;
  font-weight: Bold;
  margin-bottom: 1em;
  }
```

The result as rendered makes it clear that certain information belongs together.

Using computed text

Using computed text with @formulas that resolve to lines of text is an easy way to customize forms and pages.

Display a customized title bar

Add a simple formula to an element's Window Title property.

```
"Sandbox 1 - Time: " + @Text(@Now;"D1S1")
```

The computed text displays in the browser's title bar.

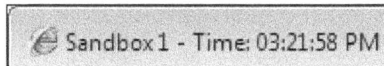

The result of a computation must be a text string. Here is computed text that fails to display on the Web.

```
"It is now: " + @Now
```

This formula generates an HTTP 500 error because the value of @Now is not text. Correct this by converting a non-text result with @Text.

```
"It is now: " + @Text(@Now)
```

Display customized messages

Customized messages can be presented on a form with computed text. Here is a simple computed text formula:

```
"Welcome " + @Name([CN];@UserName)
```

If computed text Properties formatting attributes fail to affect the look of the computed text in the browser, you can surround the computed text on the form with <span> tags and style attributes. Make sure to mark the <span> tags as Pass-Thru HTML.

```
<span style="color:Red;font-size=20pt"><Computed Value></span>
```

Using hidden computed fields

Using hidden computed fields on a form is an easy way to provide information to @formulas and JavaScript that run in support of a form. Normally, hidden fields are collected at the top or the bottom of a form. Since some fields depend upon others, the order of fields on the form may be important, with dependent fields positioned after independent ones.

Hidden fields serve many purposes. Here is a sampling of how these fields can be used.

Add fields to provide access to key document attributes

Some document attributes can be retrieved by invoking @functions in formulas. There are, however, situations in which you cannot rely on @functions and formulas to return the correct information.

For example, the name of the form used to create a document is not available until after the document has been saved. If the name of the form is important to either a form formula, some JavaScript, or an agent invoked by the WebQuerySave event, then create a hidden Computed when composed Text field (for example, named FormName) and set its value to the name of the form. Form formulas, JavaScript, and agents can refer to this value instead.

Access CGI variables

Many CGI variables are available and can be used in @formulas and JavaScript codes. See Designer help for a complete list of the CGI variables.

To access one of these variables, code a hidden Computed for display field whose name is identical to the CGI variable (for example, Server_Name). Provide a default value for the field that is also equivalent to the name of the CGI variable name.

If CGI variables are used routinely in web applications, consider creating a common subform that lists all the CGI variables; copy this subform into all your applications and insert it at the top of every form that needs it.

Improve @DbLookup and @DbColumn formulas

@DbLookUp and @DbColumn functions are powerful and often used to retrieve data from views or documents by key. These functions access a view, locate one or more documents containing the key (as displayed in the view), and retrieve either a single value or a column of values. In web applications, especially in earlier versions of Domino, errors in these formulas caused HTTP 404 errors, and forms would not display. To prevent problems like this, consider using the [FailSilent] keyword option on @DbLookup formulas.

Consider trapping errors dynamically if they do occur. A formula like this returns either valid data or the error message.

```
rv := @If(!@IsDocBeingEdited;@Return(@Unavailable);@DbLookup(...) );
@If(@IsError(rv); @Text(rv); rv)
```

Using HTML to add value to a form or page

Adding HTML tags is sometimes necessary to dress up a page or to gain control of form and page elements. But adding unnecessary HTML tags and attributes clutters up a source page, takes longer to build and transmit, and may not add any real value. If you can achieve layout or formatting effects with CSS, remove the HTML tags.

HTML can be added to a form or page in many places. While this demonstrates the flexibility of Designer, it also can make it difficult to rework a design, especially if the HTML is tucked away in many places. Look for HTML tags and attributes in any of these locations:

- The HTML Head Content area
- Forms or pages as Pass-Thru HTML
- The computed text
- The field formulas
- The field attributes
- The special $$ fields
- The properties of many elements

You need to be aware that HTML can also be found in other design elements, especially in these locations:

- View headings and columns
- LotusScript Print statements
- JavaScript code

Unless you specify a form content type of HTML, Domino automatically adds several HTML tags (and closing tags); you do not need to code any of the following:

- `DOCTYPE`
- `html`
- `head`
- `body`
- `form` (for the primary form)
- `script` (for JavaScript added in the JS Header or in field events)

You could code the following HTML tags if appropriate to your application:

- `script` (in the HTML Head Content area to identify CSS rules and JavaScript functions)
- `form` (on a form design element to identify a second form)

Here are two key recommendations:

- Avoid styling and formatting with HTML; use CSS instead
- Avoid using inline CSS and JavaScript; place CSS rules and JavaScript functions on separate pages, in stylesheet resources or in JavaScript libraries

Use special fields

If you need to supply a custom DOCTYPE declaration for a form, create a Computed for display field named `$$HTMLFrontMatter` on your form with an appropriate formula. Domino then will not automatically add a `DOCTYPE` statement; instead, it will insert the result of your formula before the `<html>` tag.

If for some reason you need to add attributes to the `<html>` tag, you can create a Computed for display field named `$$HTMLTagAttributes` on your form with an appropriate formula. The result of your formula is included as `<html>` tag attributes.

In a similar manner, you can create a Computed for display field named `$$HTMLHead` with an appropriate formula specifying items to be placed after the `<head>` tag.

- Title
- Metadata
- JavaScript global variables
- Links to CSS and JavaScript Libraries

These items can also be coded as the result of an @formula in a form or page HTML Head Content area.

Domino supports adding a field named `HTML` to a form. The value of the field is an @formula which results in valid HTML.

The primary value in using any of these special fields lies in the ability to use an @formula to dynamically modify the HTML when a document is prepared for transmission to the browser. If all HTML is static, coding tags as Pass-Thru HTML directly on the form may be the more appropriate thing to do.

Convert between Notes and HTML

If you cannot view the HTML page source with a browser, then it may be useful to look at the HTML code that Domino generates, while you are in Designer. Select a button, field or other element and then try the following menu command.

Edit | Convert to HTML

To revert, place the cursor in the middle of the HTML and try the following menu command.

Edit | Convert to Notes Format

Be sure to save the form or page before doing a conversion, as you may lose fidelity.

Creating pseudo Action Bars for the Web

Action Bars generated automatically by Domino for the Web reside at the top of a form, page, or view, just as they do in the Notes client. By default, these buttons are pretty basic, even unattractive. Here is an example of an Action Bar rendered with HTML.

Action Bars can be displayed with the **Action Bar Java applet**, and the buttons then can be styled to a certain extent, which is an improvement from a style point-of-view. But the Java applet can be slow to load and problematic in other ways.

Rendered with HTML or with the Java applet, the Action Bar is still stuck at the top of the form.

Consider moving the functions assigned to the Action Bar buttons to a set of buttons or hotspots positioned elsewhere on the form. Such buttons can be laid out in a table and styled extensively with CSS.

An independent set of buttons can then be placed above or below the banner. A second set of these buttons can be arrayed along the bottom of the form, if desired.

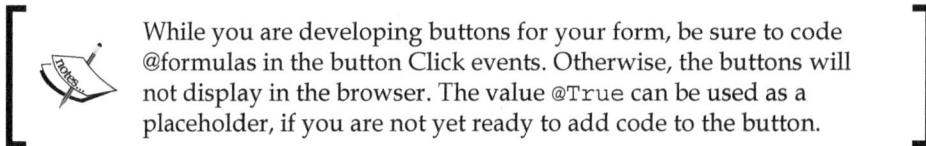

> While you are developing buttons for your form, be sure to code @formulas in the button Click events. Otherwise, the buttons will not display in the browser. The value @True can be used as a placeholder, if you are not yet ready to add code to the button.

A later chapter illustrates in more detail how CSS rules can be used to style Action Bar buttons as well as independent buttons.

Summary

Web applications rely on forms and pages extensively. Pages inform users and forms collect data from them. Creating attractive forms and pages can be challenging, especially considering the variety of tools a developer has at his disposal. This chapter has provided selected tips and recommendations applicable to designing forms and pages for Domino web applications.

4
Navigation

Navigating from page to page or from view to form and back again presents some challenges for Domino web developers. The browser menu and toolbars are of little use to an application, and almost everything required for a page to make decisions and to proceed to the next page must be contained on the page itself.

Navigation styles and strategies should be consistent within an application, and if at all possible, the same styles and strategies should be implemented across related applications. Consistency and familiarity facilitate user learning; experience with one application transfers directly to a similar application, shortening the learning curve, and improving user productivity. Development of new applications, of course, can be hastened if similar strategies are consistently employed within the organization.

Topics in this chapter highlight a number of navigational issues and how these issues can be addressed in Domino web applications:

- Launching an application
- Creating menus of links and hotspots
- Directing the browser after a document is submitted or cancelled
- Coding default error pages
- Providing directions and help

General precautions

Some design practices that seem expedient in the moment can be problematic in the long term as they create problems for managing or using an application. It is tempting to take shortcuts, especially if an application is needed quickly or if it is expected to be of only temporary value. Resist such temptations.

Do not hardcode URLs, filenames, or UNIDs

It should go without saying that applications should never hardcode specific URLs. A link to a specific website, server, directory path, or filename is almost guaranteed to break eventually, as applications move from server to server and from directory to directory.

Use @WebDbName

Links from one design element to other elements within an application are typically constructed as relative links, while links to external resources are naturally coded as absolute links. Links attached to buttons or hotspots typically derive from @formulas or JavaScript code. Of course, a button or hotspot formula also can do some processing (for example, setting the value of a field or saving a document) before passing the link to the browser.

In older code, you may find formulas that create relative links using various constructions, some of which may become problematic as your network changes. The most common problems of this sort are URLs which contain:

- Blanks (spaces)
- Backslashes
- Incorrect file path casing (depends upon the server)

Here are some examples:

This formula extracts the directory path and filename of the current database, and then opens the default view. There is nothing inherently wrong with this construction, unless the path name contains blanks or backslashes:

```
pathname := Subset(@DbName;-1);
@URLOpen("/" + pathname + "/$defaultview?OpenView");
```

To avoid any potential problems with filenames containing blanks (for example, Human Resources Records.nsf), developers can explicitly replace each blank in the path name with the string %20 or a plus sign, which is an improvement:

```
pathname := @ReplaceSubstring(@Subset(@DbName;-1);" ";"+");
@URLOpen("/" + pathname + "/$defaultview?OpenView");
```

The resulting path name contains no blanks, but it still may contain backslashes if the application resides within a subfolder on the server. Domino is very accommodating about serving URLs that contain backslashes, but some web proxies and authentication servers may not be so forgiving. So developers can account for both backslashes and blanks:

```
pathname := @ReplaceSubstring (@Subset(@DbName;-1) ; "\\":" " ;
                                                        "/":"+");
@URLOpen("/" + pathname + "/$defaultview?OpenView");
```

In the older code, written before the @WebDbName function was introduced, you may see this less elegant construction which replaces the blanks with plus signs and then replaces backslashes with forward slashes:

```
pathname := @ReplaceSubstring(@ReplaceSubstring
                    (@Subset(@DbName;-1);" ";"+");"\\";"/");
@URLOpen("/" + pathname + "/$defaultview?OpenView");
```

While these last two formulas address blanks and backslashes adequately, it is a good idea to replace such formulas when you come across them. Use the @WebDbName function, which should assure an acceptable web-encoded path name, regardless of the characters used to name the directory or file:

```
pathname := @WebDbName;
@URLOpen("/" + pathname + "/$defaultview?OpenView");
```

In a similar manner, avoid hardcoding references to the path and filenames of related databases (for example, a log file). Should the location or name of the related database change, the developer is forced to make design changes, which can interrupt production while the changes are made, tested, and rolled out. To address this issue, create a configuration or application profile document with fields to hold the names of those related databases; use @DbLookup formulas to retrieve those values as needed. Record file and application dependencies and provide that information to the Domino administrators and other interested parties. See the topic *Use configuration documents* in *Chapter 2, Design and Development Strategies*, for other suggestions.

Use $Ref

If a parent document's UNID is available in a field on a child document, then a formula for a URL can be constructed to direct the browser back to the parent document either by way of a $$Return field or a button's Click event. The parent document might be the desired "next page" if a child document is submitted or otherwise exited.

A somewhat obscure problem can arise when a response document permanently records the **UNID** of its parent document. For example, if a response document defines a field with this formula, then the UNID of the parent document is saved in the response document when the response document is saved:

```
@Text(@InheritedDocumentUniqueID)
```

Or a response document might be designed such that a field inherits the UNID of the parent from a field on the parent document (the default value of the response document field is the name of the parent document field). If the parent UNID is stored in the parent document, then when the response document is created, the parent UNID is copied into the corresponding response document field.

The parent UNID is then included in a link formula on a button on the response document, and all seems well. For example, if the response document field ParUNID contains the parent UNID, then the following formula should open the parent document from the AllDocs view. And indeed it does in the original database:

```
@URLOpen("/" + @WebDbName + "/AllDocs/" + @Text(ParUNID))
```

But if the parent and response documents are at some future time copied to another database, new UNIDs are assigned to the new parent and new response documents, but the UNID values previously saved in parent and response document fields are not changed. Clicking the response document's button fails because the link formula now refers to a UNID which does not exist in the new database.

To avoid this problem, use the reserved field **$Ref** which automatically contains the UNID of the response document's parent. This value is updated properly if parent and response documents are copied to another database. Replace the reference to the ParUNID field with a reference to $Ref as in the following link formula:

```
@URLOpen("/" + @WebDbName + "/AllDocs/"  +@Text($Ref))
```

Use a "go forward" navigational strategy on the Web

One of the most vexing navigational issues concerns the browser's **Back** button. In simple browsing from page to page, the **Back** button works well in returning the user to the previously viewed page, assuming that page is in the browser cache. But in applications that include filling in and submitting forms, the browser's **Back** button presents a number of difficulties, including the likelihood of asking the user to back through an editable version of a form and then through a read-only version of the form that displays old data. At the very least, this can be confusing and tedious. Were the changes saved or not?

Several strategies were presented in *Chapter 3, Forms and Pages,* for determining which page displays after a successful document submit or save, and several more are presented in this chapter. None of these strategies rely on using the browser 's **Back** button or JavaScript using the browser history to go back a page:

```
history.go(-1)
```

If the browser's **Back** button (or `history.go(-1)`) does exactly what you want it to do, then okay. But as a rule a web application should implement a "go forward" approach for every action, even if going forward means directing the browser to display a previous page. Never require the user to click the browser's **Back** button and do not rely on manipulating the browser history, as these provide unreliable navigation.

Avoid generating complex dynamic pages

As discussed in *Chapter 3*, a `$$Return` field is a good mechanism for specifying the URL of the next page to be displayed in the browser. The text created by the @formula in `$$Return` can be arbitrarily complex, and it is tempting to use the `$$Return` field to do more than simply direct the browser to the next page. For example, this @formula added to a `$$Return` field presents a small post-save message:

```
"<html><body>" +
"<h1>Success!</h1>" +
"<p>You have successfully saved this form.</p>" +
"<p>Please click on the following link the return to the home page.
</p>"+
"<a href='/" + @WebDbName+"' target='_top'>Home Page</a>" +
"</body></html>";
```

When the document is saved, a "page" is displayed that presents a short message and then provides a clickable link that returns to the application's launch element. Note the use of the `target=` attribute on the link, which directs the browser to open the link in the top-most window. This construction is useful when using framesets; if the target is not specified, unexpected results may occur, such as opening the homepage of an application within a frame of the homepage!

`$$Return` formulas can be very elaborate, for example displaying a customized menu of links derived from attributes of the document just saved. LotusScript agents and JavaScript functions can be coded to create and display complex pages as well.

Compared to creating a normal form or page element, using dynamically generated pages can be more difficult both to code and to debug. If you are unfamiliar with the application design, troubleshooting is more problematic as you must first determine where the page is coming from (`$$Return`, LotusScript, JavaScript, Java).

In general, if you need to display a page, create a real page element and open it with @URLOpen or any of the other techniques previously discussed. If you need to present customized messages, create a real response form that inherits values from the saved parent and open that.

Application launch options

Every application opens to some major design element when launched — a page, a frameset, the About document, and so on. Which **Default Launch Element** (DLE) to use is a topic of some discussion. Tastes and requirements differ. Fortunately, several choices exist for launching Domino applications.

Which element initially displays may depend upon organizational policy or application objectives. By default the web client launch option is the same as the Notes client launch option, but you can choose a different launch option for web users.

Check to see if there is a standard way to launch Domino applications in your organization. If not, consider several options as discussed in this section. There is no "right answer" here. Each option offers advantages and perhaps some disadvantages.

Select a web launch option from the **Launch** tab of **Database Properties**:

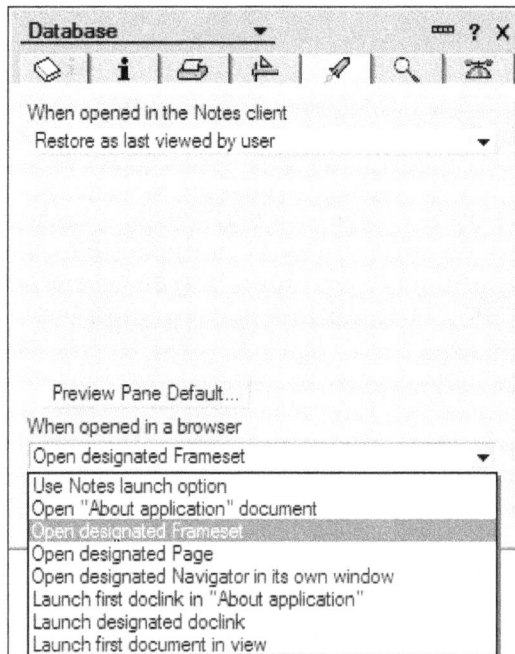

Launch the About document

The About document can present a copyright notice, organizational policy statements, or release information about the current application.

Add some meaningful "link text" to the About document. Select that text and create a **Link Hotspot** or an **Action Hotspot**. Select a design element or add a formula to the hotspot to designate the design element that should open when the hotspot is clicked:

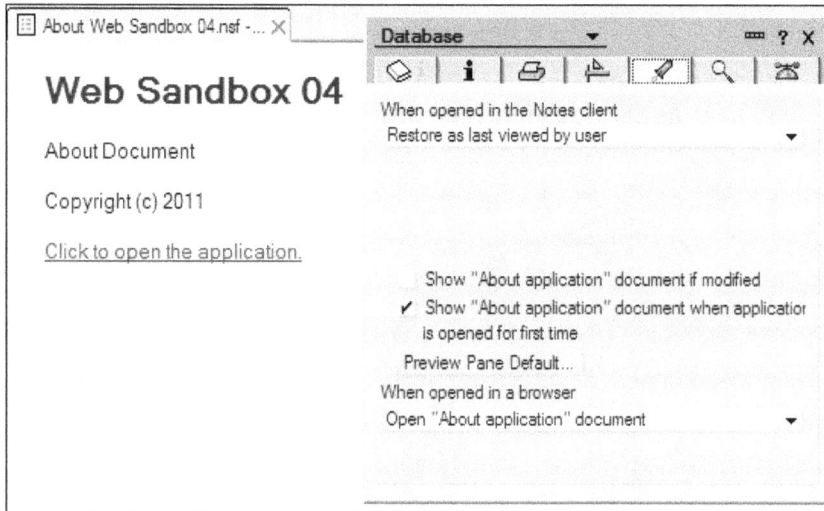

To change the hotspot, place the cursor in the hotspot and select either the Hotspot Properties or Edit Hotspot menu item (depending upon which type of hotspot you defined) from the Hotspot menu.

Select the web launch option to open the About document in **Database Properties**. When the application launches, the About document is displayed. The user clicks the hotspot to open the designated element:

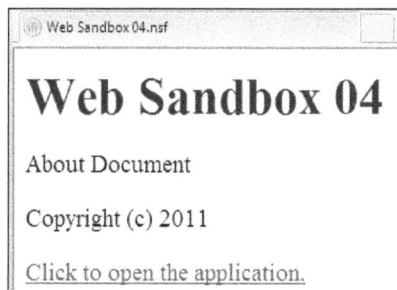

Launch a specific homepage

It might be appropriate to launch a traditional web homepage. Create the homepage. Note the page alias in **Page Properties**:

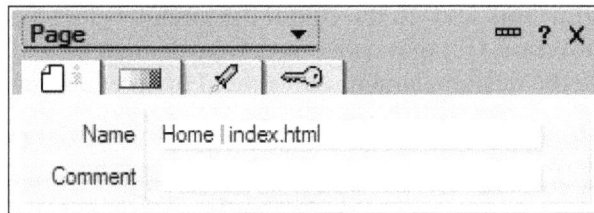

Select the homepage as the web launch option in **Database Properties**:

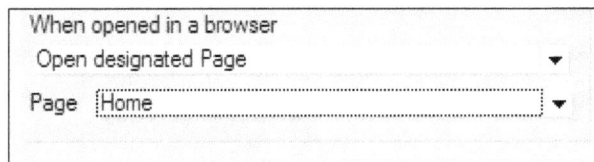

Note that the page alias can also be used in the URL:

Launch a frameset

Framesets are sometimes frowned upon as they can be problematic for screen readers, navigation, and printing. However, if the application uses (or requires) a frameset, one can be designated as the web launch option:

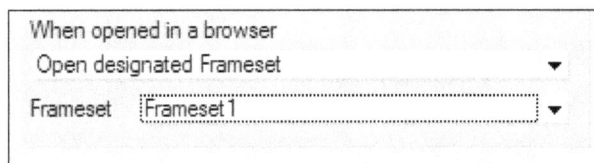

Launch a view

You may want to launch the application to a view. If you look at the list of web launch options, launching to a view is not one of them. But there are ways this can be accomplished.

View templates were discussed in *Chapter 3* as a way to associate a form with a view. If the view template is then attached to a frame within a single-frame frameset, the application can be launched to that frameset, and the view + template will open.

Another way to launch a view is a little more complicated to set up, but it avoids using a frameset.

First, create a blank Navigator element called `index.html`. Yes, this is really blank.

Second, create a form named **$$NavigatorTemplate for index.html**. Add an embedded view and whatever other form elements (for example, headings, buttons) might be required.

In the following example, a prominent heading displays at the top of the form followed by some guidance text, **Previous** and **Next** buttons, and the embedded view itself. Note that the embedded view is set to display **Using HTML** and that only 10 rows display at a time. To advance to the second 10 lines, the user clicks the **Next** button. This is the form as seen in the Designer:

Finally, select the **index.html** navigator as the web launch option in
Database Properties.

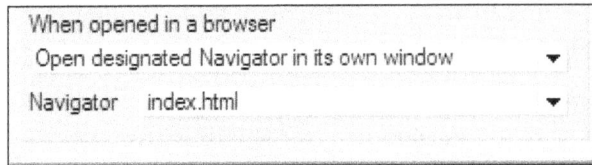

```
When opened in a browser
  Open designated Navigator in its own window        ▼

Navigator    index.html                              ▼
```

Here's how this option looks in the browser:

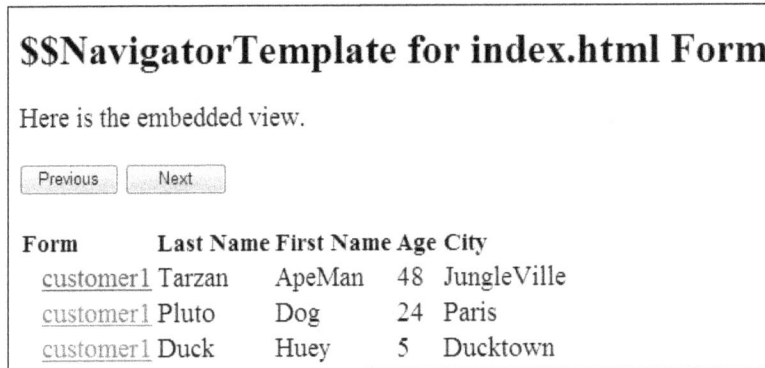

$$NavigatorTemplate for index.html Form

Here is the embedded view.

[Previous]   [Next]

Form	Last Name	First Name	Age	City
customer1	Tarzan	ApeMan	48	JungleVille
customer1	Pluto	Dog	24	Paris
customer1	Duck	Huey	5	Ducktown

Launch a form

Launching to an empty form for a survey, registration, or something similar might
be desirable, but is no specific web launch option for this. Here is one way to
launch a form without using a frameset, although there are drawbacks to this trick.

Create a blank page. In the HTML Head Content area of the page, add an @formula,
the result of which is a small JavaScript that redirects the browser to open a specific
form. Here is a formula that opens the "Survey" form:

```
url := "/" + @WebDbName + "/Survey?OpenForm";
"<script type='text/javascript'>" +
  @NewLine +
"window.location = '" + url + "'" +
  @NewLine +
"</script>"
```

Select the page as the web launch option in **Database Properties**. When the
application opens, the page loads and immediately directs the browser to open
the form.

One drawback to this approach is that the browser's **Back** button cannot be used to return to a page *before* the application was opened. As soon as the **Back** button is clicked, the page redirects the browser to display the form. Be sure to provide good post-save and post-cancel navigation with the form.

A somewhat more complicated @formula introduces a 3,000 millisecond (3 second) delay before the browser is redirected to the form. With this approach, the initial page displays for a short time, allowing the user to use the browser's **Back** button:

```
url := "/" + @WebDbName + "/Survey?OpenForm";
"<script type='text/javascript'>" +
  @NewLine +
"window.setTimeout('window.location='" + url + " ',3000);" +
  @NewLine +
"</script>"
```

If you take this approach, treat the initial page like a splash screen and dress it up with some text that explains what is going on. It is also good practice to add a hotspot to the page that the user can click to proceed manually to the form in case the JavaScript approach fails. A button with this simple @formula suffices:

```
@Command([Compose];"Survey")
```

Launch a graphical navigator

Graphical navigators, perhaps more than framesets, have fallen out of favor as entry points for web applications, although they are still found in existing applications, and some users like them. In essence, a navigator is a page-like element with images or text hotspots. The hotspots link to or launch other elements, such as views, forms, or framesets.

In general, graphical navigators are a bit harder to maintain than other design elements, and they offer fewer design options. Being graphical, they are more problematic for screen readers. As you can attach graphics and images to pages and forms, you should think about replacing graphical navigators with other design elements.

But if you choose to use one, be sure to enable the **Web browser compatible** attribute on the **Info** tab of **Navigator Properties**. Otherwise, the navigator will not display on the Web. Then select it as the web launch option in **Database Properties**.

Launch documents in context using Auto Frame

If you are using a frameset, you may want a document always to open inside a frame within the frameset. As long as users open the application using the intended launch element, things work as designed. But if a user bookmarks a specific document or perhaps receives e-mail with a URL pointing to a specific document, then clicking on that bookmark or URL may not open the document within the specific frameset as intended. To force a document to open within the frameset context, set the **Auto Frame** options on the **Launch** tab of **Form Properties**. Select a frameset and a frame:

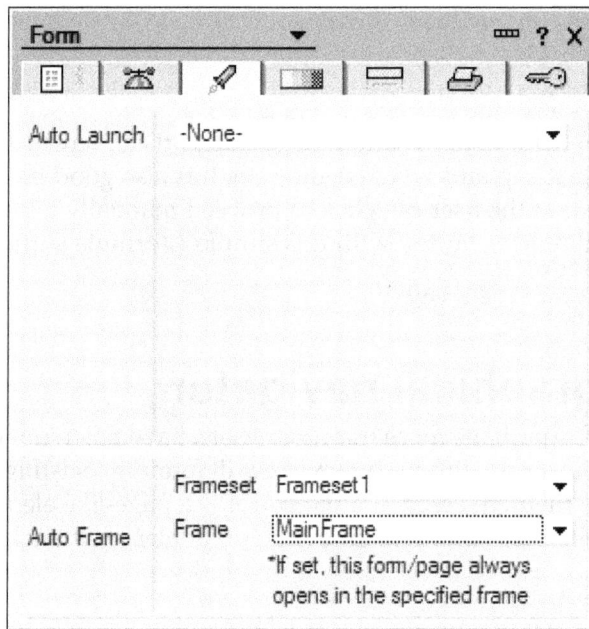

Form	▼	▭ ? X
🔳 🖇 ✒ 🔲 ▭ 🖨 🗝		

Auto Launch   -None-   ▼

Frameset Frameset 1   ▼

Auto Frame   Frame   MainFrame   ▼

*If set, this form/page always opens in the specified frame

With this option enabled, opening a document launches the designated frameset as well.

Unfortunately, if you are using a single form for both web and Notes clients, then enabling **Auto Frame** will also launch the frameset in Notes. This may not be desirable. If you want the frameset to open in a browser but not in Notes, create two forms, one for Notes and one for the Web, and then set the **Auto Frame** options differently for the two forms.

Creating a custom application login form

If parts of an application are allowed to anonymous users and other parts are reserved to authenticated users, you can implement your own "login" form. This technique requires several components to work together.

First, the server must be enabled for HTTP Session authentication. This is a setting on the server document in the Domino Directory. As a developer, you may not be privileged to change server documents, so contact your Domino administrator for assistance. Here is a sample of what the setting might look like:

| Basics | Security | Ports... | Server Tasks... | Internet Protocols... |

| HTTP | Domino Web Engine | DIIOP | LDAP |

HTTP Sessions	
Session authentication:	Single Server
Idle session timeout:	30 minutes
Force login on SSL:	No
Maximum active sessions:	1000

Second, the application's ACL should include an entry for **Anonymous** with **Author** access and any other privileges or roles that might be required:

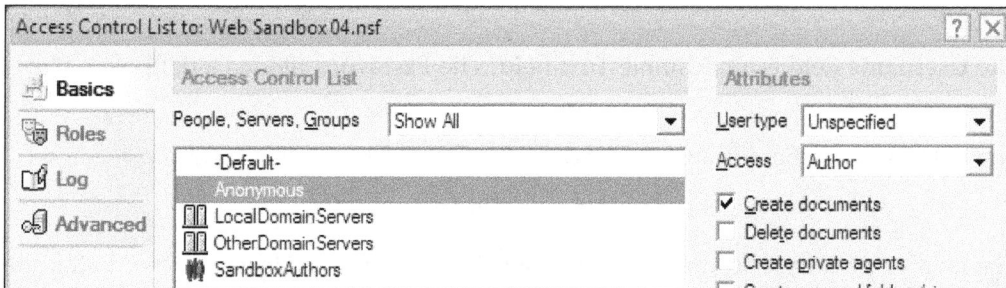

Access Control List to: Web Sandbox 04.nsf

Basics	Access Control List		Attributes	
Roles	People, Servers, Groups	Show All	User type	Unspecified
Log	-Default-		Access	Author
Advanced	Anonymous		☑ Create documents
	LocalDomainServers		☐ Delete documents
	OtherDomainServers		☐ Create private agents
	SandboxAuthors		

Third, create a customized login form. The following is an example of a login form as it might look in the Designer. Below the image are several notes about the form:

```
</form>
    SaveOptions  T   Server_Name  T

Login Form
<form method="post" action="/names.nsf?login" name="loginform" target="_top">
              UserName   Username  T

              Password   Password  *

<input value="Login" type="submit" class="button">
<input name="RedirectTo" value="  URLforLogin  T " type="hidden">
</form>

<script type="text/javascript">
document.forms[1].Username.focus();
</script>
```

Note that the Domino-generated form is closed with the first `</form>` end tag, and a new form with the name **loginform** follows. It is necessary to close the Domino-generated HTML form in order to specify a different post action, in this case, accessing the **names.nsf** application.

The hidden **SaveOptions** field is set to "0" (with quotes) so that this form is not saved. The hidden **Server_Name** field is set to **Server_Name** (no quotes), which is a CGI variable.

The **Username** field is an Editable Text field. The **Password** field is a field of type Password.

The **URLforLogin** field is a Computed for display field with this formula:

```
"http://" + Server_Name + "/" + @WebDbName
```

The JavaScript at the bottom of the form sets the focus to the **Username** field after the form loads. Form elements can be styled with CSS.

Finally, add a login button or hotspot to your default launch element (for example, the homepage) that launches the customized login form. Use a simple @formula. In this example, the customized login form is called `login`:

```
@Command([Compose];"login")
```

When the user clicks the login hotspot on the homepage, the `login` form displays with the cursor set into the **Username** field:

Login Form

UserName	
Password	

[Login]

After entering a valid username and password, the user is redirected (in this example) back to the homepage.

Control what is seen by Anonymous and what is seen by authenticated users with hide-when formulas that test the value returned by the `@Username` function. When an anonymous user logs in, his user name is "Anonymous". Here is a hide-when formula that prevents associated text or another element from being seen by Anonymous:

```
@If(@Name([CN];@UserName)="Anonymous";@True;@False)
```

Logging out from an application is even simpler than logging in. Provide an action hotspot with an @formula similar to the following. In this example, the user is logged out and returned to the homepage as an Anonymous user:

```
@URLOpen("/" + @WebDbName + "?Logout&RedirectTo=/" + @WebDbName)
```

Creating menus

Onscreen controls and menus of actions and links can be designed in very many ways using several different strategies. A few techniques are illustrated in this section as a starting point.

Create Hotspots

Some people prefer to use buttons to initiate a process and underscored text to link to another page. A **Button Hotspot** looks like a button, and clicking it runs an attached @formula or JavaScript. An **Action Hotspot** looks like a link, but like a button, clicking it executes a formula. A **Link Hotspot** looks and behaves like a traditional link, and clicking it opens the associated URL or named element:

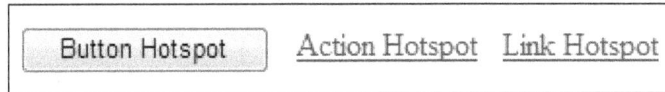

Create a button hotspot with the **Create | Hotspot** submenu. To define an action or link hotspot, select some text on the form or page and then access the same submenu.

Hotspots can be styled with Notes or CSS rules, so you can make them look the way you want them to:

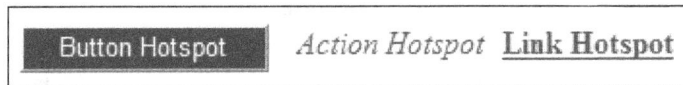

To display a screen tip when a hotspot is hovered with a mouse, add a **Title** on the **HTML** tab of **Hotspot Properties**:

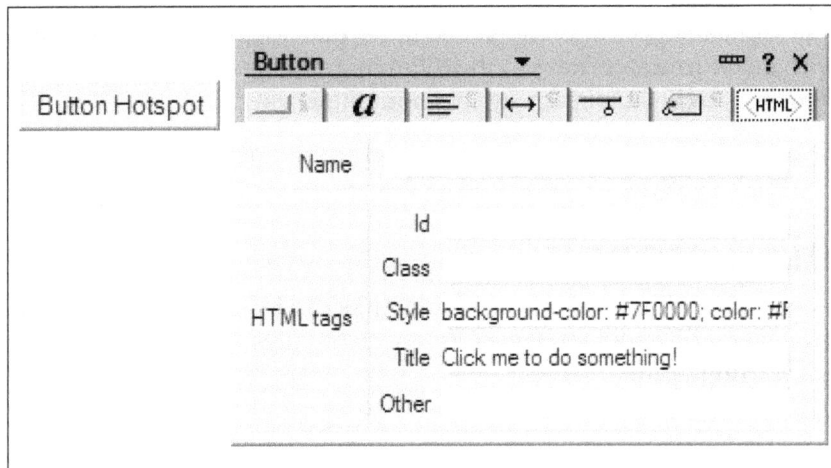

Create menus with outlines

Embedded outline controls offer a lot of flexibility, but it takes effort (and some trial and error) to get one looking the way you want it to. Here are the general steps to this approach:

1. Create an outline design element. Outline entries are similar to hotspots in that they can be links or actions. Add outline entries with links or actions to the outline.

2. Create a page and embed the outline on it with the **Create | Embedded Element** menu item.

3. With **Embedded Outline Properties,** choose to display the outline with HTML or with the Java Applet. Also style the control.

4. Create a frameset and attach the page to a frame in the frameset.

5. Using **Outline Entry Properties, Embedded Outline Properties,** or **Frame Properties**, direct links from the embedded outline to open in another frame.

Here is a sample outline displayed as HTML (essentially a clever table):

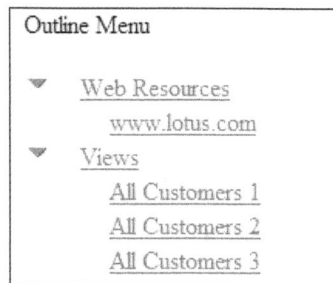

```
Outline Menu

  ▼   Web Resources
              www.lotus.com
  ▼   Views
              All Customers 1
              All Customers 2
              All Customers 3
```

Here is the outline displayed with the Java Applet:

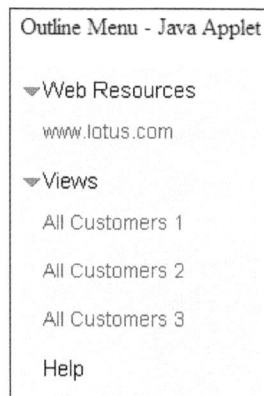

```
Outline Menu - Java Applet

▼Web Resources

  www.lotus.com

▼Views

  All Customers 1

  All Customers 2

  All Customers 3

  Help
```

While there are some drawbacks to using outlines in web applications — styling, performance, and behavior are not always what you expect — they do provide a relatively quick way to create menus.

Create menus with tables

Tables offer a convenient way to arrange hotspots on a form or page. Create a single column table, for example, and then define hotspots within each table cell. Tables and table cells are relatively easy to style with CSS. In this example, the table has a border, but the cells do not. CSS rules can be applied to cells and to the hotspots themselves:

Create menus with HTML and CSS

A little more effort is required to create menus with HTML tags and CSS rules, but this is a flexible technique with few drawbacks. In essence, hotspots are surrounded with <span>, <div>, or <li> tags which are in turn styled with CSS. HTML tags are, of course, marked as Pass-Thru HTML. Here is a simple illustration.

On a form or page, menu headings are surrounded with <div> tags. Menu items are link hotspots surrounded by <li> tags. CSS classes are attached to the <div> and <ul> tags to provide linkage to CSS rules:

The CSS rules are contained on a separate page. Menu headings are rendered in a 12 point font. Links (anchor tags) are not underscored. And when the links are hovered with a mouse, the text color and background color of the links change. A reference to the CSS rules page is contained in an @formula in the HTML Head Content area of the menu form or page, as illustrated in *Chapter 3, Forms and Pages*:

```
.menuheading {
        font-size: 12pt;
        }
.menulist a {
        text-decoration: none;
        }
.menulist a:hover {
        background-color: #DDD;
        color: #FF0000;
        }
```

The resulting menu is basic but serviceable. In this image, the **All Customers 2** hotspot is hovered with the mouse:

Menu 3 - HTML and CSS

Web Resources

- www.lotus.com

Views

- All Customers 1
- All Customers 2
- All Customers 3

Depending upon how good your CSS is, you can craft some really wonderful menus with this technique.

Create dynamic menus with views

A view can be thought of as a menu where each item (row) acts like a hotspot that opens a specific document. As views include all documents that meet specific selection criteria (the **View Selection** formula), when qualified documents are added to the database, they are automatically added to the view and therefore added to the view-as-menu.

Using a view as a dynamic menu may be appropriate in applications where documents are informational: news stories, policies and procedures, meeting minutes, and so on. Here is how this strategy can be implemented. In this example, the application collects and displays help topics.

The solution consists of these design elements:

- A form to create the help topics (for example, **HelpTopic** form).
- A lookup view to index the help topic documents (for example, **LookupHelpTopics** view).
- A page to contain the embedded lookup view menu (for example, **Help Menu** page).
- A page with instructions which is presented after new help topics are saved (for example, **HelpTopic0** page). This is the default content page.
- A frameset with a left-hand frame for the menu and a right-hand frame for the help topic documents (for example, **Help Frameset**).

First, create the **HelpTopic** form for the **Help** documents. This form consists of a subject field, a body field, a **$$Return** field, and three action buttons:

The **Cancel** button contains an @formula that re-opens the default content page:

```
@URLOpen("/"+@WebDbName+"/HelpTopic0?Openpage")
```

The **Save and Exit** button contains this @formula:

```
@Command([FileSave]);
@Command([CloseWindow]);
```

The **Edit** button is equally straightforward:

```
@Command([EditDocument]);
```

The `$$Return` field contains the same link used in the **Cancel** button:

```
"[/"+@WebDbName+"/HelpTopic0?Openpage]"
```

The **Save and Exit** and **Edit** action buttons on the form are protected with a hide-when formula that relies on an ACL role (for example, **HelpEditor**) (add this role to the application's ACL.):

```
@IsNotMember("[HelpEditor]";@UserRoles)
```

Next, create the **LookupHelpTopics** view to display text from the **HelpSubject** fields from the **HelpTopic** documents. Select the documents with an appropriate view selection formula. In this image, the left-most column is a blank (" ") to provide a little margin when the view displays:

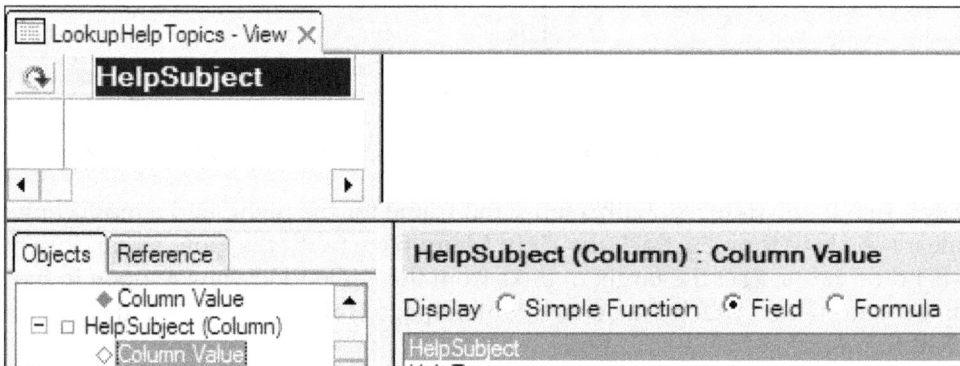

Create a new **Help Menu** page. Add a title and a **New Topic** button with the following @formula:

```
@Command([Compose];"HelpTopic")
```

Embed the lookup view on the **Help Menu** page. Adjust the attributes of the embedded view using **Embedded View Properties**. The result should look something like this in Designer:

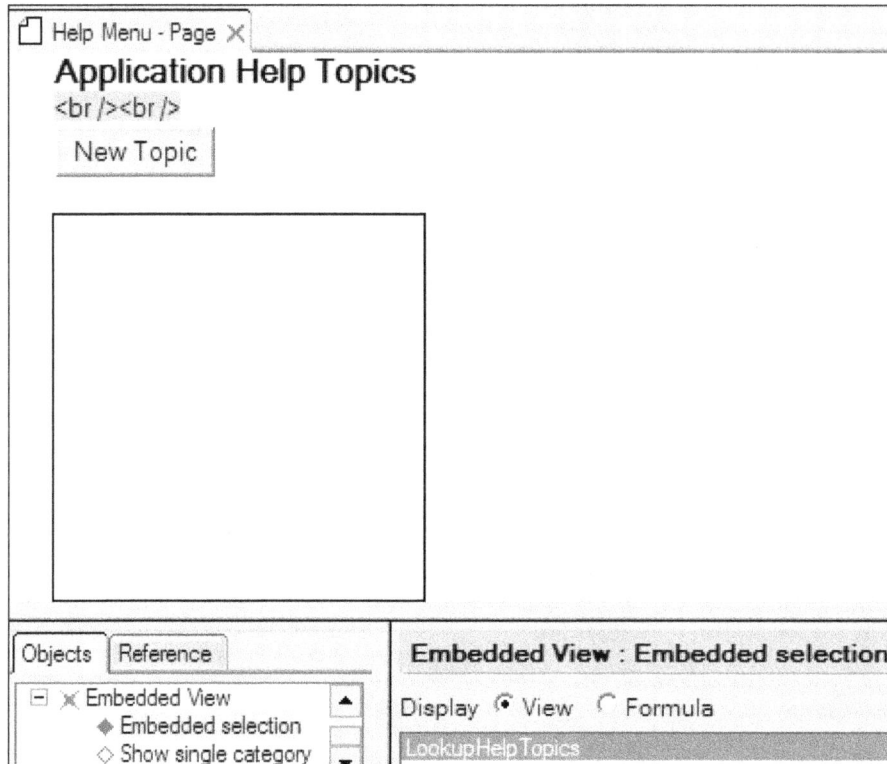

Create the default content page **HelpTopic0** with some instructions as appropriate.

Create a two frame frameset with a left-hand frame for the menu and a main content frame for the help topics. Attach the **Help Menu** page (with the view menu) into the left-hand frame, and set the target of links from the embedded view to open in the main content frame. Attach the default content page **HelpTopic0** to the main content frame.

Here is what the resulting application looks like in a browser:

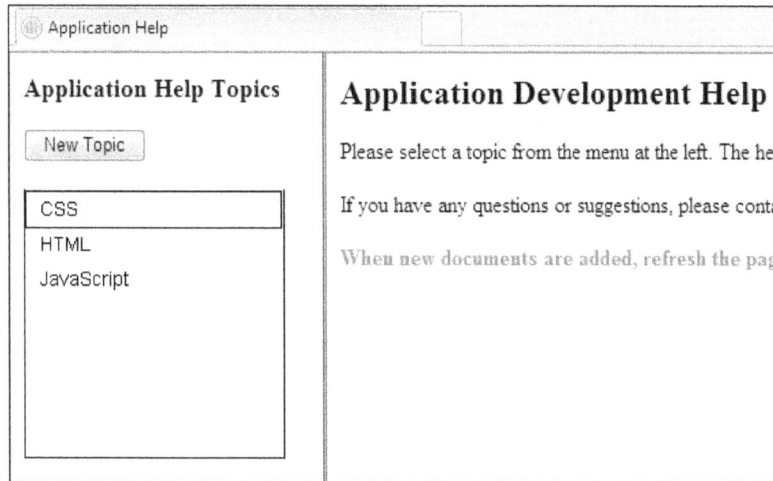

Displaying a design element after exiting a document

As discussed in *Chapter 3*, it is important to decide which design element (for example, page, view, or frameset) displays after a document is saved or cancelled. Several options were presented in that chapter including one that opens the document in Read mode and one which displays a specific view. This section illustrates some additional "post-document" options.

There are several document states or conditions to be considered. Exiting a document from each of these conditions must be handled by the application's navigation:

- New document saved
- New document cancelled
- Existing document in Read mode edited
- Existing document in Read mode cancelled
- Existing document in Edit mode saved
- Existing document in Edit mode cancelled

Here are some general strategies:

- Always display the same default view or design element after a document is saved or quit. The URL can be computed in a $$Return form field.

- Use a frameset with a menu of views and links displayed in a navigational frame, enabling the user to select a view or link regardless of what is displayed in the main content frame. The URL of a common post-document confirmation page can be computed in a form's $$Return field and displayed in the main content frame.

- On the form, code several action buttons, including possibly several mutually-exclusive **Cancel** buttons. Associate each button with a specific document state and write formulas to process the document (edit, save) as well as to determine which URL displays next. Use hide-when formulas to show the correct buttons according to the state of the document.

- Display a post-document menu of link options on a new page or response document. A user clicks a hotspot link to choose his next destination. This menu can be arbitrarily complex, and it can be customized with computed text and inherited fields. The URL of this post-document menu page or form can be computed in the original form's $$Return field.

Use $$Return to select a design element

As previously discussed, $$Return is a special form field that can contain an @formula that results in a URL to which the browser is directed after a document is exited. $$Return should be defined as a Computed for display field.

You may want to open one design element after a new document is submitted for the first time and a different element after an existing document is re-saved. Unfortunately, you cannot use the @IsNewDoc function since by the time $$Return is evaluated, the document is already saved and is no longer new. To get around this problem, create a Computed field (for example, HasBeenSaved) on the form and assign it this value:

```
@If(@IsNewDoc;"N";"Y")
```

The first time the document is saved, this field contains an N, but upon subsequent saves, the field contains a Y. Using the value of HasBeenSaved we can write a $$Return formula that works the way we want it to, displaying one page for new documents and a different page for existing documents. The square brackets inform Domino to redirect the browser to the enclosed URL:

```
@If(HasBeenSaved="N";
"[/" + @WebDbName + "/PostNewDocSave?OpenPage]";
"[/" + @WebDbName + "/PostEdit?OpenPage]");
```

Presumably each of the post-save pages contains one or more hotspot links, perhaps a little menu of them, that allow the user to select where he would like to go next.

Display the previous view

Existing documents are often shown in several views. Whichever view has focus when you open a document is the "previous view." After looking at the document, you can decide to close it without further action or you can choose to edit it and save the changes. It seems reasonable, especially if you work in the Notes environment, that after closing a document you would be returned to the previous view, regardless of whether the document is new or existing, saved or not. But on the Web, however, there is no "previous view" as such.

For an existing document, the previously displayed view can be determined with the @ViewTitle function. For a new document, however, @ViewTitle returns nothing. A new document is added to views only after it is saved, so determining which view to show after saving or cancelling a new document is problematic.

The following @formula, added to an action button, opens the previous view for existing documents and the application's default view for new documents. The first line of the formula relies on the value of the HasBeenSaved field as discussed in the previous topic. The second line extracts just the view title (not the alias) and assures that any spaces are converted to "%20" strings so that the result is valid for inclusion in a URL:

```
view := @If(HasBeenSaved = "Y"; @ViewTitle; "$defaultView" );
view := @URLEncode("Domino"; @Subset(view;1));
@URLOpen("/" + @WebDbName + "/" + view + "?OpenView");
```

Slightly modified, this formula can be set as the value of $$Return:

```
view := @If(HasBeenSaved = "Y"; @ViewTitle; "$defaultView" );
view := @URLEncode("Domino"; @Subset(view;1));
"[/" + @WebDbName + "/" + view + "?OpenView]";
```

Display the parent document

Assuming the parent of a response document is included in the allcustomers view, the following @formula, added to an action button on a response form, opens the parent document:

```
@URLOpen("/" + @WebDbName + "/allcustomers/" + @Text($Ref) +
"?OpenDocument")
```

Here is the slightly modified form suitable for `$$Return`:

```
"[/" + @WebDbName + "/allcustomers/" + @Text($Ref) + "?OpenDocument]"
```

A somewhat more generalized (and more convoluted) approach requires that the parent's `@ViewTitle` value be stored in the parent document and also inherited into the response document. Define a Computed text field named `viewtitle` on the main form and set its value to this formula:

```
@URLEncode("Domino"; @Subset(@ViewTitle;1))
```

Now create a response form that inherits values from the parent. Add a Computed text field named `viewtitle` to the response form and set its value to:

```
viewtitle
```

Assuming that the parent document is saved before the response document is created, the parent document will contain the title of the view. When the response document is created, it will inherit the `viewtitle` value from the parent document. That value can then be used in a response form button formula or in `$$Return` to reopen the parent document. Here is the `$$Return` formula:

```
"[/" + @WebDbName + "/" + viewtitle + "/" + @Text($Ref) +
"?OpenDocument]"
```

Using response forms for interim workflow steps

Some applications use temporary forms to confirm choices or to collect additional information from users. For example, suppose an application tracks work assignments on main documents. When a specific task is finished, the assigned **actionee** records comments in the appropriate main document and submits it for approval. When the manager opens that main document, an **Approve** button is displayed. If the manager clicks the button, an **Approval** response form opens that enables him to add comments and to confirm his approval. Clicking a button on the **Approval** response form launches an agent that saves the comments and changes the status of the main document.

These interim response documents inherit certain important values from a main document, including the main document's UNID, which may be passed to an agent for processing.

If the response documents should be discarded, add a hidden Text field named **SaveOptions** to the response form, with the following default value:

```
"0"
```

Setting the **SaveOptions** field to zero prevents documents from being saved.

Coding default error pages

You can create custom forms for handling error conditions. Forms using any of four reserved names can be used to provide customized messages. If these forms exist in the application, then they are displayed when conditions warrant. Otherwise, Domino presents default server forms and messages:

```
$$ReturnAuthenticationFailure
$$ReturnAuthorizationFailure
$$ReturnDocumentDeleted
$$ReturnGeneralError
```

Create a form named with one of the reserved names. Include an editable Text field named **MessageString** which Domino uses to display error messages. Add other guidance text and/or hotspots. In this example, the **Try Again** button re-launches the application:

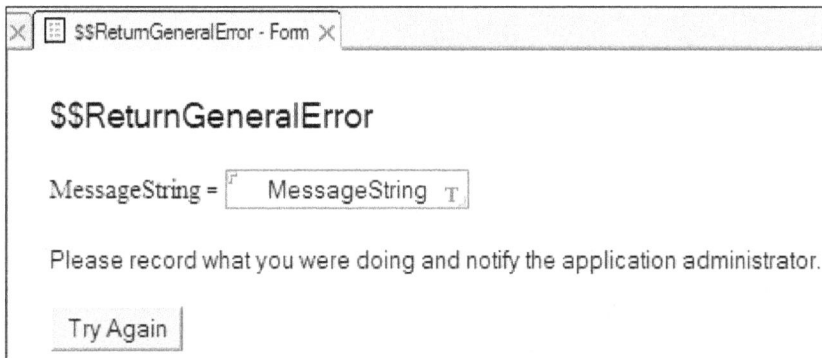

To exercise the form, code a bad @DbLookup formula on a button on some other form. Something like this should suffice:

```
@DbLookup("":"";"";"xyzview";"badkey";"fieldname")
```

Launch the application and click the button. The error form is displayed:

$$ReturnGeneralError

MessageString = HTTP Web Server: Lotus Notes Exception - A view of that name cannot be found in the specified database

Please record what you were doing and notify the application administrator.

[Try Again]

Note that **$$ReturnAuthenticationFailure** and **$$ReturnAuthorizationFailure** forms do not work if Session Authentication is enabled on the server.

Providing directions and help

Every application should provide information about itself through self-help features, and Domino applications offer several techniques to do this.

Help should answer questions and assist users in responding to features of the application. The upside of application help is that with it users can figure out for themselves what to do or what went wrong. The downside is that many of them cannot—or will not—read the help.

Nevertheless, provide as much help and guidance as possible within the constraints of the development effort. Make sure to spell and punctuate properly using words and grammar suitably plain for your users. This is a good area to ask for assistance from a technical writer, trainer, or publicist.

Add meaningful labels and guidance text

Just about every form shows labels and guidance text. Buttons, fields, column titles, and links should be sensibly named. Use common, well-understood labels for common functions (for example, "Save" instead of "Commit").

Onscreen guidance text should be simple and to the point. Use a pleasing font of sufficient size so that users need not strain to read the text. Use a color to distinguish guidance text from field labels and headings. When something is important, dress it up with a strong color, bold weight, or a small graphic. Make it clear which fields are required.

Where appropriate, consider using computed text to customize onscreen guidance. Use hide-when formulas to display appropriate error messages and other text depending upon the state of a document. Similar behavior can be implemented with CSS and JavaScript.

Add titles to design elements

Most design elements, from framesets to fields, provide for titles. Use them to provide help. For fields, buttons, and other hotspots, add titles on the **HTML** tab of **Properties**:

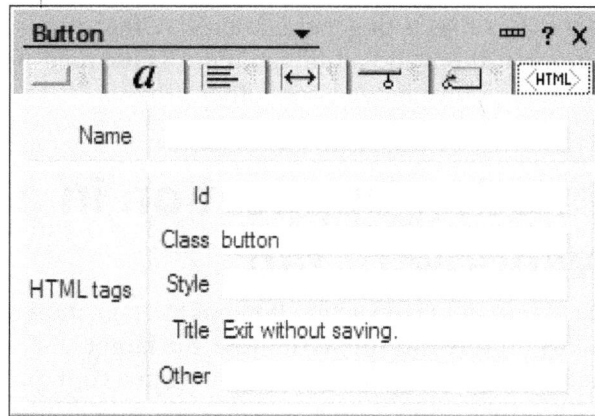

When a field or hotspot is hovered with a mouse, its title is displayed as a screen tip:

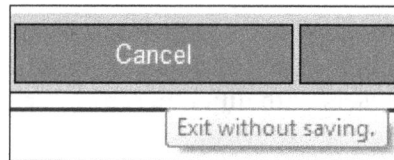

Link to the About and Using documents

Perhaps the oldest way to provide written assistance within a design is with the About and Using documents. The About document can provide a copyright notice, a summary of the application, contact information and perhaps release notes. The Using document can provide more lengthy explanations with drawings and images where appropriate. Consider using collapsible sections in these documents to separate content into meaningful units.

Provide hotspots to open these documents. For the About document, code this @formula for the value of the URL link:

```
"/"+ @WebDbName + "/$about?OpenAbout"
```

A similar @formula is used for the URL link for the Using document:

```
"/"+ @WebDbName + "/$help?OpenHelp"
```

Add customized help pages

If time permits and you are up to the task, create a little companion application filled with pages of information about the application. This is a good exercise to do while you are discovering an application or doing a significant overhaul. You should write what you learn about the application in a way that users will find helpful. Many pages will deal with subjects of general interest. Other pages will deal with application set up, configuration, and administration. These notes form an invaluable reference useful long after you've moved onto other projects.

Opening another application in a separate window or tab

At times it may be useful to define an action hotspot to open another application in a separate tab or window. In this @formula example, the target URL is hardcoded. In a real application, the target URL should be retrieved from a configuration document with an @DbLookup formula:

```
@SetTargetFrame("_blank");
@URLOpen("http://domino01.mycompany.com/application1.nsf");
```

Whether the second application opens in a tab or in a separate window depends, of course, upon the browser being used and how it is configured. Remember that users may use different browsers with different settings, factors that can impact your navigational strategy.

Summary

In all but the simplest applications, considerable care should be taken to design and implement a robust navigational scheme. Crafting the navigational aspects of an application requires understanding the overall architecture and workflow. Getting it right early is very important since correcting fundamental navigational flaws later on can be time-consuming.

Work on navigation early in the project, using form, page, and view placeholders that can be fleshed out later on. Adhere to the "go forward" principle so that buttons and hotspots clearly specify the next page or design element that should be displayed. Anticipate, prevent, and trap error conditions. Provide as much context-sensitive and other help as possible within the constraints of your project.

The suggestions and examples provided in this chapter should provide a good understanding of fundamental navigational issues and techniques relevant to a wide range of Domino web applications.

Cascading Style Sheets

5

Cascading Style Sheets (CSS) are used to style web pages, and this is the de facto standard technology used for this purpose. CSS rules define the way page elements look and, to some limited extent, where they reside and how they behave. There are many CSS techniques, most of which work with web-enabled Notes applications. As soon as possible, developers should achieve moderate to excellent CSS skills.

Current conventional wisdom tells us that HTML is for structure (what an element is), CSS is for styling (how an element looks), and JavaScript is for behavior (how an element behaves). In practice, these three technologies work synergistically to display and capture information. Oftentimes interesting effects are accomplished by combining CSS rules with JavaScript code, so it is impossible to discuss some styling strategies without discussing relevant JavaScript.

In this chapter, we look at how CSS is incorporated into classic web applications. Examples illustrate the use of CSS rules in a Domino context. There are also general recommendations regarding styling that may be of interest. Topics include:

- Incorporating CSS rules within an application design
- Using CSS to style fields, buttons, and menus
- Working with images
- Providing CSS rules for printing

Using CSS for styling design elements on the Web

There are two strategies which you can use to apply style to design elements. You can work with Designer-applied styles and you can work with CSS-applied styles. Of course, you can also use both techniques on a form or page, although I would generally recommend against doing so.

With Designer features alone, you can add style to design elements. Text, for example, can be colored, sized, aligned, and styled in several ways. The method is straightforward—select the text and then select the style options with **Text Properties**. Likewise, most design elements can be styled with **Properties**. For a Notes application, Designer-applied styles work very well. They are simple to use and there are many pleasant options. And in most cases, what you see is what you get.

Many Designer-applied style properties are translated into HTML formatting tags and attributes when a design element is served to a web browser. As an example, here is the HTML source generated by Domino for the title of a form. The text is bold, colored blue-green, and set to the 12 point Times New Roman font:

```
<b><font size="4" color="#008080" face="Times New Roman">This is a
Form Title</font></b>
```

However, not all Designer-applied style attributes are translated for the Web. Many style attributes, drop-shadows for instance, are not supported and are therefore simply ignored when a form or page is composed for the Web. So maintaining strict fidelity between the "Notes version" and the "web version" of a form can be difficult. The Notes version may look just right, but then the web version turns out to be only an approximation of the Notes version. Oftentimes the web version is just not good enough.

The other way to apply style to design elements is to use CSS which provides extensive control over the look of design elements when displayed in a browser. Stunning web pages can be created using relatively few rules. So using CSS to style web pages is highly recommended.

Traditionally, CSS rules do not apply to design elements when they display in the Notes client; rules applied to a form when it displays on the Web are ignored when the form opens in Notes. Worse, if you add style to some design elements with Designer (for example, text font size or color) then any CSS rules also applied to those design elements are overridden by the Designer-applied styles (HTML formatting tags) when a browser displays those design elements on the Web. Worse yet, which styling technique takes precedence (HTML tags or CSS rules) is inconsistent—sometimes HTML formatting tags have priority and sometimes CSS rules win out. This is not so much an issue with Domino, but rather with the way browsers render pages sent to them.

These fundamental incompatibilities between Designer-applied styles / HTML formatting tags and CSS styles are mitigated in later versions of Lotus Notes and Domino. If you do not face these issues, great. Otherwise, either stick with Designer-applied styles or use CSS. The balance of this chapter assumes you will use CSS for styling.

Learn basic CSS coding

Web application developers must learn at least the basics of CSS, which is a standard language for specifying how documents (composed with markup languages like HTML and XML) are presented. Many good books and web-based tutorials about this technology are readily available. This chapter highlights some key concepts, but it is not intended as a CSS primer.

A CSS rule consists of a **selector** followed by one or more **declarations**. Each declaration consists of a property and value(s) for that property.

Rules can be written for specific HTML tags. For example, the following CSS rule applies a specific set of style characteristics to all `<h1>` HTML tags on a form or page. Each property is assigned a specific value. The selector in this case is called a **type selector**:

```
h1  {
    color: red;
    font-family: Verdana;
    font-size: 16pt;
    font-weight: bold;
    }
```

A set of declarations can be associated with a **class name**. In CSS, a class name is preceded by a period; the class name does not include the period. The class rule itself consists of the declarations associated with the class name, and these property values are applied to any design element assigned the particular class name. In this example, two property values are associated with the `requiredtext` **class selector**:

```
.requiredtext {
    color: #7F0000;
    font-weight: bold;
    }
```

A set of declarations can be associated with an **identifier** or ID. A name preceded by a hash or the pound sign is defined as an identifier. The property values associated with an **ID selector** are applied to the one and only one design element assigned that particular identifier:

```
#toprow {
    background-color: gray;
    color: white;
    }
```

If an identifier is assigned to a design element, then JavaScript programs can access that element (by ID) and apply CSS style to it (or otherwise manipulate it).

When writing CSS rules, punctuation matters (braces, colons, semicolons), but layout and (most) spaces do not. The preceding declarations for the `toprow` element can be laid out in other ways:

```
#toprow {background-color:gray;color:white;}
```

Code your CSS so that it is easy to read and understand.

Associate CSS rules with design elements

Assuming a set of CSS rules is available to a form or page, you must associate specific CSS rules with specific design elements. There are two ways to do this. Most often you will use design element properties, as in the next two illustrations. Sometimes you will assign CSS classes and IDs directly to elements with Pass-Thru HTML.

Here the `PhoneNumber` field is associated with the `requiredtext` CSS class on the **HTML** tab of **Field Properties**. Note that only the class name is entered into **Properties** (no preceding period):

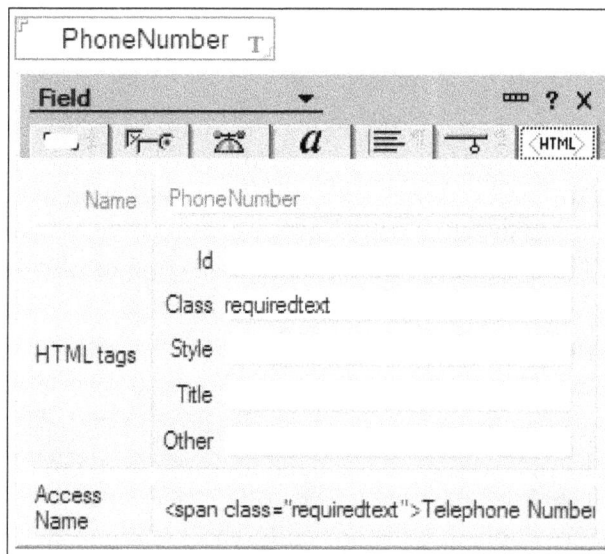

In a similar manner, if the ID of a design element is set equal to a CSS ID selector, then that element is styled according to the rules assigned to that CSS selector. From the previous topic, recall that `toprow` is associated with two properties:

```
#toprow {
    background-color: gray;
    color: white;
    }
```

Here, the ID of a single table cell (the top row) is set to `toprow` (the hash mark or pound sign is omitted, since it is not part of the identifier). This table cell property creates the linkage between the design element and the CSS rule:

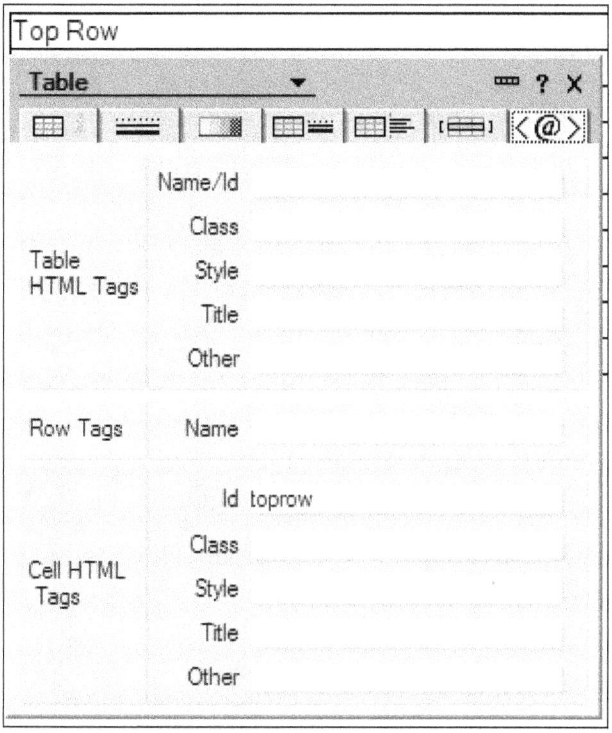

Here is the rendered table cell:

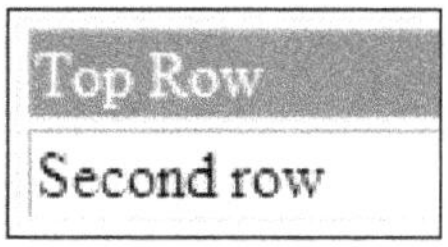

If you are working directly with text on a form or with HTML elements that are not design elements (for example, `<fieldset>`, `<span>`), then you can link that text or HTML to CSS rules with the HTML `id` and `class` attributes. Here is an example which associates a field label with a CSS class. The gray text is marked as Pass-Thru HTML:

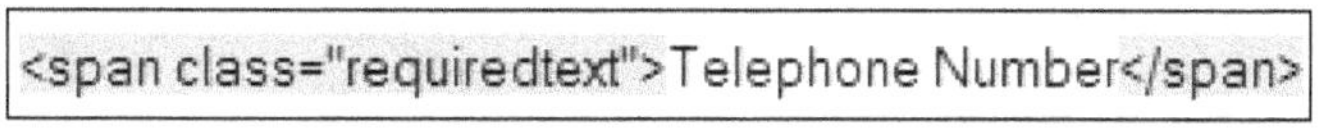

Locating style rules in applications

CSS rules can be coded in many places within an application, and in some ways that is unfortunate. Several CSS rules that define the same property can be targeted to the same design element; the browser figures out which rule applies and then renders the element accordingly. If an element is not styling the way you expect it to, you may have to look in several places to find the rogue rule. You will find CSS easier to work with if you co-locate all rules in the same place.

The following topics illustrate several ways in which CSS rules can be inserted into forms and pages.

Use a page design element

A page design element can be used to store CSS rules. Create the page and use Designer to edit the rules. The page name can be anything you like, but it is well to name the page in a way that identifies it as containing CSS rules, as in this example:

```
Web Sandbox 05 CSS | websandbox05.css
```

It is critical to identify the content type of the page as text/css on the **Page Info** tab of **Page Properties**. Otherwise, Domino will not serve the CSS rules page properly and the rules will not be applied to forms or pages for which they are intended:

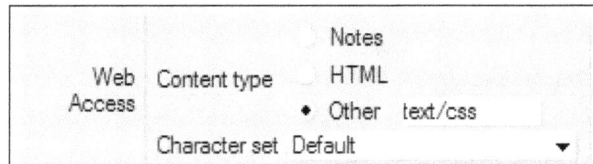

To make the CSS rules page available to other forms and pages, you must explicitly code a linkage in the HTML Head Content area of those other forms and pages. This linkage is coded as an @formula. In this example, the @Newline functions force the resulting HTML onto its own line(s):

```
@NewLine+
"<link rel='stylesheet' type='text/css' "+
"href='/"+@WebDbName+"/websandbox05.css' />"+
@NewLine
```

The link to the CSS rules page is placed in the form's head section:

```
<link rel='stylesheet' type='text/css'
href='/ellisits/websandbox05.nsf/websandbox05.css' />
```

CSS rules can be rather complex, so sometimes it might be easier to create several CSS pages. There are many reasons why you might want to do this. For example, you might want one style sheet just for Action Bars, a second for embedded views, and a third for everything else. Or you might need to code different CSS rules for different browsers. Or you may want to place rules for printing on a different page.

Add a comment to the top of each page to indicate the intent of the style sheet:

```
/* CSS Rules for Action Bars */
```

If several style sheets contain rules that apply to elements on a form or page, code a link to each style sheet in the @formula in the element's HTML Head Content area. In this example, two style sheets are included in the @formula:

```
@NewLine +
"<link rel='stylesheet' type='text/css' " +
"href='/" + @WebDbName + "/websandbox05.css' />" +
@NewLine +
"<link rel='stylesheet' type='text/css' " +
"href='/" + @WebDbName + "/datatable.css' />" +
@NewLine
```

Use Style Sheet Resources

External CSS editors offer several advantages to developers working with CSS style sheets, and you may want to try out one or two of these tools; browse the Web for options. CSS editors provide features such as automatic formatting, integrated help, and syntax validation.

If you prefer to use an external CSS (or text) editor, create the CSS file externally to the Domino application and then import it as a **Style Sheet Resource**:

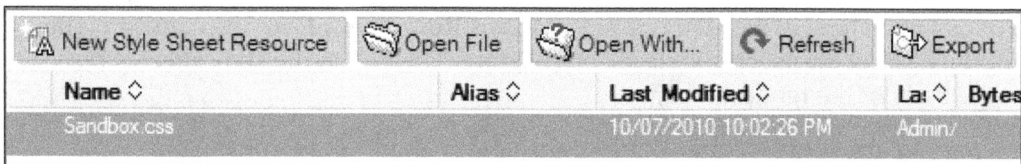

To create the linkage between a form or page and a Style Sheet Resource, insert the resource into the element's HTML Head Content area. Select the area, and then select **Insert Resource...** from the context menu (right-click). Several style sheets can be inserted into the HTML Head Content area as needed:

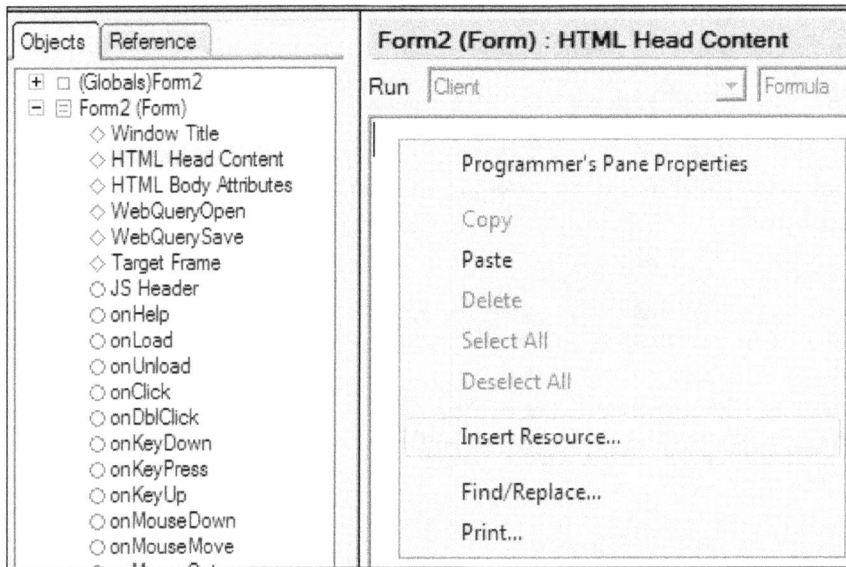

Objects	Reference	Form2 (Form) : HTML Head Content

```
⊞ ☐ (Globals)Form2
⊟ ⊟ Form2 (Form)
     ◇ Window Title
     ◇ HTML Head Content
     ◇ HTML Body Attributes
     ◇ WebQueryOpen
     ◇ WebQuerySave
     ◇ Target Frame
     ◯ JS Header
     ◯ onHelp
     ◯ onLoad
     ◯ onUnload
     ◯ onClick
     ◯ onDblClick
     ◯ onKeyDown
     ◯ onKeyPress
     ◯ onKeyUp
     ◯ onMouseDown
     ◯ onMouseMove
```

Run Client ▼ Formula

Programmer's Pane Properties

Copy

Paste

Delete

Select All

Deselect All

Insert Resource...

Find/Replace...

Print...

Select the resource from the list of available style sheets in the **Insert Resource** dialog. The link to the Style Sheet Resource is placed in the head section of a page like the following:

```
<link rel="stylesheet" type="text/css"
href="/ellisits/websandbox05.nsf/Sandbox.css?OpenCssResource">
```

You can also insert a Style Sheet Resource elsewhere on a form or page. Position the cursor somewhere in the element, select **Insert Resource...** from the context menu, and then select the specific style sheet as before. The link to the style sheet is placed in the body of the rendered page:

```
<style type="text/css">
@import url(/ellisits/websandbox05.nsf/Sandbox.css?OpenCssResource);
</style>
```

It is recommended that Style Sheet Resources be co-located toward the top of a form or page to avoid rendering issues.

Add style (sparingly) to Properties

Individual style rules can be added on the **HTML** tab of **Properties**. In this example, a field's CSS class is set to **InputColor** which defines the foreground color as 'Blue'. Unfortunately, the color **Red** has been applied inline to this particular field via the **Style** attribute also in **Properties**. As styles **cascade**, the inline style takes precedence and the input field text is rendered in red:

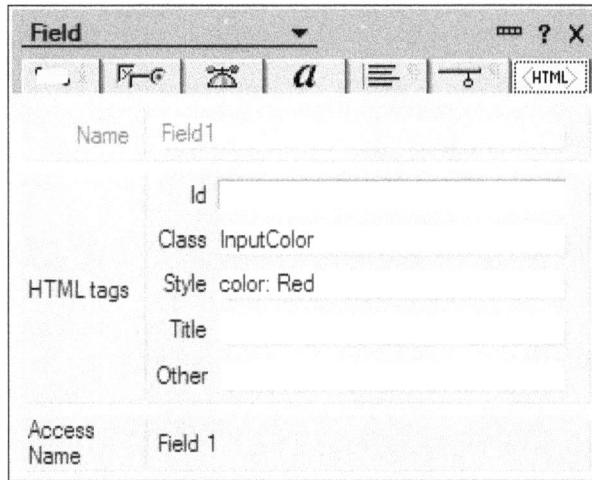

The HTML composed for this field includes both `style` and `class` attributes. Style takes precedence over class:

```
<input name="Field1" value="" class="InputColor" style="color: Red">
```

In general, avoid using the **Style** property, especially if there exists the possibility of conflicting CSS values in a style sheet. Sometimes during development you might toss in an inline style like this as a quick test, perhaps as a way to adjust a margin. But if you forget to remove the inline style, debugging later on can be frustrating.

Minimize the use of internal and inline styling

At the top of a form you might see **internal CSS**, marked as Pass-Thru HTML. Internal CSS consists of CSS rules wrapped in `<style>` tags. Internal CSS is, of course, limited in scope to the current form or page:

```
<style type="text/css">
h1  {
    color: Blue;
```

```
        font-family: Tahoma;
        font-size: 24pt;
        font-style: Italic;
        }
</style>
```

As mentioned previously, **inline CSS** can be found as the value of the `style` attribute coded on HTML tags:

```
<span style="color: Red; font-style: Italic">Telephone Number</span>
```

You might also find internal or inline CSS in many other places including these:

- HTML Head Content area
- HTML field
- `$$Return` field

Scattering CSS rules all around like this can result in a confusing and difficult-to-debug form. Do yourself and other future developers a great favor and avoid internal and inline CSS.

Use common style sheets

If your organization supports the use of common style sheets for multiple applications, by all means use them. Common style sheets promote a sense of cohesiveness and brand identity. A pleasing, uniform style can contribute to user productivity and satisfaction.

Use a Domino application as a style sheet repository

Common Style Sheet Resources can be stored in a central repository. Because applications link to style sheets in the repository, when a style sheet is updated, then those dependent applications immediately take advantage of the changes. To include a link to a common style sheet in another database, select the application and resource from the **Insert Resource** dialog. Browse to another application if it is not immediately available:

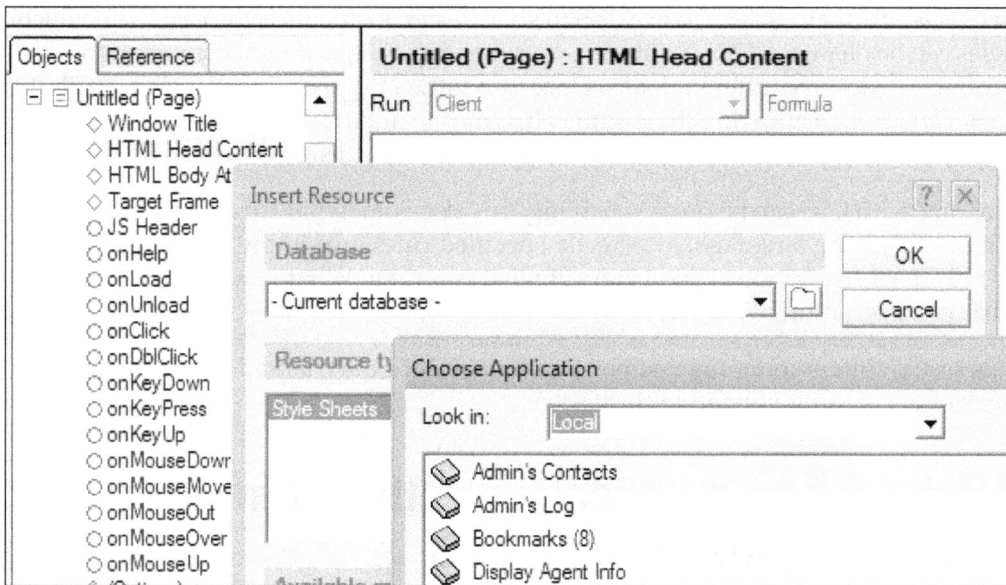

Use the HTML directory on the server

Common style sheets can be stored in the HTML subfolder on the Domino server, usually by the Domino administrator. To access a common style sheet, code an @formula in an HTML Head Content area. Code a relative or absolute link, but do not refer to the current database. In this example, the @formula results in a relative link to a style sheet file located on the same server as the current application:

```
@NewLine +
"<link rel='stylesheet' type='text/css' href='/Sandbox2.css' />" +
@NewLine
```

When composed for the browser, the link refers to the correct server-based file:

```
<link rel='stylesheet' type='text/css' href='/Sandbox2.css' />
```

Developing CSS rules

Decide where to place the CSS rules for your application and then stay with that strategy. Mixing strategies during development may be expedient, but failing to clean up and standardize can lead to debugging issues down the road.

Of course, the main reason to use CSS to style design elements is the ease with which styles can be changed. CSS facilitates experimenting with different combinations of attributes to achieve different looks. Once you settle on a specific set of style attributes for a feature, then applying those same attributes to another design element amounts only to assigning the same CSS class name to that other design element.

Working with CSS can be quite satisfying, but also somewhat frustrating at times. CSS is a forgiving language; incorrectly specified rules are simply skipped. There are no error messages or other indicators of what is wrong. What you wanted was not what you got, and that's about it.

This section offers some suggestions that may reduce the frustration and hasten the work of developing your style sheets.

Work with an application rather than a template while writing CSS

Tweaking CSS rules is often an iterative process that can be very time-consuming. If you normally design a template and then apply the template to a test application, you will spend a lot of time unnecessarily manipulating the template. Instead, consider working directly with the test application while you fine-tune the CSS page.

Try using this development sequence while working out the CSS rules:

1. Open the application in a browser.
2. Open the application in Designer.
3. Update the CSS rules page in the application and save.
4. Refresh the browser.
5. View the result.

When the CSS rules are done, complete the job by transferring the CSS page from the application to the template:

1. Open the template.
2. Copy the CSS rules page from the application to the template.
3. Save the template.
4. Close the application from Designer.

Make sure you have control over the style of an element

Often enough when you first start writing CSS rules for a design element, nothing seems to work; rule changes are not reflected in the look of the form or page. There may be an error but you just don't see it right away.

When this happens, start by making sure you have control over the style of the element, perhaps a field or a cell in a table. If your browser includes developer tools, take a look at the CSS applied (or not applied) to the problematic design element. Otherwise, pick one attribute—I usually choose "color" because color is easy to see—and write just one rule to change that one attribute. If the rule does not change the element, you do not have control over the style of the element. Before you can make any real progress, you must gain control.

Your first step should be obvious: check spelling and punctuation for the rule. If the rule is correctly coded, try these suggestions.

Clear the browser cache

CSS is cached. Just because you changed a CSS rule in the application and reloaded the page, you have no guarantee that the most recent CSS rules are being applied. Clearing the browser cache can be a quick way to reestablish control. Clear the cache and reload the page. If the design element displays with the new rule, you have control over the style of the element.

Remove HTML formatting

As mentioned previously, some Designer-applied styles are translated into HTML formatting tags, such as `<b>` and `<font>`. If you apply any style with Designer, the resulting HTML is likely to include HTML formatting tags, and these tags may take precedence over CSS rules.

In this example, the CSS rule for `<h1>` tags specifies a green color for text. But the title `Meeting Topics` was changed to red with Designer. The composed HTML contains a `<font>` tag with an attribute that overrides the CSS rule. As a result, the heading is rendered red by the browser. (In this example, the `<h1>` tags were coded directly on the original page and marked as Pass-Thru HTML.):

```
<h1><b><font color="#FF0000">Meeting Topics</font></b></h1>
```

Use Designer to create the structure of a form or page with design elements. Do not style design elements if you intend to use CSS. If a design element is already styled with Designer, then reset the styles to their defaults. The default text styles are as follows:

- Default Sans Serif
- 10 points
- Black

If text formatting is problematic, view the page source to identify the problem. Setting the text formats back to their defaults clears out many undesirable HTML format tags and allows CSS rules to rule.

Remove conflicting inline and internal CSS rules

Remember that CSS rules can be placed inline as attributes on an HTML tag and also as the value of the **Style** property on the **HTML** tab of **Properties**. Inline rules take precedent over rules coded on a CSS page or Style Sheet Resource. Likewise, internal CSS rules coded on a form or page override external rules. If you do not have style control over a design element, look for conflicting inline and internal CSS rules and remove them.

Use fully qualified CSS selectors

A CSS class name should stand alone as a selector, but on occasion it may be necessary to more fully qualify a selector in order to gain control of an element. For example, a simple selector like the following should be sufficient to select table cells within a table whose ID is `actions`:

```
#actions td
```

But if you cannot gain control over the subordinate element (`<td>` in this example), then you might try fully qualifying the selector as follows:

```
table#actions td
```

You can fully qualify elements with class names as well:

```
table.actions td
```

Accommodate different browsers

Even if your users all use the same browser, it is useful to view your forms and pages in more than one browser to assure cross-browser functionality or to gain insight into a styling problem. Certainly use one or more versions of Internet Explorer, as that browser is widely installed. But also use Chrome, Firefox, Opera, Safari, or another popular browser to verify results.

Historically, different browsers rendered certain CSS rules in slightly different ways. So website developers learned different tricks or **hacks** to accommodate these differences.

If your users work with different browsers and you discover that common CSS rules do not render elements satisfactorily for all browsers, then you can elect to create a separate CSS page for each browser. Each form or page in your application would then detect the browser in use and load the appropriate CSS page(s). The `@BrowserInfo` function can provide details about the browser being used.

Because Internet Explorer has been a problematic browser, Microsoft introduced **Conditional Comments** as a technique that can be used to select one or another CSS page for different versions of IE. Non-IE browsers should ignore conditional comments; IE evaluates the comments and then includes or does not include additional HTML specified within the comment. For example, in this snippet, the browser includes the statement `Hello IE !` if the browser is IE. Otherwise, the whole thing is ignored:

```
<!--[if IE]>
Hello IE !
<![endif]-->
```

In a similar manner, style sheet links can be selected with conditional comments. In this example, two style sheet links are selected. The first style sheet page, `Sandbox.css` is always included; this is the primary CSS page and contains rules applicable to all browsers. After that, three conditional comments provide alternate or supplemental CSS pages for IE6 or earlier, IE7, and IE8. One and only one of these additional pages will be selected, depending upon which version of IE is being used:

```
<!-- CSS Stylesheets, different css for IE -->
<link rel='stylesheet' type='text/css' href='/ellisits/websandbox05.nsf/Sandbox.css' />
<!--[if lte IE 6]>
<link rel='stylesheet' type='text/css' href='/ellisits/websandbox05.nsf/Sandbox-ie.css' />
<![endif]-->
<!--[if IE 7]>
<link rel='stylesheet' type='text/css' href='/ellisits/websandbox05.nsf/Sandbox-ie7.css' />
<![endif]-->
<!--[if IE 8]>
<link rel='stylesheet' type='text/css' href='/ellisits/websandbox05.nsf/Sandbox-ie8.css' />
<![endif]-->
```

An @formula in the HTML Head Content area of a form or page creates HTML with conditional comments as shown in the previous illustration. Here is the code:

```
LTag := "<link rel='stylesheet' type='text/css' href='/"+
@WebDbName+"/";
"<!-- CSS Stylesheets, different css for IE -->"
+@Newline+LTag+"Sandbox.css' />"
+@Newline+"<!--[if lte IE 6]>"
+@Newline+LTag+"Sandbox-ie.css' />"
+@Newline+"<![endif]-->"
+@Newline+"<!--[if IE 7]>"
+@Newline+LTag+"Sandbox-ie7.css' />"
+@Newline+"<![endif]-->"
+@Newline+"<!--[if IE 8]>"
+@Newline+LTag+"Sandbox-ie8.css' />"
+@Newline+"<![endif]-->"
```

Note that at the time of this writing, if IE 8 is toggled into **compatibility mode**, then conditional comments for IE 7 are honored and conditional comments for IE 8 are ignored.

Over time, browsers and browser usage change. Web application developers should keep an eye on browser usage trends by visiting web monitoring sites, such as that provided by Net Applications: http://marketshare.hitslink.com.

Adding style to form and page elements

Most of the CSS rules you write for an application relate to design elements on forms and pages. Suggestions and examples in this section just scratch the surface of CSS possibilities. Browse the Web for additional ideas. Here we focus on the mechanics of how elements are styled, rather than on specific recommendations about what looks good, which is largely a matter of taste.

Use color effectively

Use pleasing, complementary colors. If your organization requires a specific set of colors, then of course find out what that palette is and conform to it as much as possible. Color tastes change over the years, primary colors dominating at times and lighter pastels in vogue at others. Here are a few generalities to consider:

- Use white or very light colors for backgrounds
- Use stronger colors such as dark red to make important elements stand out
- Use no more than three or four colors on a form
- Use black or dark gray text on a light background for lengthy text passages

If you have paid little attention to the matter of color in your applications, do some web work on the subject. Once you select a color scheme, provide some samples to your customers for their opinions and suggestions.

Style text

Typography is a complex topic with a rich history and strong opinions. For web application design purposes, consider using **web safe** fonts which are likely to be available on most or all personal computers. If you use a font that is not available to a browser, then text is rendered with a default font.

Fonts with serifs are usually considered easier to read on paper, and less so as web page text. Experiment with the following fonts:

- Bookman Old Style
- Cambria
- Garamond
- Georgia
- Times New Roman

Common fonts without serifs (sans serif) are considered easier to read on the Web. Some examples include:

- Arial
- Calibri
- Helvetica
- MS Sans Serif
- Tahoma
- Trebuchet MS
- Verdana

Mono-spaced fonts are useful when you want text to line up — columns of numbers in a table, perhaps:

- Courier New
- Courier

Establish a common font style with CSS rules applied to the `body` type selector or to a main division using a type selector, a class selector, or an ID selector:

```
body {
    color: #555555;
    font-family: Verdana;
    font-size: 8pt;
    }
```

Style headings and labels

If headings and labels are bracketed with HTML heading tags (for example, `<h1>` or `<h2>`), they can be styled with type selectors:

```
h1   {
    color: Blue;
    font-family: Arial;
    font-size: 18pt;
    font-weight: bold;
    }
```

If headings and labels are bracketed with `<span>` tags, use CSS classes:

```
<span class="highlight1">October News</span>
```

Underline links in text but not in menus

When browsers and the Web first appeared in the early 1990's, hyperlinks were a novelty. To distinguish a link from normal text, the convention developed to underscore the text containing the link, and often the link text was colored blue. There is no magic associated with underscoring and making text blue — it was just the convention adopted at the time.

Today links in text passages are usually distinguished from adjacent text with color, weight or underscoring. In a menu, however, each item is understood to be a hotspot link. Underscores and blue text are not required. So if you feel like underscoring a link, do so if the link appears within some text, but don't underscore links in menus.

At the same time, refrain from highlighting important text with underscoring, which implies that that text is a hyperlink. Use another highlighting technique; italics, bold, or an alternate color work well for this purpose.

Style fields

Fields can be styled with CSS either with the **Style** attribute in **Field Properties** or with CSS rules. An example of using the **Style** attribute was shown previously in this chapter.

The key to understanding how CSS rules can be applied to fields is to understand that fields are translated to the Web using `<input>` tags. Here is how a simple text field translates into HTML:

```
<input name="FirstName" value="">
```

Here is how a radio button field translates:

```
<input name="%%Surrogate_Gender" type="hidden" value="1">
<label><input type="radio" name="Gender" value="M">M</label><br>
<label><input type="radio" name="Gender" value="F">F</label><br>
```

CSS rules can be defined for the `<input>` tag, an ID, or a class. For example, assume that a CSS class named `requiredtext` is defined. If that class name is entered in the **Class** attribute of **Field Properties**, the resulting HTML might look like this:

```
<input name="FirstName" value="" class="requiredtext">
```

CSS style rules coded for the `requiredtext` class are applied to the field.

Highlight required fields

Required fields are validated, most likely with JavaScript code, so that complete and good data is saved into the database when a document is submitted. If entered values fail validation, the user is presented with a message of some sort that identifies the problem and requests correction.

Web forms typically identify which fields are required. Any of several techniques can be used. Required field labels can be styled with a more prominent color or a special marker such as an asterisk or a checkmark can be positioned near the field. Required fields also can be co-located and set apart using the `<fieldset>` and `<legend>` tags.

If a field value fails validation, it is common practice to provide an error message and then to set the **focus** into the field; the cursor is positioned in the field to facilitate an immediate correction. As the cursor can be difficult to spot on a busy form, it is also possible to change the background color of the incorrect field as a way of drawing the user's attention to the field. In this illustration, the background color of the field has been changed to yellow:

Telephone Number

Implementing this technique requires writing a small JavaScript function that changes the background color of the field, and then calling that function when field validation fails. This technique is fleshed out in a later chapter.

Style buttons

Every form uses one or more hotspot buttons to initiate actions. The basic button hotspot is not unattractive, but it can be styled as desired with CSS class or ID rules, just like other design elements. But some buttons do need a little more work.

Replace the default Action Bar buttons with hotspot buttons

Action Bar buttons added to forms or views work the same way on the Web as they do in Notes, as long as the `@Commands` associated with the actions work on the Web. By default, Domino-generated Action Bar buttons look like the following:

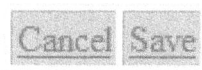

The Action Bar and Action buttons can be styled when displayed in Notes, but that styling does not translate to the Web. Displaying the Action Bar with the Action Bar Java Applet improves the look of the Action Bar somewhat, but the Java Applet can be slow to load and may not initialize properly at times.

One alternative is to create a set of hotspot buttons, styled with CSS and arranged in a table across the top of a form. The @formulas associated with the Action Bar buttons are recoded to the hotspot buttons' click events. CSS classes (for example, `button` and `buttontable`) can be defined and applied to these buttons and to the table which contains them. The end result is more pleasing:

Style the default Action Bar buttons

A Domino-generated Action Bar displays on the Web as an HTML table, each cell of which contains an Action button. It turns out that the Action Bar table is typically the first table on the form. That fact can be used to locate this table element in the DOM. Once the Action Bar table is located, a CSS class name can be added to it dynamically. CSS rules then style the table elements.

Note that in Domino and Designer 8.5, a new option was added that simplifies this technique somewhat by automatically adding class names into the HTML for the Action Bar table and buttons. In Designer 8.5, check the **Enable enhanced HTML generation** option on **Basic Properties** for the application:

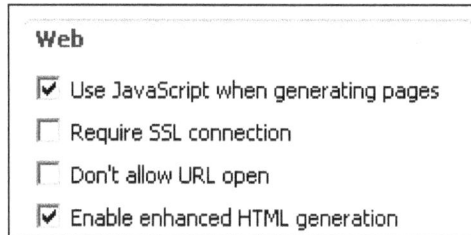

```
Web

☑ Use JavaScript when generating pages

☐ Require SSL connection

☐ Don't allow URL open

☑ Enable enhanced HTML generation
```

With this option enabled, the class domino-actionbar is added to the <table> tag, the class domino-action is added to the <td> tags, and the class domino-actionbar-sep is added to the <hr> tag. CSS rules can then be styled for these classes. View the page source to verify the class names attached to the Action Bar table and other elements:

```
<table border="1" cellspacing="2" cellpadding="2"
class="domino-actionbar">
<td class="domino-action". . .
<hr class="domino-actionbar-sep" />
```

If you work with versions of the software prior to 8.5, here is a way to apply CSS rules to the Action Bar. The solution described here consists of five components. If you are using Designer 8.5 in a Domino 8.5 environment, you can skip the steps related to JavaScript, and use the Domino-generated class names instead of the class names in the example. Here are the components required for this strategy:

- A CSS style sheet named ActionBar.css containing rules for an actionbar class and other HTML tags

- A JavaScript library named ActionBar.js containing a JavaScript function named styleActionBar that sets the Action Bar table class name property to actionbar

- A link to the ActionBar.css style sheet in the form's HTML Head Content area

- A link to the ActionBar.js JavaScript library in the form's JS Header

- A short JavaScript placed at the bottom of the form that invokes the styleActionBar JavaScript function after the page loads

Reshuffling the parts, here is (roughly) how this works:

1. The form loads into the browser.

2. The last line of the form fires the `styleActionBar` JavaScript function fetched from the `ActionBar.js` JavaScript library.

3. The `styleActionBar` function locates the Action Bar table at the top of the form and sets its class name property to `actionbar`.

4. The browser restyles the Action Bar table according to the rules in the `ActionBar.css` style sheet.

5. The form displays in the browser viewport.

The `ActionBar.css` page contains the following rules. Note that all rules apply to a table whose class name is `actionbar` or to elements (for example, `<td>`) within that table:

```css
/* Rules for Action Buttons */
table.actionbar {
    border-collapse: collapse;
    border: none;
    margin: 0;
    padding: 0;
    }
table.actionbar td {
    background-color: rgb(0,0,128);
    border: solid 2px #555;
    border-top: solid 2px #DDD;
    border-left: solid 2px #DDD;
    font-family: Verdana;
    font-size: smaller;
    font-weight: normal;
    height: 2em;
    margin: 0;
    padding: 0;
    text-align: center;
    width: 11em;
    }
table.actionbar td a {
    color: White;
    float: left;
    padding: .5em 0;
    text-decoration: none;
    width: 100%;
    }
table.actionbar td a:hover {
    background-color: #DDD;
    color: red;
    }
```

The `styleActionBar` JavaScript function in the `ActionBar.js` JavaScript library contains just a few lines. An array of the form's tables is created, and then the **className** property of the first table in the array is set to `actionbar`, forming the linkage between the Action Bar table and the aforementioned CSS rules:

```
function styleActionBar() {
  var form = document.forms[0] ;
  var tables = form.getElementsByTagName("TABLE") ;
  var actionbar = tables[0] ;
  actionbar.className += " actionbar" ;
  }
```

The link to the `ActionBar.css` page in the form's HTML Head Content area results from a simple @formula:

```
@NewLine+
"<link rel='stylesheet' type='text/css' href='/"+
@WebDbName+"/actionbar.css' />"+
@NewLine
```

The link to the **ActionBar.js** JavaScript library in the form's **JS Header** results from inserting that resource with the context menu:

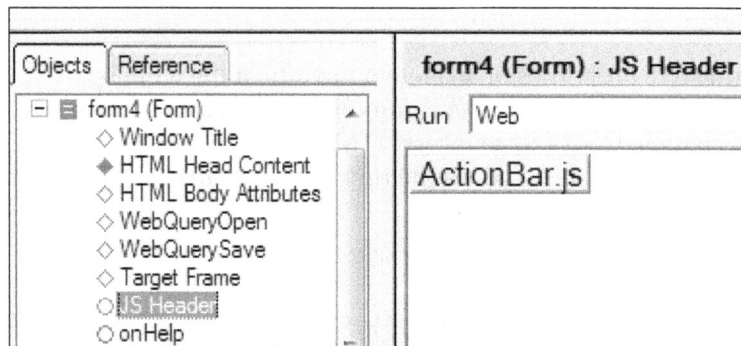

The JavaScript added to the end of the form is marked as Pass-Thru HTML:

```
<script type="text/javascript">{styleActionBar();}</script>
```

With these pieces in place, the default Action Bar buttons that look like this:

Cancel Edit

are restyled. Here the **Edit** button is shown in a mouse hovered state:

Cancel   Edit

Style borders and margins

If you examine closely the CSS rules in the previous illustration, you can see how to create borders with a three dimensional look. In the illustration, the table cells which contain the "buttons" are styled with three border declarations. The first declaration sets all the borders to the same width and color (a dark gray). The second and third declarations change the top and left-hand borders to a lighter color:

```
border: solid 2px #555;
border-top: solid 2px #DDD;
border-left: solid 2px #DDD;
```

Use the **margin** style properties of an element to adjust the whitespace between it and other elements. Without CSS, the common way to create white space above a table or between table rows was to insert HTML tags (`<p>`, `<br>`, ` `). With CSS, a margin or padding declaration does the trick. Here, a table is positioned 10 pixels below the element above it on the page:

```
margin-top: 10px;
```

Note that adjacent elements share a margin, so you may have to adjust the margins of both elements. Use the **padding** style properties to provide white space between an element and its border or container.

Work with images

As discussed in *Chapter 2*, select, refine, and scale down images externally before importing them into your application as shared image resources. You can of course copy and paste an image directly onto a form or page, but this technique is not recommended, especially if the image is used on more than one design element.

Once in the template, you have several ways to incorporate images. The easiest technique is to position the cursor on the form and then to select the menu item **Create | Image Resource...** which opens the image selection dialog. Note that you can browse to other Domino applications and even to the file system:

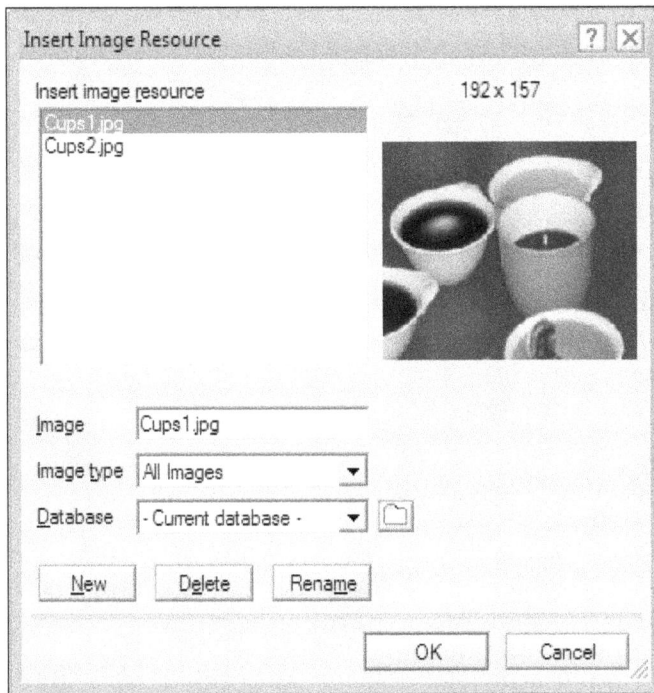

Alternately, you can embed an image with an HTML `<img>` tag marked as Pass-Thru HTML:

```
<img src="cups1.jpg" alt="Easter Eggs">
```

But since this chapter is about using CSS, let's look at how CSS rules can be written to attach images to design elements. Let's start by attaching an image (for example, a watermark) to a form as a background. Assuming there is an imported `cups2.jpg` image in the template, here is the relevant CSS rule:

```
body{
    background: url("cups2.jpg");
    }
```

The image serves as a background for the entire form or page. In this illustration, note the use of **Lorem Ipsum** which often serves as a placeholder for real text during the design process. Be mindful that placing text over an image may make the text more difficult to read:

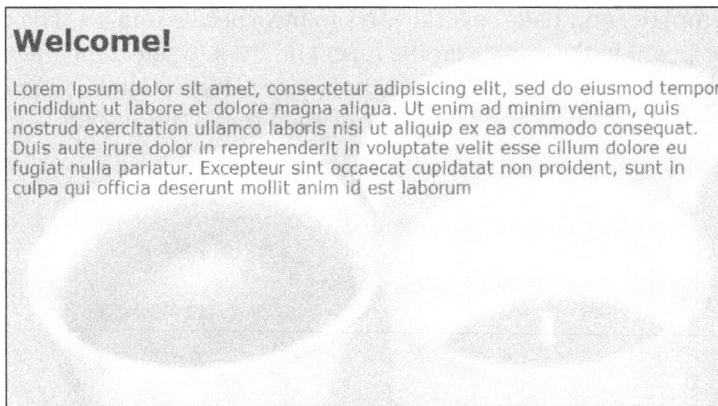

You can attach an image as background to many elements. Here a somewhat more pale `cups3.jpg` image is attached as background to a `<div>` element whose ID is `maintext`. The text color is black in an attempt to provide more contrast between the background image and the text:

```
#maintext {
    background: url("cups3.jpg");
    color: #000;
    font-family: Verdana;
    font-size: 12pt;
    }
```

Unfortunately, the value of an image can degrade behind text, so further adjustments may be required:

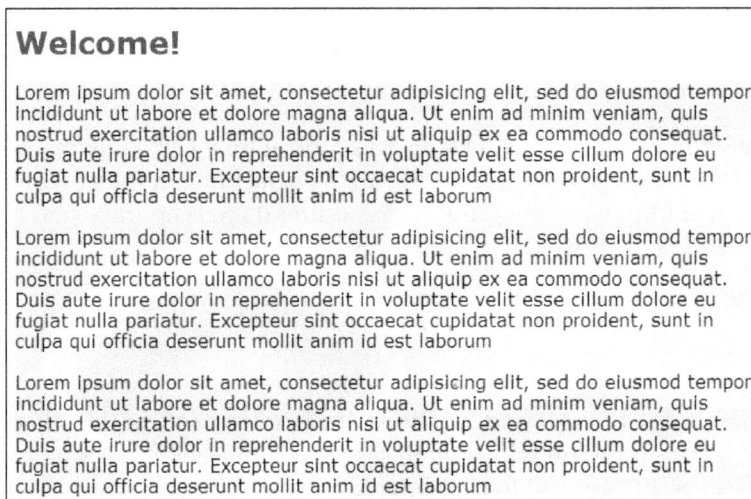

As a final example, let's add an image to a button. The problem of background images interfering with the readability of foreground text exists with buttons as well, and it may take some finagling to achieve a reasonable result, especially with colorful or busy images. Attaching the background image is fairly straightforward, as we have seen in the previous examples.

It is important to assure that the size of the button (height and width) are less than or equal to the size of the image. A too-large image is cropped when rendered, but a too-small image will not fill the entire button. Unless the image is a pattern, it should not repeat on the button. In this next illustration, the cups4.jpg image is 100 pixels wide and 82 pixels high.

The real effort—which can take considerable experimentation—is in finding a good set of properties for the button text. Color is most important, as the color of the text should make it stand out clearly from the background image.

Here is the CSS rule for a button with an ID of sub. Note the inclusion of border properties to achieve some sense of three dimensionality:

```
input#sub {
    background: url("cups4.jpg") no-repeat center center;
    border: solid 2px #555;
    border-top: solid 2px #DDD;
    border-left: solid 2px #DDD;
    color: #FFFF00;
    font-family: Verdana;
    font-size: 16pt;
    font-weight: bold;
    height: 40px;
    width: 100px;
    }
```

The button displays with a colorful background image dominated by greens, white, and deeper blue. The text is a bright yellow. Altogether this is not a bad solution, but the readability of the text is still not what it should be—there is too little contrast between the letters and the objects in the picture:

Working with images is both pleasurable and frustrating. In general, try to work with images whose internal colors are fairly similar, without a lot of contrast. Use bright, grayscale images if at all possible since these will interfere less with dark foreground text.

Style menus

Chapter 4, Navigation, introduced the idea of creating menus with HTML tags and CSS rules. This topic elaborates a bit on that earlier discussion.

If you browse the Web for CSS menus, you will find many, many examples. You will also find menus created with CSS and JavaScript, jQuery, and any number of other techniques. Getting a menu just right takes time. Here is one example, which should whet your appetite. Walk through the example carefully to understand how all the pieces work together.

In this example, there is a heading, and below the heading are three menu items, each of which contains a link to a view. When hovered with a mouse, these menu items change color as a visual cue to the user. The final result looks like this:

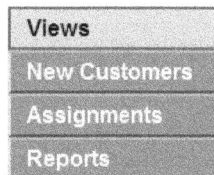

The menu on the form is structured as an unordered list within an unordered list. This arrangement of HTML elements is a bit more complicated than using just a single unordered list, but it does enable us to apply some unique styling to the inner list if we so desire.

The list item in the outer unordered list contains a link to itself. This convention provides us with an `<a>` (anchor) tag that can be styled. Clicking the link does nothing.

The list items in the inner unordered list contain Hotspot Links to views. The hotspots translate to the Web as `<a>` tags:

```html
<div id="menuA">

<ul>
  <li class="item"><a href="#">Views</a>
    <ul>
        <li class="subitem">New Customers</li>
        <li class="subitem">Assignments</li>
        <li class="subitem">Reports</li>
    </ul>
  </li>

</div><!--end of menuA div-->
```

Now the CSS rules are rather lengthy. Style is applied to each HTML element, starting with the menuA division. In order, rules are laid out for the division, the unordered lists, the list items, the anchor tag links, the outer list item anchor tag (the menu heading), the inner list item anchor tags (the menu items), and finally the inner list item anchor tags when hovered. Whew! Here it is:

```
#menuA {
    margin: 0;
    }
#menuA ul {
    list-style: none;
    margin: 0;
    padding: 0;
    }
#menuA li {
    width: 10em;
    }
#menuA a {
    display: block;
    font-family: Arial;
    font-weight: bold;
    padding: .25em;
    text-align: left;
    text-indent: .5em;
    text-decoration: none;
    width: 100%;
    }
#menuA li.item a {
    background: #CCC;
    border: solid 2px #555;
    color: #000;
    }
#menuA li.subitem a {
    background: #F00;
     border-top: solid 2px #AAA;
    border-right: solid 2px Maroon;
    border-bottom: solid 2px Maroon;
    border-left: solid 2px #CCC;
    color: #FFF;
    }
#menuA li.subitem a:hover, #menuA li.subitem:hover {
    color: #F00;
    background: #FFF;
    }
```

The intent of this example is to demonstrate how CSS alone can be used to create some simple yet stylish menus. Browse the Web for even more complex and challenging examples.

Style printed pages

Styles appropriate for a web page are not necessarily the best choice for a printed page. For example, fonts without serifs may be easier to read on a computer screen, while fonts with serifs are generally more pleasing when printed on paper. A web page with a dark background and light text might better print as black text on a white background.

Then again, forms and pages often contain guidance text, buttons, menus and hotspots—even whole sections—which are unnecessary when the form or page is printed. To style elements differently when printed or to avoid printing certain elements, create a second style sheet with alternate CSS rules. Alter the style of some elements for printing and hide those elements that should not print at all. In this example, text in the `maintext` division prints in a black, 10 point Times New Roman font, and any element (for example, buttons and hotspots) assigned the `NoPrint` class do not print:

```
#maintext {
    color; #000;
    font-family: "Times New Roman";
    font-size: 10pt;
    }
.NoPrint {
    display: none;
    }
```

In the form or page HTML Head Content area, code an @formula that includes both the primary and the printing style sheets. The `media` attribute on the second `<link>` tag signifies that the style sheet should be included only when the form or page is printed:

```
@NewLine +
"<link rel='stylesheet' type='text/css' " +
"href='/" + @WebDbName + "/websandbox05.css' />" +
@NewLine +
"<link rel='stylesheet' type='text/css' href='/"+
@WebDbName+"/noprint.css' media='print' />"+
@NewLine
```

Add more than one class to an element

If an element is already styled with a specific class, you can simple add another class to designate that the element should not print. In this example, a button is styled with two classes, the second of which is the NoPrint class.

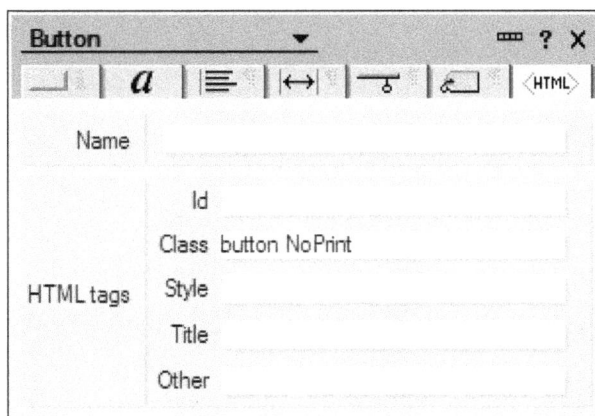

Summary

Contemporary web applications should look good as well as perform well. Web-savvy users — that means just about everyone — expect well-styled pages, and developers should attend to this aspect of applications, both new and old.

Expect to spend some time polishing and fine-tuning the layout and style of forms and pages as your development or redesign project rolls toward completion. Finding just the right balance of fonts, colors, images, borders, margins, and so on can be challenging, but applying good-looking style to a design can really impress your customers.

The suggestions and examples in this chapter provide a good understanding of how CSS rules can be used to style and enhance design elements within Domino web applications.

6
JavaScript

JavaScript is the programming language used to manipulate web pages in browsers. It is the technology that puts the "dynamic" into Dynamic HTML. Learning JavaScript is essential for anyone enhancing or developing web applications, and of course, it is well integrated into the fabric of Domino web development.

If you already have a good grasp of JavaScript, your focus should be on how to incorporate JavaScript into Domino applications. There is no special version of JavaScript for Domino, but how you work with JavaScript in this environment may seem a little foreign.

In classic Domino applications, JavaScript worked only in browsers. Version 8.5 changed this, and set the stage for using JavaScript in server-side agents. This chapter focuses on using JavaScript in the classic sense, to manipulate form and page elements in browsers. Code samples are intended to illustrate concepts and strategies but not finished products. Use the samples as starting points for your own work, and certainly go on to explore JavaScript frameworks like Dojo and JQuery.

This chapter includes these topics:

- Inserting JavaScript code into Domino applications
- Using JavaScript to enhance forms and pages
- Writing your own Ajax functions

Using JavaScript in web applications

JavaScript is used pervasively in web applications. Of course, you can write Domino applications without coding a line yourself—Domino will insert the few lines it needs anyway.

JavaScript provides another coding option for many tasks. Field validation, for example, can be done with @formulas or with JavaScript. Unfortunately, not everything you might want to do can be done with a single language, so web applications end up as a mixture of @formulas, LotusScript (or Java), HTML, CSS, and JavaScript.

Contemporary web applications use JavaScript extensively to improve performance and page behavior, so if you don't know much about the language, grab a book or look through one of the many online JavaScript tutorials. A few hours of study should be enough to get you going. Full mastery of JavaScript will take considerably longer as it is a rich and powerful scripting language.

It is also useful to grasp the essentials of the **Document Object Model (DOM),** which is intended to represent and organize elements of a web page and also to provide an API for accessing those elements with a programming language like JavaScript. The structure and naming conventions for the DOM are fairly standard across all browsers, but there are a few differences; some objects and methods are supported by some browsers and not by others. A few illustrations of such differences are presented in this chapter.

Also, spend a little time learning about the **Browser Object Model (BOM),** which is similarly intended to represent the browser and to provide access to browser objects (like the **window** object). Although there is good similarity here, browsers are less standardized than we might like, and this can impact how you write your JavaScript. For this reason, it is important to test your JavaScript with multiple browsers.

The primary purpose of this chapter is to focus on using JavaScript within a Domino Designer context. The examples may help you to learn some JavaScript, but this chapter is not intended as a primer for the language.

Keep it simple, comment the complex

Programming is half engineering and half art. Be kind to the next developer who has to work with your code. Format your scripts with indentations, use sensible variable names, and keep statements and functions relatively simple.

Also leave tracks. Add a few comments in your functions. Use a page within the template to document complex strategies. Yes, it takes a bit of time, but it is the professional thing to do.

Be alert for disabled JavaScript and other options in browsers

In the past, some users disabled JavaScript in their browsers, and older Domino applications may have provided workarounds or notices that were displayed whenever JavaScript support was disabled or unavailable. Those days are long gone; enabled JavaScript support in browsers should be assumed.

Of course, there is always the possibility that someone has turned it off by mistake or otherwise. If JavaScript is disabled, even basic functionality like opening an application or toggling into the Edit mode may be lost. Also be aware that users have considerable control over how their browsers operate; locally disabled browser features can impact how well an application appears to function.

If you suspect a user has turned off support for JavaScript, have him look around his browser for an appropriate setting with which to turn it back on. In this example, JavaScript is disabled in Google's Chrome 8 browser:

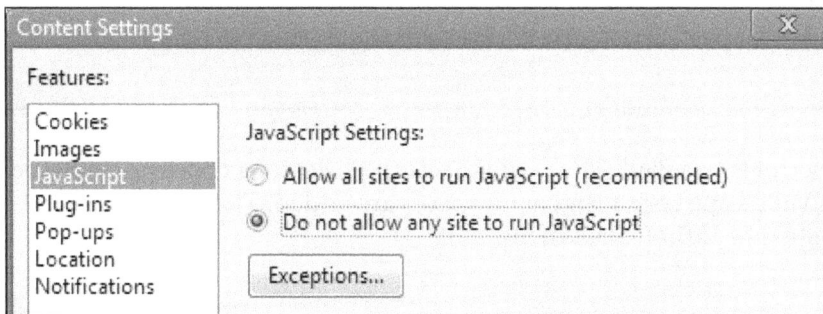

Be alert for inconsistent JavaScript behavior in different browsers

Except for browser extensions, JavaScript behavior should be consistent across all major browsers, but this is not completely so. The following example walks through a specific example in which only minor changes are required to achieve a good result.

This simple script is attached to a button's onClick event:

```
alert(
  "Server Name:\tMY SERVER\r"+
  "Web DB Name:\tMY DATABASE\r"+
  "User ID:\t\tMY USERID")
```

IE 8 displays the alert this way, with the text lined up as expected:

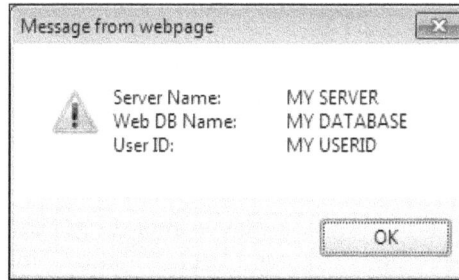

Firefox 3.6 displays the alert unacceptably. It appears that Firefox does not handle the carriage return escape code **\r** in the same way as does IE 8:

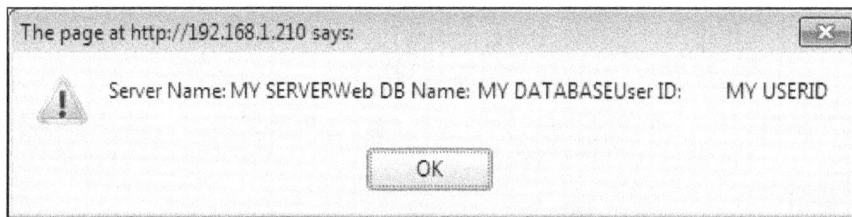

Here the script is tweaked. The carriage return (**\r**) escape codes are replaced with new line (**\n**) escape codes, and extra spaces are added. The result is much better, although still not entirely consistent:

```
alert(
   "Server Name:   \tMY SERVER\n"+
   "Web Name:      \tMY DATABASE\n"+
   "User ID:          \tMY USERID")
```

This example illustrates that even simple scripts can behave quite differently in different browsers. Inconsistent rendering and behavior across browsers has been a problem for a long time, one which Domino web application developers must keep in mind during development and testing. Minor tweaks may result in acceptable behavior, but sometimes more effort is required to achieve the same result in different browsers.

Use browser object detection

While recent browsers support common objects, methods, and properties, there are exceptions. As much as possible, use techniques that behave the same way in all the common browsers.

There may be occasions, however, when you need to use features that are implemented differently in different browsers. If so, use **browser object detection** to determine whether or not a feature is supported by a browser; code an alternate strategy if support is lacking.

Use the **typeof** operator to test for the existence of an object, method, or property. Here is an example:

```
if ( typeof document.implementation.createDocument != "undefined" ) {
alert("'document.implementation.createDocument' IS available.");
}
else {
alert("'document.implementation.createDocument' IS NOT available.");
}
```

IE 8 indicates that the feature is not available:

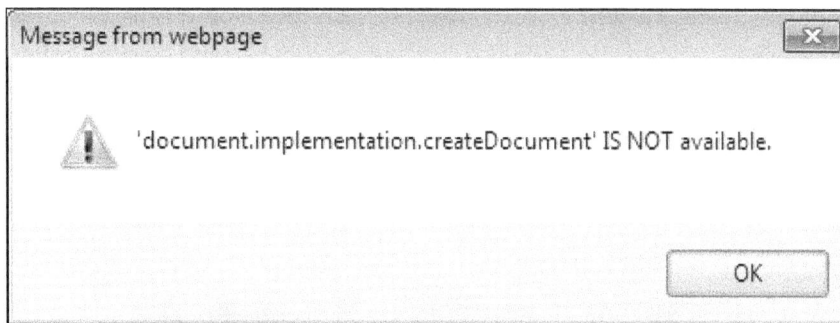

Firefox 3.6 supports the feature:

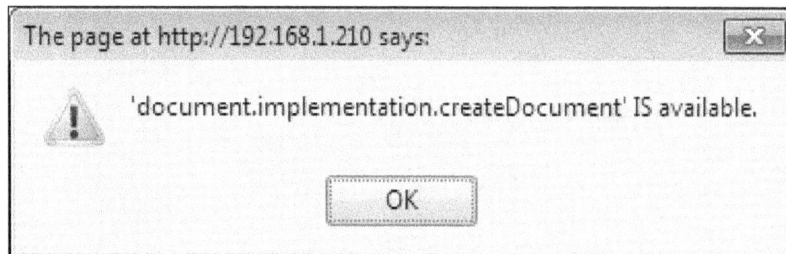

Use browser detection only when really necessary

It is possible to detect a specific browser, but since browser support for various objects changes over time, it is better to detect the support for an object rather than a specific browser. But if there is a need to detect and accommodate Internet Explorer (in the past, a more standards-deviant browser), here is a simple way to do it:

```
if (typeof window.ActiveXObject != 'undefined') {
  alert("Microsoft Browser") ;
  }
else {
  alert("Non-Microsoft Browser") ;
  }
```

If more specific information about a browser is required, the **navigator** object can be interrogated. Three properties contain the information you might need. Parse the results as required:

```
alert (
  "navigator.appName:\n\n" + navigator.appName + "\n\n" +
  "navigator.appVersion:\n\n" + navigator.appVersion + "\n\n" +
  "navigator.userAgent:\n\n" + navigator.userAgent )
```

Here are details provided by Chrome:

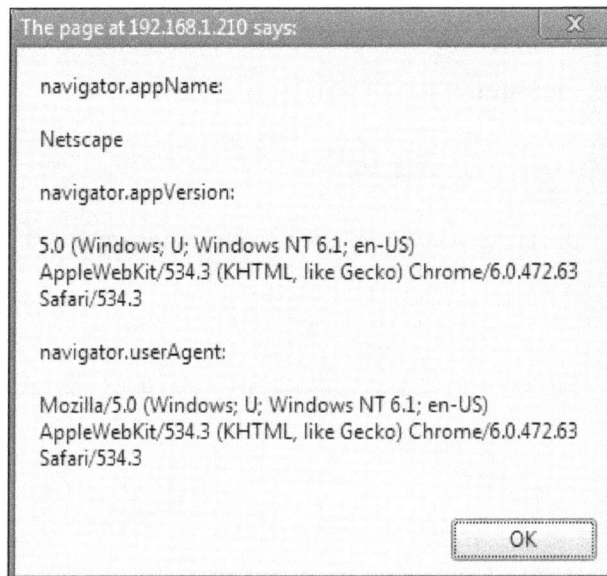

Locating JavaScript in applications

JavaScript can be inserted into various locations within a Domino application, and that flexibility is both a boon and a problem. Follow-on developers may have to go hunting to find an errant function.

JavaScript can be placed on forms or pages in many locations, including these:

- A JavaScript library
- The HTML Head Content area
- The JS Header
- A Web event, like onClick
- Inline as Pass-Thru HTML
- Inline attached to an HTML tag as Pass-Thru HTML
- A separate page or subform
- Form fields (forms only)
- Computed text

Place functions in JavaScript libraries

Unless there is a very good reason not to do so, JavaScript functions should be co-located in one or more JavaScript libraries. Scripts in a library can be shared by all forms and pages in the application, and co-location makes it easier to find functions for maintenance. Function calls, of course, exist in other places.

Create a JavaScript library with Designer. Open **Script Libraries** as in the following screenshot.

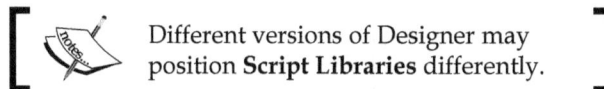

Different versions of Designer may position **Script Libraries** differently.

To add a library, click the **New Javascript Library** button:

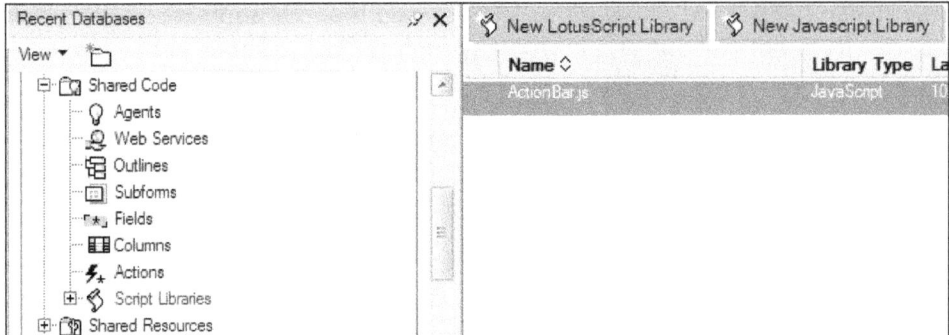

A page opens up. Enter well-formed JavaScript functions. Name and save the library
with **Script Library Properties**. If you have many functions, you may want to create
several libraries, each storing related functions:

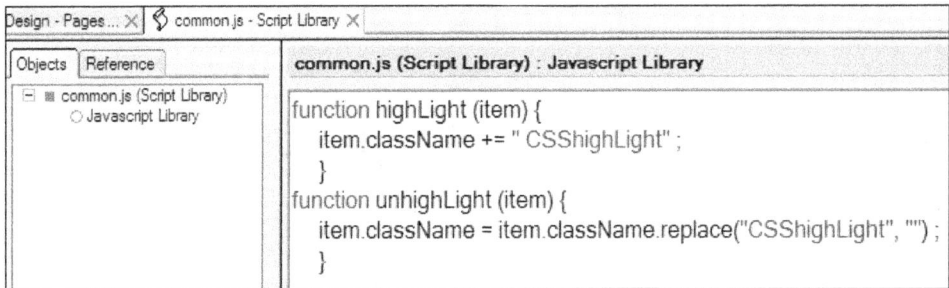

```javascript
function highLight (item) {
    item.className += " CSShighLight" ;
    }
function unhighLight (item) {
    item.className = item.className.replace("CSShighLight", "") ;
    }
```

To link a JavaScript library to a form or page, open the element's **JS Header** and
insert the JavaScript Library Resource from the context menu. Multiple JavaScript
Library Resources can be inserted into the **JS Header**:

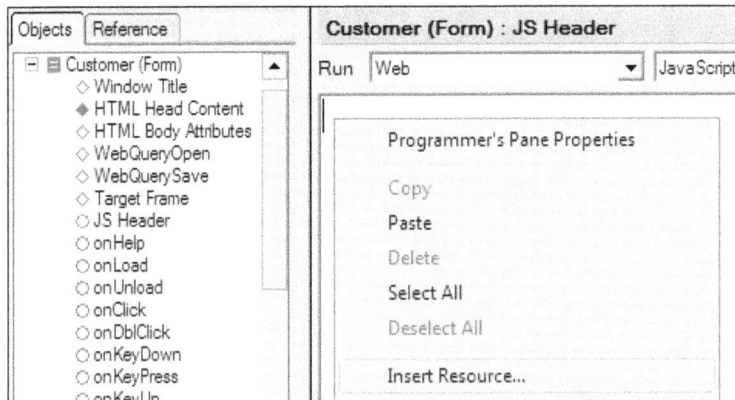

Now add function calls on your form or page wherever appropriate.

Add JavaScript in the JS Header

If a script should run when a form is first loaded, perhaps to set some JavaScript global variables, then you can add code directly into the JS Header. When the header is loaded, the JavaScript executes. In this example, the variable `greeting` becomes available throughout the form, including to any functions located in the JavaScript libraries:

```
var greeting = "Welcome!" ;
```

Add JavaScript to web events

JavaScript can be added to field, form, page, and button events, either as complete scripts or as function calls. For ease of maintenance, code in these events only calls to functions saved in JavaScript libraries. Have I said this enough by now?

Here are some of the web events that accept scripts. The scripts themselves are entered in the Programmer's Pane:

- onHelp
- onLoad
- onUnload
- onClick
- onDblClick
- onKeyDown
- onKeyPress
- onKeyUp
- onMouseDown
- onMouseMove
- onMouseOut
- onMouseOver
- onMouseUp
- onReset
- onSubmit

Of these, onClick, onLoad, onUnload, onReset, and onSubmit may be the most useful. Consider using the onMouseOver and onMouseOut events to add visual cues and other dynamic behavior when an object is mouse hovered.

For example, suppose you want to add some guidance text that is displayed when a form field is mouse hovered.

First, add the field and a message bracketed by `<span>` tags . Remember to mark the HTML tags as Pass-Thru HTML:

Address: Address T `<span id="addressmsg">Enter a complete street address here.</span>`

Next, in the onMouseOver event for the field, code a call to a function containing this JavaScript (or for demonstration purposes only, code this script in the onMouseOver event itself):

```
var item = document.getElementById("addressmsg") ;
item.style.visibility = "visible" ;
```

Now in the onMouseOut event for the field, code this JavaScript:

```
var item = document.getElementById("addressmsg") ;
item.style.visibility = "hidden" ;
```

Finally, code this CSS rule that sets the initial visibility attribute for the span:

```
#addressmsg {
    color: #7F0000;
    visibility: hidden;
    }
```

When the field is mouse hovered, the message displays, and when the field is exited, the message disappears. The following screenshot shows the result with the mouse hovered over the `Address` field; the guidance text is displayed to the right. When the mouse is moved away from the field, the text is hidden:

Address: Enter a complete street address here.

Use a page for JavaScript

In older applications, you may find JavaScript on a separate page element. Using a page element to segregate JavaScript may have been the personal preference of the developer or it may be an artifact from days before JavaScript libraries were available within application designs. JavaScript segregated this way can include JavaScript functions as well as the inline code.

Coding JavaScript on a separate page makes the JavaScript page serve rather like a JavaScript library and a JavaScript header all rolled into one. Forms and pages that reference the JavaScript page remain smaller and cleaner.

While for reasons stated earlier it is a good idea to co-locate JavaScript functions in JavaScript libraries and to minimize inline JavaScript, there may be good reasons to consider creating a separate JavaScript page for your application.

Consider the issue of initializing JavaScript global variables to hold values derived from @formulas. One solution is to code @formulas in fields on a form; JavaScript can access those fields and manipulate those values. If you use non-editable Text fields, remember to enable **Generate HTML for all fields** on the **Defaults** tab of **Form Properties**; otherwise the values of such fields render as simple text and cannot be accessed by JavaScript.

In this example, the default formula for a field named URoles contains this formula:

```
@Implode(@UserRoles)
```

A JavaScript variable roles is set equal to the result of the @UserRoles function with this JavaScript statement:

```
roles = document.forms[0].URoles.value ;
```

But remember that this solution requires adding a field to every form. If you need many temporary fields like this, then each field must be added to every form. The forms are not as simple and clean as they might be, and updating those fields later on might be time-consuming.

An alternative solution requires the use of a separate page element that contains JavaScript statements that initialize JavaScript global variables. A form that requires access to these global variables links to the JavaScript page, and the global variables are then available to any scripts on the form or called from the form.

> This technique is intended for forms accessed with a web browser. Care should be taken to prevent JavaScript errors when the form is opened with the Notes client.

To implement this strategy, create a page within the design to hold the JavaScript variable assignment statements. Use computed text to supply values for the variables.

In this example, several global variables are defined on a page (`startup.js`). Note that the terms on the right-hand side of the assignments include computed text. The @formulas generally resolve to text strings, which are then surrounded by quotation marks:

```
// startup.js
var NotesName = "<Computed Value>" ;
var NotesCName = "<Computed Value>" ;
var NotesRoles = "<Computed Value>" ;
var ServerName = "<Computed Value>" ;
var ServerDomain = "<Computed Value>" ;
var AppTitle = "<Computed Value>" ;
var WebDbName = "<Computed Value>" ;
```

Here is the computed text for each of these JavaScript variables. Most of these @formulas should be familiar to you:

- **NotesName**:
  `@UserName`

- **NotesCName**:
  `@Name([CN];@UserName)`

- **NotesRoles**:
  `@Implode(@UserRoles)`

- **ServerName**:
  `@ServerName`

- **ServerDomain**:
  `svr := @ServerName ;`

  `@DbLookup("":"";svr:"names.nsf";"($servers)";svr;"SMTPFullHost Domain")`

- **AppTitle**:
  `@DbTitle`

- **WebDbName**:
  `@WebDbName`

By the book, the content type of a JavaScript page should be set to `text/javascript` although as a practical matter, setting the **Content type** to **HTML** in **Page Properties** seems to work as well:

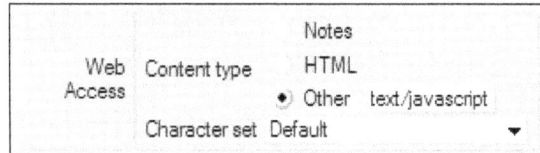

```
                            Notes
       Web   Content type    HTML
       Access               ● Other   text/javascript
             Character set  Default                 ▼
```

Link a form to the JavaScript page with an @formula in the form's HTML Head Content area. More than one JavaScript page can be included. Here is how a form would link to a single JavaScript page:

```
"<script type='text/javascript' src='/" +
@WebDbName + "/startup.js?OpenPage' />" +
"</script>" +
@NewLine
```

To verify that the JavaScript global variables are, indeed, created and available to the form, create a button on the form and add this JavaScript to its onClick event:

```
alert(
  "NotesName = \t" + NotesName + "\n" +
  "NotesCName = \t" + NotesCName + "\n" +
  "NotesRoles = \t" + NotesRoles + "\n" +
  "ServerName = \t" + ServerName + "\n" +
  "ServerDomain = \t" + ServerDomain + "\n" +
  "AppTitle = \t" + AppTitle + "\n" +
  "WebDbName = \t" + WebDbName + "\n"
  );
```

Clicking the button displays the computed JavaScript variables:

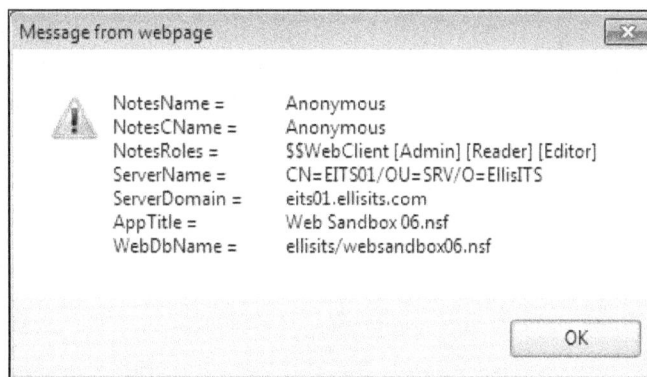

```
Message from webpage                                    [X]

    ⚠    NotesName =      Anonymous
         NotesCName =     Anonymous
         NotesRoles =     $$WebClient [Admin] [Reader] [Editor]
         ServerName =     CN=EITS01/OU=SRV/O=EllisITS
         ServerDomain =   eits01.ellisits.com
         AppTitle =       Web Sandbox 06.nsf
         WebDbName =      ellisits/websandbox06.nsf

                                              [    OK    ]
```

Note that for this example, user Anonymous was granted Read access to `names.nsf` on the server, which would normally not be allowed.

To assign a Domino Boolean value to a JavaScript variable as a Boolean value, use a computed text formula that returns either the string **true** or the string **false**:

```
var JSSupport = <Computed Value> ;
```

The computed text in this example consists of an @formula that returns either **true** or **false,** which are Boolean primitives in JavaScript:

```
@If(@BrowserInfo("JavaScript");"true";"false")
```

Computed text formulas on the JavaScript page can also include JavaScript formatting characters (for displaying in an alert box) as in the following example where new line escape codes are appended to each user role in the string that is assigned to the JavaScript variable.

```
@Implode(@UserRoles;"\\n")
```

When this string is displayed in an alert, each user role is written to a separate line:

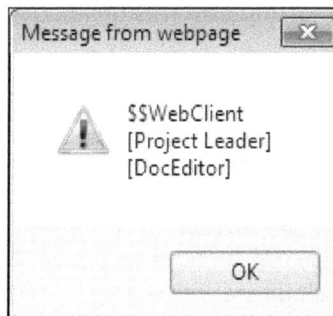

Use a subform for JavaScript

An alternative to placing JavaScript and computed text on a separate page is to place the same JavaScript and computed text on a subform, which is then included with each form. An advantage with this technique over the JavaScript page technique is that it works with the Notes client.

There are two minor disadvantages, however. The subform—and consequently the JavaScript—cannot be included on page elements. Secondly, the subform must be inserted at the top of the form in order for other scripts on the form to access global variables or functions defined on the subform.

Make sure the JavaScript *and the computed text* coded on the subform is all marked as Pass-Thru HTML. Also assure that the option **Render pass through HTML in Notes** is selected on the **Form Info** tab of **Form Properties**.

Consolidate and co-locate JavaScript

Whenever possible during a design refresh, follow these guidelines:

- Convert most or all inline JavaScript into a JavaScript functions.
- Consolidate JavaScript functions into one or more JavaScript libraries in the template and then insert those libraries into the JS Headers of forms and pages as needed.
- If your application uses many JavaScript global variables, pull that code together into a small JavaScript page or library and then add an appropriate link to that page or library on forms and pages as needed.

With all inline JavaScript converted to functions, all functions tucked into script libraries and all global variables co-located on one page, future developers need to look in only a few places to make changes. And they may thank you for it.

Developing and debugging scripts

JavaScript code runs when browser events occur—typically in response to something that the user does (for example, clicks a button). Developers should test all the scripts by exercising all the functionality of the application. Sometimes the result of a script is obvious because something moves or changes color. Sometimes nothing obvious happens or perhaps an unexpected **page not found** error is displayed. Scripts can fail without displaying error messages or any other indication of failure, and the developer is left wondering where to start troubleshooting.

In addition to inserting JavaScript **alert** function calls into suspect scripts and viewing the page source in the browser, here are two general techniques that can help during script development.

Use browser debugging tools

Get to know your browsers' developer tools and other options. For example, IE displays a warning icon (and sometimes a message) in the lower left-hand corner of the browser window. Click the icon to display additional information:

Firefox provides some information with its Error console that provides a quick view of detected errors:

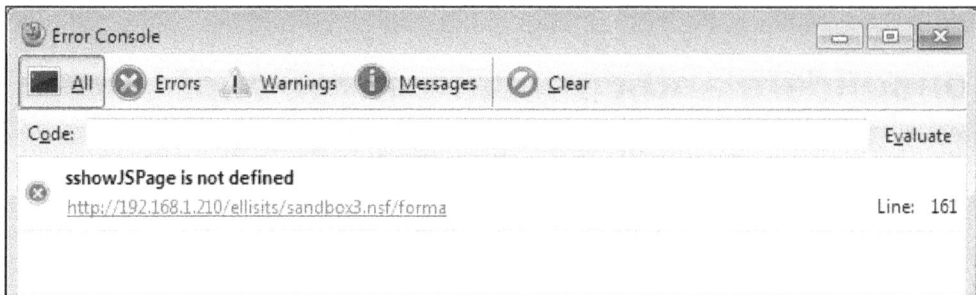

Chrome provides some information in its Developer Tools frame:

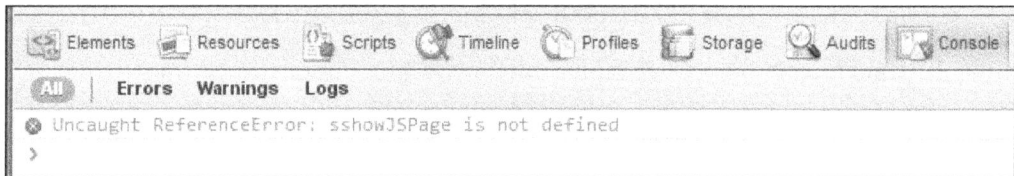

Explore the browsers with which you work, along with developer aids and plug-ins that are freely available on the Web. Such tools may save you considerable development time.

Validate JavaScripts

JavaScript, like HTML and CSS, can be validated. Results may suggest improvements to your code, which can prevent problems when the application goes into production. One online validation service is located at: `http://www.javascriptlint.com`

Simply paste a script or script snippet into the text area and click the **Lint** button. Detected errors are highlighted. The process is iterative, so changes can be made directly in the Lint text area. When finished, copy the modified JavaScript back into your design element. Like all tools, use this with caution and circumspection. Error messages, as in this example, may not be correct, but they can point you in the right direction:

Using JavaScript to enhance forms and pages

As we have seen already, there are many ways in which JavaScript can be added into web applications. In this section, we explore some additional ways that scripts can be used to enhance forms and pages.

Run JavaScript on load

Not uncommonly, you may want to run some JavaScript when a form first loads into the browser. This can be a bit tricky since documents can open in Read or Edit mode, and in Edit mode documents are often refreshed from the server. You may want to run a script only with a document in Read mode or only in Edit mode. And you probably want an initialization script to run only once even if the document is refreshed from the server. These kinds of situations need to be addressed and tested carefully to assure a good final product.

There are some obvious places to insert JavaScript so that it runs when a form first loads:

- The JS Header
- The onLoad Event
- Inline on the form

Positioned in any of these locations, a script might possibly run before the document is completely loaded, and depending upon what the script does, this could produce erroneous results.

Another issue concerns the edit mode of the document. As mentioned, it may be that a script should run when a document is in Edit mode, but not when it is in Read mode. Here is a technique that can be used to address this issue:

At the bottom of the form, add some computed text with this @formula as a value:

```
mode := @If(@IsDocBeingEdited;"Edit" ; "Read") ;
"[<script type='text/javascript'>" +
"{" + "runOnLoad('" + mode + "');}"+
"</script>]"
```

As Domino composes the source for the form, the value for the Formula variable `mode` is set to `Read` or `Edit`, and then the JavaScript code is composed with the appropriate argument. Here is what the computed source looks like when the document opens in Read mode:

```
script type='text/javascript'>{runOnLoad('Read');}</script>
```

When the form loads into the browser, the script runs and invokes a `runOnLoad()` function with a single argument. Here is the skeleton of a `runOnLoad()` function, with two alerts inserted for debugging purposes:

```
function runOnLoad(mode) {
  if ( typeof mode == "undefined" ) { var mode = "Read" ; }
  if ( mode == "Edit" ) {
    // Insert code here which runs if document is in Edit mode
    alert("Document is in Edit mode") ;
    }
  else {
    // Insert code here which runs if document is in Read mode
    alert("Document is in Read mode") ;
    }
  }
```

Variations can include tests for new or existing documents, or for any set of field values or attributes.

Access CGI variables

A previous topic covered the idea of JavaScript global variables and how they could be set when a document or form is opened. Another common set of global variables are the CGI variables that are standard values available in web browsers. CGI variables define a number of web browser, page, and server properties. CGI variables, like other JavaScript global variables, are available when a document is in the Read mode as well as in Edit mode.

Typically, a subform is designed to hold all the CGI variables, and then that subform is inserted at the top of forms as required. If the fields are named and initialized properly, then Domino sets the variables for you. For example, here are three relatively useful CGI variables:

- Path_Info
- Query_String
- Server_Name

If the CGI subform contains three fields with these names, and if the default value for each field is its own name, then those values become available when a document opens. Because these are Domino fields, they can be referenced in @formulas. The following @formula recreates the URL required to open a specific document or form:

```
"http://" + Server_Name + Path_Info
```

CGI variables are available to JavaScript code as well. This JavaScript snippet creates the same URL string as above:

```
var path = document.forms[0].Path_Info.value ;
var server = document.forms[0].Server_Name.value ;
var url = "http://" + server + path ;
```

Note that these variables are specifically available to web browsers, and not to the Notes client. Provision must be made to handle missing values or JavaScript errors when such documents or forms are opened with the Notes client. See Designer help for more information, including a complete table of CGI variables that can be used.

Validating fields

Client-side JavaScript is perhaps most commonly used to validate values entered by users into fields on a form. Validations can be done when a user exits a required field or when he submits the document. Field-level validations occur immediately upon exiting a field. Form-level validations occur when a user clicks a button (for example, **Submit**) to save a document.

Consider the following general purpose function coded in a field's onBlur event. In this example, assume the field is named `Address` and that it is required:

```
detectBlanks(this, "Address field is required.") ;
```

The first argument in the function call's argument list refers to the field itself; the second argument is an optional message that is displayed if the field is blank. When the user tabs away from the field or moves the cursor to another location with the mouse, the onBlur event fires and the `detectBlanks()` function runs.

The `detectBlanks()` function contains logic to detect nothing (or blanks) in the calling field. In this case, if no address is entered, then the field's background color is set to yellow as a visual cue, and an alert is displayed:

```
function detectBlanks(field, message) {
  var string = field.value;
  if ( typeof message == "undefined" || message == "" ) {
    message = "Blank field detected." ;
  }
  string = string.split(' ').join('') ;
  if ( string=="" ) {
    field.style.backgroundColor = "Yellow" ;
    alert( "Warning: " + message ) ;
    return false ;
  }
  field.style.backgroundColor = "White" ;
  return true ;
}
```

Some developers set the focus into a field upon validation failure with the following line of code. Here, `fieldname` is a placeholder for the real field name:

```
document.forms[0].fieldname.focus() ;
```

By coding this line in a field validation function, the cursor is set back into the field whose validation just failed; the user is essentially captive until he enters the required information. I find this behavior fairly annoying, so I do not recommend it. Use this technique only if it is really, really necessary.

Validating all required fields upon submission is generally a good strategy. JavaScript in the form's onSubmit event calls a general purpose field validation function:

```
if( !validateForm() ) { return(false); }
```

If the validation function fails (returns `false`), then the onSubmit event fails and the document is not submitted.

This sample `validateForm()` function validates only two fields and those only for blanks; it can easily be expanded to analyze many more fields. Note that only a single alert displays at the end:

```
function validateForm() {
  var message = "" ;
  var string ;
  f = document.forms[0] ;
  string = f.Address.value ;
  string = string.split(' ').join('') ;
  if ( string == "" ) { message += "Address\n" ; }
  string = f.City.value ;
  string = string.split(' ').join('') ;
  if ( string == "" ) { message += "City\n" ; }
  if ( message != "" ) {
    alert( "Please enter information for required field(s):\n\n" +
    message ) ;
    return false ;
    }
  return true ;
  }
```

Field validations can be much more complex of course, but the basic strategy presented here can be expanded to serve your own validation requirements.

Validate number fields

A field on a Domino form intended to store numeric data can be defined as a number field rather than as a text field. Using the Notes client, a user enters **numeric text,** which is automatically converted to a true number before being stored in the number field.

On the Web, all values typed into fields are submitted to the server as text. If non-numeric text (for example, "ten") is entered for a number field and then the document is saved, an error is detected by the server and the document is not saved. Instead, a generic **HTTP 500** message is displayed—not very helpful in determining what is wrong:

The website cannot display the page

HTTP 500

Most likely causes:
- The website is under maintenance.
- The website has a programming error.

The solution to this problem is to validate that the entered text is indeed numeric, before allowing the form to be saved. Here a function call is added to the Age field's onBlur event:

```
detectNumber(this,"Age must be a number.")
```

This detectNumber() function is also relatively simple and straightforward. If non-numeric text is entered into the Age field, then a warning displays.

The first argument in the function call's argument list refers to the field itself; the second argument is an optional message that displays if the field is non-numeric or blank. When the user tabs away from the field or moves the cursor to another location with the mouse, the onBlur event fires and the detectNumber() function runs.

The detectNumber() function contains logic that detects non-numeric text or nothing or blanks in the calling field. In this case, if no age is entered, then the field's background color is set to yellow as a visual cue, and an alert is displayed:

```
function detectNumber(field, message) {
  if ( typeof message== "undefined" || message == "" ) {
    message = "Non-numeric data detected." ;
    }
  var data = field.value ;
  var b = isNaN(data) ;
  var string = data.split(' ').join('') ;
  if ( b || string == "" ) {
    field.style.backgroundColor = "Yellow" ;
    alert( "Warning: " + message ) ;
    return false;
    }
  field.style.backgroundColor = "White" ;
  return true ;
  }
```

Numeric field validations can be more complex—an entered value must be an integer and within a certain range, for example.

Use a date picker for date fields

A field on a Domino form intended to store a date may be defined as a date field. Using the Notes client, a user enters text in a date format (for example, 01/01/2020), and the text is automatically converted to a true date value before being stored in the date field. But on the Web, as mentioned previously, all values typed into fields on a form are submitted to the server as text. If text is entered for a date field, but that text is not in an acceptable date format, then an error is detected by the server when the document is submitted and the document is not saved. A generic **HTTP 500** message is displayed.

The best solution to this problem is to use a **date picker** rather than to allow manual entry of dates.

The strategy explained in this topic refers to a date picker written by Julian Robichaux and freely available at the following website. Search the site for **datepicker** to locate the sample page.

```
www.nsftools.com
```

This date picker tool consists of five components:

- A date field on a form
- A button on the form that activates the date picker feature
- Several date picker global JavaScript variables
- Several date picker JavaScript functions in a JavaScript library
- A date picker CSS style sheet

Here's how the feature might look on a form. Note that a previously selected date is displayed in the date field to the right of the button. Clicking a date in the control saves that new date to the field and hides the control:

This should take about an hour or less to get running. Here are the steps required to incorporate Julian's JavaScript datepicker into a form:

1. Browse to the website listed above and search for **datepicker**.
2. Select the sample date picker page and read the instructions.
3. View the source code of the sample datepicker page.
4. Copy the JavaScript global variables to a new `DatePickerVars.js` page, as suggested in a previous topic, or to the HTML Head Content area of a form as an @formula.
5. Copy the JavaScript functions to a new `DatePicker.js` JavaScript library.
6. Copy the CSS rules to a new `DatePicker.css` page.
7. As necessary, add links to the `DatePickerVars.js` and `DatePicker.css` pages in the form's HTML Head Content area.
8. Insert the `DatePicker.js` JavaScript library into the form's JS Header.
9. Add a date field to the form (for example, `StartDate`).
10. Add a button to the form with this JavaScript function call (where `StartDate` is the name of the date field):

```
displayDatePicker("StartDate")
```

In this particular case, there are options regarding how the date might be returned to the date field. Also, the CSS rules can be modified to style the date picker elements as desired. Comments in the source code provide additional details.

Explore the Web for other available datepickers.

And thank you, Julian Robichaux!

Warn users before leaving an un-submitted form

One of the more frustrating web experiences is entering data into a form and then losing it by browsing away from the document before the data is submitted. Here is one *partial* solution to this issue, inspired by the write-up on this page:

```
http://www.webreference.com/dhtml/diner/beforeunload/bunload4.html
```

This example can provide a good mechanism to warn users before they inadvertently lose the data already entered into form fields. I want to emphasize that this is a *partial* solution because there may be cases where it breaks down. You should check the code in a variety of browsers and proceed accordingly. As of this writing, the technique works with IE, Firefox, and Safari, while results with Chrome are mixed.

The technique relies on a browser's `onbeforeunload` event that fires whenever a user begins to leave a page, perhaps by clicking a link to another page, by clicking the browser refresh button, or by toggling into Read mode.

In this solution, when a field loses focus, the `onbeforeunload` event is initialized with a warning message. If the user then attempts to leave the page without saving the data, then the warning confirmation is displayed. Firefox displays the message like this:

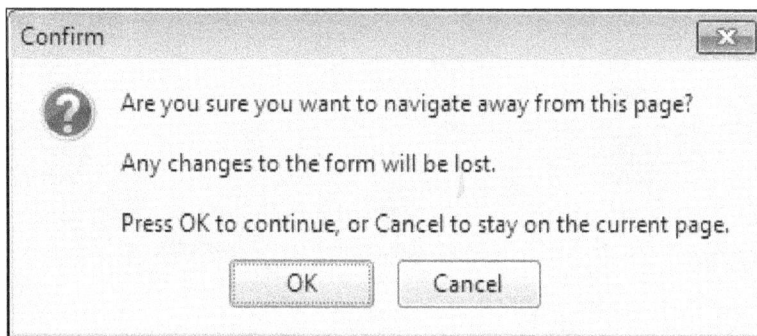

There are a number of pieces to this solution. In summary, here are the steps:

1. Create a JavaScript library and add five functions to it.
2. Link to the JavaScript library from the form's JS Header.
3. Add a hidden field to the form (`FormChanged`).
4. Add a function call to the form's onLoad event.
5. Add function calls to the onClick events of form fields that refresh the form automatically when changed.
6. Add function calls to the onBlur events of form fields that do not refresh the form automatically when changed.
7. Add a function call to the form's **Save** or **Submit** button.
8. Set the value of the `FormChanged` field to `no` before saving a document.

Here are the details:

Step 1: Create a JavaScript library.

Add these five functions to the JavaScript library:

- SetFormChanged()
- GetbeforeunloadMsg()
- RefreshingForm()
- Setbeforeunload()
- Initbeforeunload()

Here is a summary of what each of these functions does:

The SetFormChanged() function sets the FormChanged field to yes and that's about it.

```
function SetFormChanged() {
    document.forms[0].FormChanged.value = "yes" ;
    }
```

The GetbeforeunloadMsg() function checks the value of the FormChanged field and returns a message if the field's value is yes or returns null otherwise:

```
function GetbeforeunloadMsg() {
    var msg = "Any changes to the form will be lost." ;
    var chg = document.forms[0].FormChanged.value ;
    if (chg == "yes") { return msg ; }
    else { return null ; }
    }
```

The RefreshingForm() function sets the FormChanged field to yes and then sets the onbeforeunload event to null, which essentially gives the event nothing to do. This function is added to the onClick events of fields that automatically refresh the form when changed:

```
function RefreshingForm() {
    document.forms[0].FormChanged.value = "yes" ;
    window.onbeforeunload = null ;
    }
```

The `Setbeforeunload()` function receives an argument, `true` or `false`, and then either initializes the onbeforeunload event or sets it to null. If the argument is `true`, it also calls `SetFormChanged()` to change the value of the `FormChanged` field to `yes`:

```
function Setbeforeunload(onoff) {
   window.onbeforeunload = (onoff) ? GetbeforeunloadMsg : null ;
   if (onoff) { SetFormChanged() ; } ;
   }
```

The `Initbeforeunload()` function checks the value of the `FormChanged` field. If the field is `yes` (indicating that one or more fields on the document were previously changed) then this function calls the `Setbeforeunload()` function with the argument of `true` and causes `Setbeforeunload()` to initialize the onbeforeunload event. If the value of the `FormChanged` field is `no` (indicating that the document is loading for the first time or it is being refreshed, but no fields have been changed), then `Initbeforeunload()` calls the `Setbeforeunload()` function with the argument of `false` and causes `Setbeforeunload()` not to initialize the onbeforeunload event:

```
function Initbeforeunload() {
   if (document.forms[0].FormChanged.value == "yes" ) {
      Setbeforeunload(true) ; }
   else { Setbeforeunload(false) ; }
   }
```

Step 2: Link the JavaScript library to the form.

Add a link in the form's JS Header to the JavaScript library by inserting the JavaScript Library Resource, as discussed earlier in this chapter.

Step 3: Add a hidden, editable Text field to the form.

Add to the form a hidden Text field named `FormChanged` with `no` as its default value. If this name is changed, then the JavaScript functions must be changed to match.

Step 4: Add a function call to the form's onLoad event.

Code the following function call in the form's onLoad event:

```
Initbeforeunload() ;
```

The result is that the onbeforeunload event is either initialized or it isn't, depending upon whether fields on the document were previously changed. When a document is loaded for the first time, the value of the `FormChanged` field should be `no` and the function `Initbeforeunload()` therefore sets the onbeforeunload event to null. But if a field on the form caused the form to refresh, then the value of the `FormChanged` field should be `yes` in which case the function `Initbeforeunload()` initializes the onbeforeunload event with a message.

Step 5: Add function calls to the onClick events of form fields that refresh the form automatically.

For each field that refreshes the form automatically when changed, code the following function call in the field's onClick event:

```
RefreshingForm();
```

The logic assumes that a clicked field might have been changed.

Step 6: Add function calls to the onBlur events of form fields that do not refresh the form automatically.

For each field that does not refresh the form automatically when changed, code the following function call in the field's onBlur event:

```
Setbeforeunload(true) ;
```

The logic assumes that if the cursor was placed in the field and then moved, then that field may have been changed.

Step 7: Add a function call to the form's Save or Submit button.

When a user clicks the **Save** or **Submit** button on the form, a warning message is unwarranted. To prevent the warning, add this function call to one or more events on the button:

```
Setbeforeunload(false) ;
```

In this example, the function is added to button events using the **Other** option of the **Button Extra HTML** tab of **Button Properties**:

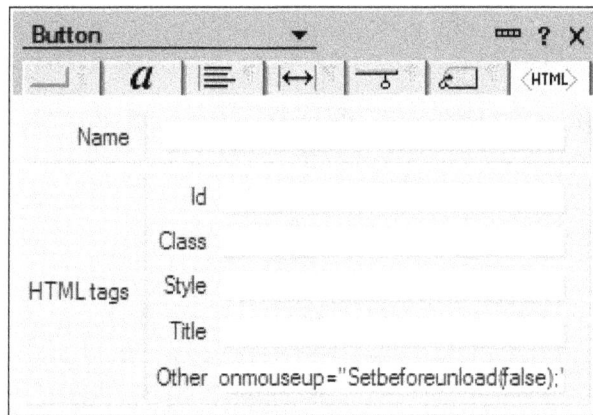

The full value of **Other** sets values for both mouse clicks and key clicks:

```
onmouseup="Setbeforeunload(false)";
onkeypress="Setbeforeunload(false)"
```

Step 8: Set the value of the FormChanged field to no before saving a document.

Set the value of the `FormChanged` field to `no` before a document is saved. There are several ways to do this. For example, the **Save** button's `Click` event might be coded with this @formula:

```
@SetField("FormChanged";"no");
@Command([FileSave]);
@Command([FileCloseWindow]);
```

Use Ajax calls to avoid server round trips

Ajax is the name of a significant JavaScript technique used in the browser to retrieve data from a server. Ajax calls can dramatically improve the performance and behavior of forms on the Web, leading to a more satisfying end user experience.

(There is some debate about whether **AJAX** is an acronym or not. For those who believe it is, it stands for **Asynchronous JavaScript And XML**.)

In traditional Domino applications, some action on the part of a user may require data displayed in a form in the browser to be refreshed from the server. The server re-computes the form and sends the new version to the browser. Unfortunately there can be a noticeable time-delay while this happens. The screen may blink or jiggle up-and-down, and often the form is repositioned in the browser window. The refresh delay and form movement can be a bit annoying.

With Ajax calls, response is much, much quicker and the form does not move around on the screen. An Ajax call retrieves only a relatively small amount of information from the server, and that information is then inserted quickly into the visible form as directed by JavaScript functions doing the work. The full form itself is not recomputed or reloaded.

At a high level, let us say the user clicks a button that invokes a JavaScript function. That function invokes several other scripts as needed. A request for specific data (perhaps a column of data from a view) is sent from the browser to an agent in the application on the server. The agent performs a lookup for the required data and sends that data back to the browser where another JavaScript function retrieves it. The data is formatted as needed and inserted into the visible form where it may appear as a drop-down list of options or in some other manner.

The key browser component that enables all this to work is called the **XMLHttpRequest Object**. This object serves as a communication link between JavaScript running in the browser and an agent running on the server. The flow can be summarized like this:

1. A script creates an instance of the request object and tell it what to do.
2. The request object sends the request to the agent on the server.
3. The agent returns data to the request object in the browser.
4. Another script receives data from the request object and then inserts it into the current page.

Like any complex strategy, a number of components must be installed together for this to work. There is a form with elements that call JavaScript functions; there are several interdependent JavaScript functions which run in the browser; there is an agent that runs on the server; and of course, there is a view or other data source in the application that holds retrievable data.

Here are the components used in this example:

- A form used to create keyword documents
- A lookup view that indexes the keyword documents
- A form that interacts with the user in the web browser
- A button on the user form that initiates the request for data
- A target field or location on the form where the retrieved data displays
- Hidden Computed for display fields that define the location of a LotusScript agent and the source of the data
- A wrapper function that requests data, formats the response into HTML, and then inserts that HTML into the target field or location on the form
- A function that manages the XMLHttpRequest Object
- Four primitive Ajax functions:
    ◦ A function to create an XMLHttpRequest Object
    ◦ A function to send the request for data
    ◦ A function to receive the data
    ◦ A function to delete the XMLHttpRequest Object
- A LotusScript agent that receives the request, fetches the data, and sends it back to the browser

This example is not a complete application. Use the sample scripts as a starting point for writing your own Ajax functions and agents.

Here are the steps required to implement this strategy.

Step 1: Create a JavaScript library.

Create a JavaScript library. In this example, the library's name is **Ajax Functions**. Shortly we will add functions to the library.

Step 2: Create a keyword form and lookup view.

Create a simple form that composes keyword documents. Create a lookup view that selects only the keyword documents, and displays those keywords in the first column. Assure that the first column sorts in ascending order. In this example, the name of the view is **AjaxLookupView**.

Add several keyword documents. In this example, each keyword is the name of a sport.

Step 3: Create a user form.

Create a form with which the web user interacts. Several values are required for the Ajax functions, so these are added to the form as hidden Computed for display fields. There are other ways to provide these values to the JavaScript functions, of course, but for simplicity, defining these values in fields should suffice.

Remember to enable **Generate HTML for all fields** in **Form Properties**.

These are the hidden Computed for display fields we need, along with the @formulas required to compute their values:

- **AgentName:**
  `"XMLHttpResponseAgentdbColumn"`
- **AgentPathName:**
  `"/"+@WebDbName+"/"+AgentName+"?OpenAgent"`
- **ServerName:**
  `@Name([Abbreviate];@ServerName)`
- **DbPathName:**
  `@Left(@Subset(@DbName;-1);"\\")+"\\"+"\\"+@RightBack(@Subset(@DbName;-1);"\\")`
- **ViewName:**
  `"AjaxLookupView"`

This is the name of the lookup view that indexes the keyword documents. In this example, the name of the view is computed.

ColumnNo: `"1"`

This is the column in the lookup view from which the data is retrieved. In our example, this is column one, computed as a string.

Add an Editable field to the form that will receive the data. In this example, the field named Keyword1 is a checkbox field whose value is computed from a formula. Values saved in the field appear as checked options when a document is reopened. Here is the specific formula for the choices:

```
@If(Keyword1="";"All Sports";Keyword1)
```

Also, surround the `Keyword1` field with the HTML `<span>` tags marked as Pass-Thru HTML. The retrieved data, with appropriate HTML tags, will be inserted into the **innerHTML** property of this span.

Add a button to the form. Add this JavaScript function call to the button's onClick event:

```
getDbColumnData() ;
```

The `getDbColumnData()` function resides in a JavaScript library. This script, along with other scripts, retrieves data from the server, reformats it appropriately and inserts it into the innerHTML property of the `Keyword1` span, as mentioned above.

Insert a link the Ajax Functions library in the form's **JS Header**.

Add some Action buttons to cancel, edit, and save the document as appropriate.

Add a `$$Return` field if necessary.

Here is what the user form should look like in Designer:

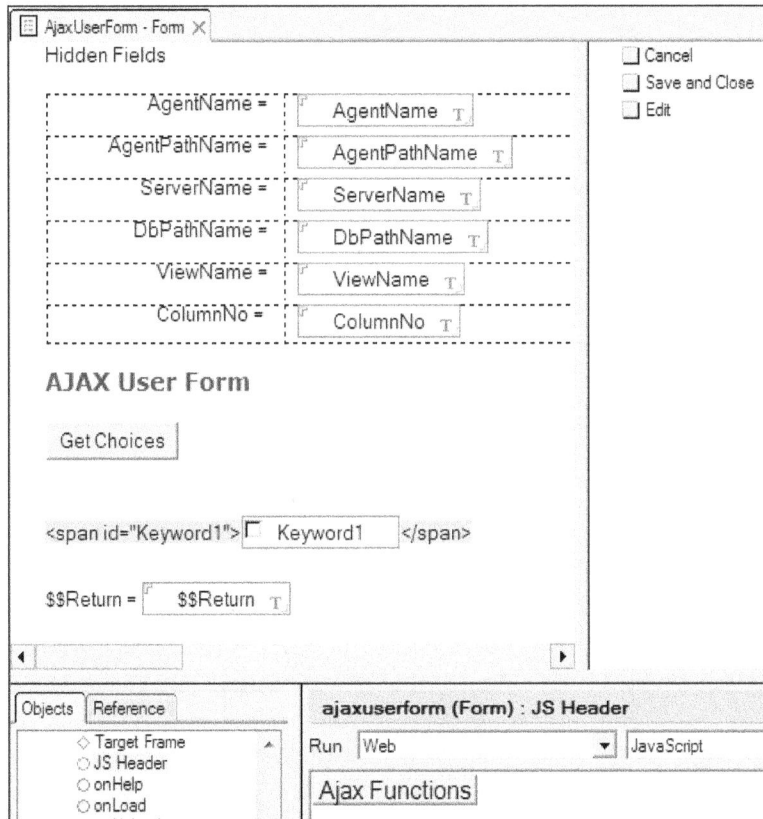

Step 4: Create a wrapper function.

Create a JavaScript wrapper function in the Ajax Functions library. This function requests data, wraps the returned data in HTML tags, and inserts the result into the Keyword1 span:

```
function getDbColumnData() {
  var data ; var i ; var j = 0 ;
  var ihtml = "" ;
  var items = new Array ;
  // Retrieve the hidden field values from the user form
  f = document.forms[0] ;
  var AgentPathName = f.AgentPathName.value ;
  var ServerName = f.ServerName.value ;
  var DbPathName = f.DbPathName.value ;
  var ViewName = f.ViewName.value ;
  var ColumnNo = f.ColumnNo.value ;
  // Create a parameter string and full url
```

```
      var parms = "&server=" + ServerName + "&pathname=" + DbPathName +
        "&view=" + ViewName + "&column=" + ColumnNo ;
      var url = AgentPathName + parms ;
      // Retrieve the data and check for failure
      data = DbColumn(url) ;
      if (! data) {
        alert("Error: No data found.") ;
        return false ;
        }
      // Split the returned list into array elements
      items = data.split('\n') ;
      // Surround each list item with HTML tags
      for (i = 0; i<items.length; i++) {
        if (items[i] != "") {
          ihtml = ihtml + "<input type='checkbox' name='Keyword1'" +
            " value='"+items[i]+ "'>"+items[i]+"<br>" ;
          }
        }
      // Write the HTML into the Keyword1 SPAN
      document.getElementById("Keyword1").innerHTML = ihtml ;
      return;
      }
```

Take some time to look through this wrapper function. Your wrapper functions may be similar. The key to making this useful is in wrapping the retrieved list items in the proper HTML tags.

Step 5: Create a function to manage the Request Object.

This short JavaScript function is called by the wrapper function. Its job is to create the XMLHttpRequest Object and to organize the data retrieval. The single argument it receives consists of the reference to the LotusScript agent in the database along with the parameters that tell the agent where to get the required data:

```
function DbColumn(url) {
  reqObject = false ;
  createXReq() ;
  sendXReq(url) ;
  var response = reqObject.responseText ;
  deleteXReq() ;
  return response ;
  }
```

Step 6: Create functions to support the XMLHttpRequest Object.

These are the four scripts that create the request object, initiate the request to the agent, receive the data back, and delete the request object.

The createXReq() function creates the XMLHttpRequest Object. Note that different browsers instantiate this object with different syntax:

```
// Create an XMLHttpRequest object
function createXReq() {
  try { // most browsers
    reqObject = new XMLHttpRequest() ;
    }
  catch(ms1) {
    try { // newer Microsoft browsers
      reqObject = new ActiveXObject("Msxml2.XMLHTTP") ;
      }
    catch(ms2) {
      try { // older Microsoft browsers
        reqObject = new ActiveXObject("Microsoft.XMLHTTP") ;
        }
      catch(failed) {
        reqObject = false ;
        }
      }
    }
  return reqObject ;
  }
```

The sendXReq() function passes the request for data (as a URL string) to the XMLHttpRequest Object. Note that the receiveXReq() function is set to fire when the request object achieves the **ready state**—when it has received data back from the agent:

```
// Send an XMLHttpRequest request
function sendXReq(url) {
  if( !url ) {
    alert( "No URL specified." ) ;
    return false ;
    }
  reqObject.open("Get", url, false) ;
  reqObject.onreadystatechange = receiveXReq ;
  reqObject.send(null) ;
  return reqObject.responseText ;
  }
```

The `receiveXReq()` function waits for the XMLHttpRequest Object to receive data back from the server.

```
// Receive an XMLHttpRequest request response
function receiveXReq() {
  if(reqObject.readyState != 4) {
    return ;
    }
  if (reqObject.status == 200) {
    return ;
    }
  return false ;
}
```

The `deleteXReq()` function deletes the XMLHttpRequest Object:

```
// Delete an XMLHttpRequest object
function deleteXReq() {
  if ( !reqObject ) {
    alert("Cannot delete undefined XMLHttpRequest object.") ;
    return false ;
    }
  reqObject = null ;
  return true ;
}
```

Step 7: Create a LotusScript agent.

Here is a LotusScript agent named `XMLHttpResponseAgentdbColumn` that is invoked with the request from the XMLHttpRequest Object. Some code has been removed for brevity, but the essential components are here. Note that the result of the query is returned to the request object in the browser with `Print` statements:

```
Sub Initialize
%REM
Purpose: Simulates DbColumn for XMLHttpRequest from browser
Invoked: From an AJAX JavaScript
%END REM
  Dim msgPrefix As String
  msgPrefix = "XMLHttpResponseAgentdbColumn: "
  On Error Goto ErrorSection

  Dim session As New NotesSession
  Dim argstring As String
  Dim argarray As Variant
  Dim argcount As Integer
```

```
Dim column As String
Dim errmsg As String
Dim formula As String
Dim parm As String
Dim result As Variant
Dim pathname As String
Dim server As String
Dim value As String
Dim viewname As String
Dim e As Integer, i As Integer

' Retrieve the arguments

argstring = session.DocumentContext.Query_String(0)
argarray = Split(argstring,"&",-1)
argcount = Ubound(argarray)

For i = 1 To argcount
  parm = argarray(i)
  e = Instr(parm,"=")
  value = Mid$(parm,e+1)
  parm = Left$(parm,e-1)
  Select Case Ucase(parm)
  Case "SERVER"   : server = value
  Case "PATHNAME" : pathname = value
  Case "VIEW"     : viewname = value
  Case "COLUMN"   : column = value
  Case Else       : errmsg = "Yes"
  End Select
Next

' Print the headers

Print "Content-Type:text/plain"
Print "Cache-Control:No-Cache" 'attempting to avoid caching IE
Print "Expires: -1" 'attempting to avoid caching in IE

If errmsg="Yes" Or pathname="" Or viewname="" _
Or column="" Or Not Isnumeric(column) _
Then
  Print "Error detected in the agent parameter list."
  Goto ExitSection
End If
```

```
' Convert %20 to blank

formula = |@ReplaceSubstring('|+pathname+|';'%20';' ')|
result = Evaluate(""+formula+"")
pathname = result(0)

' Get the data from either the view column or the document

server = |"|+server+|"|
pathname = |"|+pathname+|"|
formula = |@DbColumn("":"";|+|server|+|:|+|pathname|+|;"|+ _
viewname+|";|+column+|)|

result = Evaluate(""+formula+"")

' Send the results to the browser

If Isscalar(result) Then
  If result = "" Then
    Print "Error detected."
    Print "Server: " & server
    Print "Pathname: " & pathname
    Print "Viewname: " + viewname
    Print "Column: " + column
    Print "Formula: " & formula
    Print "Result: " & result
  Else
    Print result
  End If
Else
  i = 0
  Forall z In result
    Print Cstr(result(i))
    i = i + 1
  End Forall
End If

Goto ExitSection
'******************* E R R O R   H A N D L I N G ************
ErrorSection:
  Msgbox(msgPrefix & "**** E R R O R **** "_
  & Cstr(Err()) & " at line: " + Cstr(Erl) + " : " + Error() )
  Exit Sub
ExitSection:
End Sub
```

The trickiest part about this script is in creating the formula that includes the @DbColumn function call. It is more challenging than it appears to put quotation marks in all the right places.

Step 8: Test the solution

The proof is in the pudding, as they say. Here is the user form before the Ajax call:

After the **Get Choices** button is clicked, more options are displayed:

If you choose to incorporate Ajax functionality into your applications, you can indeed write your own functions as shown in this topic. But these more advanced techniques require quite a bit of work to prepare and to debug. If you have the time, go for it. You may want to play around with this example until you understand basically how Ajax calls work, and then look for some canned functions in one of the major JavaScript frameworks.

Summary

Learning basic JavaScript programming is not particularly difficult, but there are an enormous number of ways in which scripts can be composed and used within the context of a browser. This chapter has barely scratched the surface of possibilities.

If you are relatively new to JavaScript, expect to spend considerable time studying the language and the ways in which it can be used to spruce up web applications. Learn the basics and how to incorporate those basics in Domino applications. Then continue to explore this technology with one or more of the script libraries or frameworks: Dojo, ExtJs, jQuery, MooTools, Prototype, script.aculo.us, YUI. Of these, Dojo may be more important in the context of Domino, although jQuery is by far the most popular in general web applications.

The suggestions and examples in this chapter have introduced ways in which JavaScript can be inserted into designs to improve performance and other behavior of classic Domino web applications.

7
Views

Views serve as indexes to documents in a database. Virtually all Domino applications that contain composed documents also contain one or more views that facilitate locating and re-opening previously saved documents. Some views are intended for users, and some views are intended to be used only by internal processes or by formulas to look up values. Of course, you can use the same view for both users and lookups, but doing so can be problematic.

As seen with the Notes client, views look and operate similarly. Clicking on a document (a row) in the view opens the document, usually on a separate tab. The view remains open. Closing the document returns focus to the view. Of course, on the Web, things are not quite so simple.

In a standard non-categorized view, each row represents a document, and each column contains data from the documents listed in the view. Overall a view looks like a table, and on the Web that is how they are usually rendered — as HTML tables. As the rows and cells of an HTML table can be styled with CSS and modified with JavaScript, the look and behavior of views can be improved using these standard web technologies as well.

This chapter addresses issues related to displaying views on the Web. Crafting views for the Web is challenging, as there are several options and many aspects to consider. There is no right or perfect way to display a view on the Web; each option provides benefits, but also comes with draw-backs. Understanding the options and experimenting a little with them will help you to choose the most appropriate techniques for your applications.

Topics in this chapter include the following:

- Creating diagnostic views
- Using view templates

- Inserting HTML into views
- Styling views for the Web
- Creating view navigation buttons

General guidelines

Here are a few general guidelines that most web applications should follow. These are not strictly necessary, of course, but you can improve your application and avoid certain problems if you follow them.

Create some diagnostic views

Especially if you inherit maintenance responsibility for an existing application, it may be a bit difficult at first to understand the application just by examining it with a browser. With the Notes client, look through the existing views to gain an understanding of what documents exist and how they are organized.

If the existing views do not provide the answers you need, consider adding one or more new views that present the documents in ways that are useful to you. These diagnostic or troubleshooting views are intended only for you, and perhaps the application administrator. Do not design them for the end user, and probably not even for display on the Web. Do not use them for lookups or any other processing. Identify them clearly. If you name these views with a hierarchical name, they will cluster together in the Notes navigational pane:

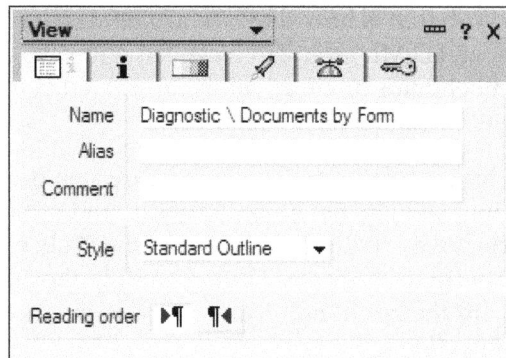

The views themselves should contain only data you find useful. Here the **Diagnostic \ Documents by Form** view is a categorized view that displays all documents categorized by form name:

		Form	Doc No	Creation Date	Name
Contacts with Scrollbars	▲	▼ contact			
Contacts2			1	01/30/2011 06:46:44 AM	ApeMan
Contacts			2	01/30/2011 06:40:25 AM	Charming
▼ 📁 Diagnostic			3	01/30/2011 07:19:32 AM	Lamb
Documents by Creation Date			4	01/30/2011 06:40:51 AM	Little
Documents by Form			5	01/30/2011 06:41:07 AM	Quinn
Documents in Hierarchy		▼ contact2			
Rep Save Conflicts			1	02/01/2011 05:51:13 PM	
Files					

Categorizing a view by form name facilitates examining the documents created by different processes within the application.

In this example, the **Doc No** column indicates how may documents exist for each form. The column value is computed:

```
@DocNumber("")
```

Additional columns that display the document author, last modified date, and key values, such as title or status, can provide diagnostic insight not easily gained by looking at the functional and lookup views.

Display documents in a hierarchy

If your application uses response documents, it may be useful to display the parent and child documents in the natural hierarchy, with child documents displayed below parent documents. You must set the view attribute **Show response documents in a hierarchy** on the **Options** tab of **View Properties**:

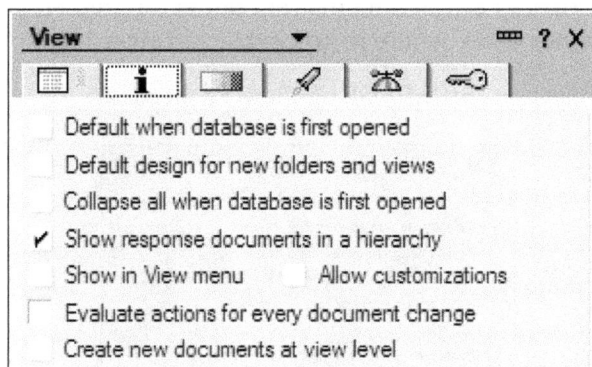

In this example, a keyword that exists on both forms serves as the category:

The column labeled **#Child** is computed:

```
@DocChildren
```

The column labeled **UNID or $Ref** is also computed. This computation displays the parent's UNID if the document is a response document, and its own UNID if it is a main document:

```
@If(@IsResponseDoc; @Text($Ref); @Text(@DocumentUniqueID))
```

A view like this might include other fields containing stored document IDs as well.

Display Replication or Save conflict documents

Another useful view highlights Replication or Save conflicts that might appear in your application. Column headings and values will depend upon the fields in the documents. The key to this type of view is setting the **View Selection Formula**:

```
SELECT @IsAvailable($Conflict)
```

Specify a default view

One view can be selected as the default view for the application. As such, it can serve as a point of return after a new document is submitted or after errors are detected. If the application does not know where to go next, it can always go to the default view.

Specify the default view on the **Info** tab of **View Properties**:

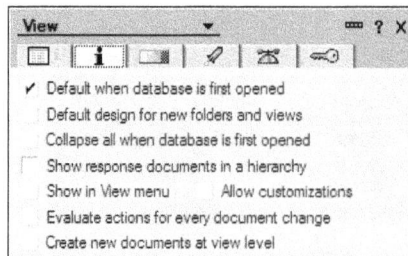

Refer to the default view with a computed URL. An @formula like this will do:

```
@URLOpen("/" + @WebDbName + "/$defaultView?OpenView")
```

Note that a default view applies to both web and Notes clients. Check to see if this view displays acceptably in Notes, and if not, consider hiding it from Notes users.

Use view templates

The technique of using view template forms as containers for displaying views on the Web was introduced in *Chapter 3, Forms and Pages*. Here we extend that discussion.

Use the same view template for several views

If your application includes a view template form named $$ViewTemplateDefault, then all views use that view template by default. If you want to tailor a view template for a specific view, you create a specific view template for that view, and you name it appropriately. Here is the format for the name of the special view template: $$ViewTemplate for name.

"Name" refers to the name or alias of the associated view. For example, a view template for the **Reports** view would be named $$ViewTemplate for Reports. The view name or view alias alone indicates a special relationship between the view and the view template.

If a second view, for example a view named **Files**, requires something other than the default view template, then another view template can be created for that second view ($$ViewTemplate for Files). And so on.

But if the view templates for the **Reports** and **Files** views are identical (but different from the default view template), then you need create only a single alternate view template to serve both views. The trick here is to code one or more aliases for the single view template. In this example, the special view template would be named like this:

```
$$ViewTemplate for Reports | $$ViewTemplate for Files
```

Code the name | alias values in the **Info** tab of **Form Properties**. Multiple aliases can be included if appropriate:

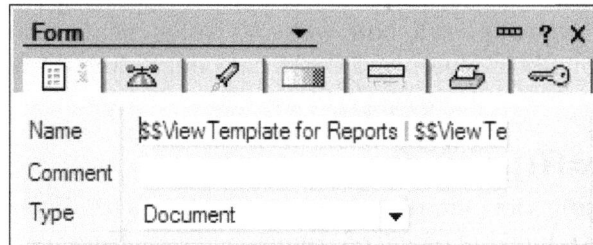

Compute the view title

You may want to display the name of the view on the view template. If so, add some computed text to the view template with a formula that includes the name of the view but omits any aliases:

```
@Subset(@ViewTitle; 1)
```

Exploring view options for the Web

Views are important to most Domino applications. They provide the primary means by which documents are located and retrieved. But working with views on the Web is often more complicated or less satisfactory than using views with the Notes client. Several classic view options are available for web applications, all of which have draw-backs and implementation issues.

A specific view can be displayed on the Web in several different ways. So it is helpful to consider view attributes that influence design choices, in particular:

- View content
- View structure
- How a view is translated for the Web
- How a view looks in a browser
- Whether or not a view template is used
- View performance
- Document hierarchy

In terms of content, a view contains:

- Data only
- Data and HTML tags

In terms of structure, views are:

- Uncategorized
- Categorized

In terms of the techniques used by Domino to translate views for the Web, there are four basic methods:

- Domino-generated HTML (the default)
- Developer-generated HTML (the view contains data and HTML tags)
- View Applet (used with data only views)
- XML (the view is transmitted to the browser as an XML document)

The first three of these methods are easier to implement. Two options on the **Advanced** tab of **View Properties** control which of these three methods is used:

- **Treat view contents as HTML**
- **Use applet in the browser**

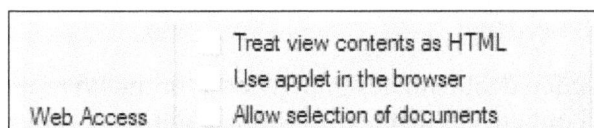

	Treat view contents as HTML
	Use applet in the browser
Web Access	Allow selection of documents

If neither option is checked, then Domino translates the view into an HTML table and then sends the page to the browser. If **Treat view contents as HTML** is checked, then Domino sends the view to the browser as is, assuming that the developer has encoded HTML table tags in the view. If **Use applet in the browser** is checked, then Domino uses the Java View Applet to display the view. (As mentioned previously, the Java Applets can be slow to load, and they do require a locally installed JVM (Java Virtual Machine)).

Using XML to display views in a browser is a more complicated proposition, and we will not deal with it here. Pursue this and other XML-related topics in Designer Help or on the Web. Here is a starting point:

```
http://www.ibm.com/developerworks/xml/
```

In terms of how a view looks when displayed in a browser, two alternatives can be used:

- Native styling with Designer
- Styling with Cascading Style Sheets

In terms of whether or not a view template is used, there are three choices:

- A view template is not used
- The default view template is used
- A view template created for a specific view is used

Finally, view performance can be an issue for views with many:

- Documents
- Columns
- Column formulas
- Column sorting options

Each view is indexed and refreshed according to a setting on the **Advanced** tab of **View Properties**. By default, view indices are set to refresh automatically when documents are added or deleted. If the re-indexing process takes longer, then application response time can suffer. In general, smaller and simpler views with fewer column formulas perform better than long, complicated and computationally intensive views.

The topics in this section deal with designing views for the Web. The first few topics review the standard options for displaying views. Later topics offer suggestions about improving view look and feel.

Understand view Action buttons

As you work with views on the Web, keep in mind that Action buttons are always placed at the top of the page regardless of how the view is displayed on the Web (standard view, view contents as HTML) and regardless of whether or not a view template is used. Unless the Action Bar is displayed with the Java applet, Action buttons are rendered in a basic HTML table; a horizontal rule separates the Action buttons from the rest of the form. Bear in mind that the Action buttons are functionally connected to but stylistically independent of the view and view template design elements that display lower on the form.

Use Domino-generated default views

When you look at a view on the Web, the view consists only of column headings and data rows. Everything else on the page (below any Action buttons) is contained on a view template form. You can create view templates in your design, or you can let Domino provide a default form.

If Domino supplies the view template, the rendered page is fairly basic. Below the Action buttons and the horizontal rule, standard navigational hotspots are displayed; these navigational hotspots are repeated below the view. **Expand** and **Collapse** hotspots are included to support categorized views and views that include documents in response hierarchies. The view title displays below the top set of navigational hotspots, and then the view itself appears.

If you supply a view template for a view, you must design the navigational hotspots, view title, and other design elements that may be required.

View contents are rendered as an HTML table with columns that expand or contract depending upon the width of cell contents. If view columns enable sorting, then sorting arrows appear to the right of column headings. Here is an example of how Domino displays a view by default on the Web:

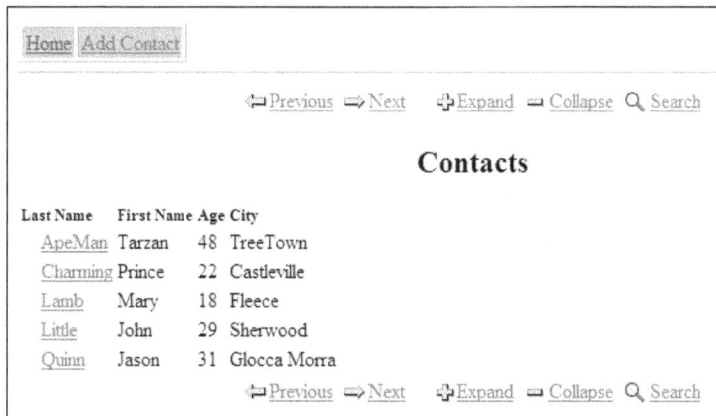

In this example, clicking the blue underscored values in the left-most **Last Name** column opens the corresponding documents. By default, values in the left-most column are rendered as URL links, but any other column—or several columns—can serve this purpose. To change which column values are clickable, enable or disable the **Show values in this column as links** option on the **Advanced** tab of **Column Properties**:

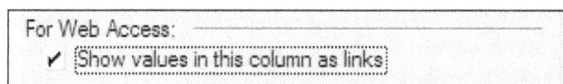

Typically a title, subject, or another unique document attribute is enabled as the link.

Out of the box default views are a good choice for rapid prototyping or for one-time needs where look-and-feel are less important. Beyond designing the views, nothing else is required. Domino merges the views with HTML tags and a little JavaScript to produce fully functional pages.

On the down side, what you see is what you get. Default views are stylistically uninspiring, and there is not a lot that can be done with them beyond some modest Designer-applied styling. Many Designer-applied styles, such as column width, are not translated to the Web. Still, some visual improvements can be made. In this example, the font characteristics are modified, and an alternate row background color is added:

Last Name	First Name	Age	City
ApeMan	Tarzan	48	TreeTown
Charming	Prince	22	Castleville
Lamb	Mary	18	Fleece
Little	John	29	Sherwood
Quinn	Jason	31	Glocca Morra

Include HTML tags to enhance views

Some additional styling and behavior can be coded into standard views using HTML tags and CSS rules. Here is how this is done:

In this example, `<font>` tags surround the column **Title**. Note the square brackets that identify the tags as HTML:

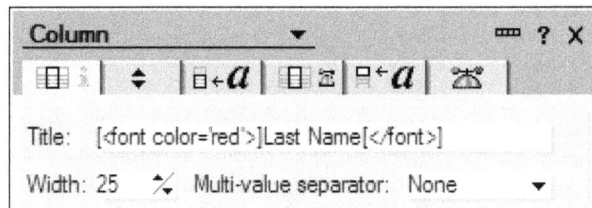

Tags can also be inserted into column value formulas:

```
"[<font color='darkblue'>]" + ContactLast + "[</font>]"
```

When viewed with a browser, the new colors are displayed as expected. But when the view is opened in Notes, it looks like this:

Web Sandbox 07.nsf	This is the Reports view	
Contacts2		
Contacts	**[<font color='red'>]Last Name[</font>]**	**[<font color='black'>]First Name[</font>]**
Diagnostic	[<font color='darkblue'>]ApeMan[</font>]	[<font color='black'>]Tarzan[</font>]
Docs with Responses	[<font color='darkblue'>]Charming[</font>]	[<font color='black'>]Prince[</font>]
Files	[<font color='darkblue'>]Lamb[</font>]	[<font color='black'>]Mary[</font>]
Reports	[<font color='darkblue'>]Little[</font>]	[<font color='black'>]John[</font>]
	[<font color='darkblue'>]Quinn[</font>]	[<font color='black'>]Jason[</font>]

The example illustrates how to code the additional tags, but frankly the same effects can be achieved using Designer-applied formatting, so there is no real gain here. The view takes longer to code and the final result is not very reader-friendly when viewed with the Notes client.

That being said, there still may be occasions when you want to add HTML tags to achieve a particular result. Here is a somewhat more complicated application of the same technique. This next line of code is added to the Title of a column. Note the use of `<sup>` and `<font>` tags. These tags apply only to the message **See footnote 1**:

```
Last Name[<sup><font color='red'>]See footnote 1[</font></sup>]
```

The result achieves the desired effect:

Last Name ^{See footnote 1} **First Name**

More challenging is styling values in view columns. You do not have access to the `<td>` or `<font>` tags that Domino inserts into the page to define table cell contents. But you can add `<span>` tags around a column value, and then use CSS rules to style the span. Here is what the column formula might look like:

```
"[<span class='column1'>]" + ContactLast + "[</span>]"
```

Here is the CSS rule for the `column1` class:

```
.column1 {
  background-color: #EEE;
  cursor: default;
  display: block;
  font-weight: bold;
  text-decoration: none;
  width: 100%;
  }
```

These declarations change the background color of the cell to a light gray and the pointer to the browser default. The `display` and `width` declarations force the span to occupy the width of the table cell. The text underscoring (for the link) is removed and the text is made bold.

Without the CSS rule, the view displays as expected:

Last Name[See footnote 1]	First Name
ApeMan	Tarzan
Charming	Prince
Lamb	Mary
Little	John
Quinn	Jason

With the CSS rule applied, a different look for the first column is achieved:

Last Name[See footnote 1]	First Name
ApeMan	Tarzan
Charming	Prince
Lamb	Mary
Little	John
Quinn	Jason

Use the "Treat view contents as HTML" option

Setting the view option **Treat view contents as HTML** on the **Advanced** tab of **View Properties** enables considerably more control over view headers, rows and columns, but at a price. Once you select this option, you are responsible for the structure and style of the view. While not strictly necessary, you should always create view templates for this kind of view.

Remember that a view is typically translated into an HTML table when composed for the Web. A little further on, an alternative to rendering a view as a table is illustrated.

Structure HTML views as tables

On the view template, surround the `$$ViewBody` field or the embedded view element with `<table>` tags that have been marked as Pass-Thru HTML. Note here that the **border** attribute has been coded:

```
<table border=1>
      $$ViewBody  T
</table>
```

Add `<tr>` and `<th>` (or `<td>`) tags and attributes into your column titles. It is not necessary to identify the tags as HTML with square brackets. In this example, the **Last Name** column title sets the width of the column to 90:

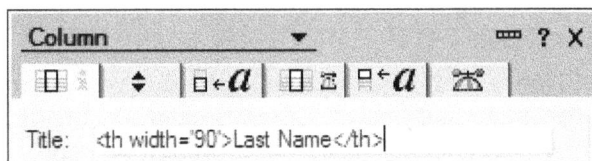

Often the `<tr>` tag is added to the title of the left-most column, and a corresponding `</tr>` tag is added to the end of the title of the right-most column. Alternatively, you can add additional left-most and right-most columns whose values are set to the `<tr>` and `</tr>` tags respectively. Separating the row tags from the data columns in this manner offers more flexibility in terms of rearranging columns in the view.

Next, change column values from simple field names to computed strings that include HTML tags. For example, the column value of the **Last Name** column would usually be a simple referent to a document field name:

```
ContactLast
```

But in an HTML view, you modify the simple column value formula to include the required HTML tags:

```
"<tr><td>" + ContactLast + "</td>"
```

Again, if you added the left-most and right-most columns to accommodate the `<tr>` and `</tr>` tags, code column value formulas for those columns appropriately and do not include the `<tr>` tag in the **Last Name** column value formula.

In this example, the width of the first column is set explicitly with the `WIDTH=` attribute in the column title; the result is a rendered table with a slightly wider left column compared to the default. Note that the browser assigns some style (centering, bold) to the `<th>` tags inserted in the column titles:

Last Name	First Name	City
Lamb	Mary	Fleece
Charming	Prince	Castleville
ApeMan	Tarzan	TreeTown
Quinn	Jason	Glocca Morra
Little	John	Sherwood

Code links to open documents

To open a document from a view, the contents of the table cell must contain a valid HTML link coded with an anchor (`<a>`) tag. In this example, the formula for the `ContactLast` column is modified to include a computed `<a>` tag:

```
db := "/" + @WebDbName ;
vw := "/" + @Subset(@ViewTitle;1) ;
doc := "/" + @Text(@DocumentUniqueID) + "?OpenDocument" ;
link := db + vw + doc ;
"<tr><td><a href=\"" + link + "\">" + ContactLast + "</a></td>" ;
```

> Caution: Complex column formulas impact view performance.

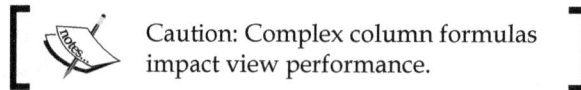

After looking at this computed column formula, you might be thinking about the performance penalty being paid here, since these formulas are recomputed each time the view is updated. For static views that do not change much, this may not be a concern, but for larger views that change frequently, performance can be problematic.

A better alternative to computing a URL in a column formula is to compute and store the URL for a specific document in the document when it is saved. The view column formula then becomes a reference to the form field containing the URL, rather than a computation.

On the form, add a Computed Text field (for example, `docURLcell`) with this formula:

```
db := "/" + @WebDbName ;
vw := "/" + @Subset(@ViewTitle;1) ;
doc := "/" + @Text(@DocumentUniqueID) + "?OpenDocument" ;
link := db + vw + doc ;
"<td><a href=\"" + link + "\">" + ContactLast + "</a></td>"
```

In the view column formula, code just the name of the field:

```
docURLcell
```

This is a much cleaner solution and will improve the view performance.

Structure HTML views as lists

In some cases, you may prefer to display a view as a list. On the view template, surround the `$$ViewBody` field or the embedded view element with `<ul>` or `<ol>` tags that have been marked as Pass-Thru HTML. In this example, the `<ul>` tag also includes a CSS class name:

```
<ul class='viewaslist'>
    $$ViewBody T
</ul>
```

Add `<li>` and other HTML tags as needed to the column title(s) and to the column value formula(s). Create CSS rules as appropriate and link to the page containing those rules from the view template's HTML Head Content area.

In this example, the view contains two columns. The first column is hidden, and its value is the `contactLast` field. This column is sorted in ascending order by last name. The second column displays both the `contactLast` and `contactFirst` names, and it is this column that displays to users.

A CSS class name is added to the title of the second column:

```
<li class='columntitle' >Contact Name</li>
```

The value of the second column references a Computed field in the documents named `docURLItem`. This field's formula computes the URL to the document, as in the previous topic. Note that in the formula the link (`<a>`) is enclosed by `<li>` tags:

```
db := "/" + @WebDbName ;
vw := "/" + @Subset(@ViewTitle;1) ;
doc := "/" + @Text(@DocumentUniqueID) + "?OpenDocument" ;
link := db + vw + doc ;
"<li>" +
"<a href=\"" + link + "\">" + ContactLast + "</a>" + ", " +
ContactFirst +
"</li>"
```

The view template links to a CSS page that includes the following CSS rules. The first rule applies to the list as a whole. The second rule applies to all `<li>` tags within the list. The third rule applies just to the column title:

```
ul.viewaslist {
   background-color: #EEEEEE;
   border: solid 1px black;
   font-family: Verdana;
   font-size: 10pt;
   padding: 10px;
   width: 15em;
   }
ul.viewaslist li {
   color: darkblue;
   list-style-type: none;
   }
li.columntitle {
   font-weight: bold;
   margin-bottom: 5px;
   }
```

The list displays in a browser as follows:

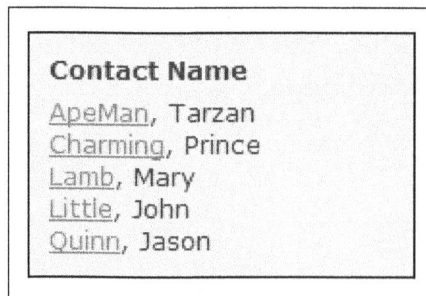

Set the view line count

Using the `$$ViewBody` field with HTML views works well, but the number of rows that display may be quite large. If you need to limit the number of lines that are rendered at one time, use an embedded view element on the view template instead of a `$$ViewBody` field.

Set several properties on the **Info** tab of **Embedded View Properties**. Especially, set the **Display** option to **Using HTML** and set the **Lines to display** value to control the line count. You will also need to include navigational buttons or hotspots on the view template to enable users to page back and forth through the view, as described later in this chapter:

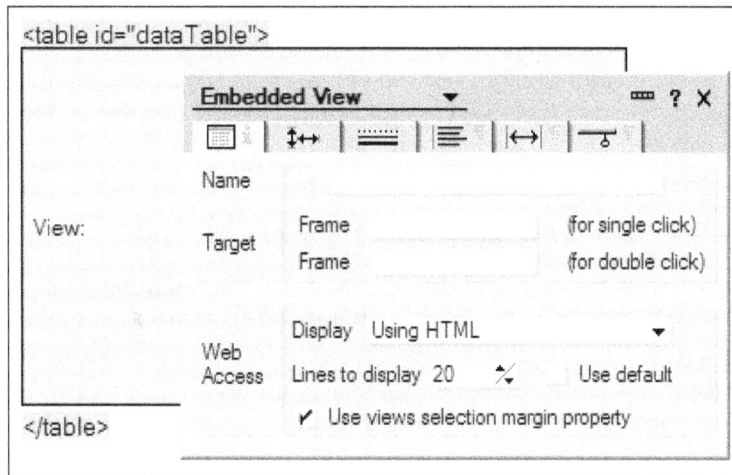

Note that the default and maximum number of lines that are displayed in views depend upon server settings controlled by the Domino administrator. Check settings on the **Domino Web Engine** tab on the **Internet Protocols** tab on the server document in the Domino Directory. In this example, the **Default lines per view page** is set to **30**, and the **Maximum lines per view page** is set to **1000**:

Conversion/Display	
Image conversion format:	GIF
Interlaced rendering:	Enabled
Default lines per view page:	30
Maximum lines per view page:	1000

Create Notes versions of HTML views

An HTML view intended for the Web is difficult to read with the Notes client. Here is what such a view might look like in Notes:

Add Contact			
<tr>	<th width='90'>Last Name</th>	<th width="90">First Name</th>	<th width="90">City</th>
<tr>	<td><a href="/Ellislts/WebSandbox[	<td>Mary</td>	<td>Fleece</td>
<tr>	<td><a href="/Ellislts/WebSandbox[	<td>Prince</td>	<td>Castleville</td>
<tr>	<td><a href="/Ellislts/WebSandbox[	<td>Tarzan</td>	<td>TreeTown</td>
<tr>	<td><a href="/Ellislts/WebSandbox[	<td>Jason</td>	<td>Glocca Morra</td>
<tr>	<td><a href="/Ellislts/WebSandbox[	<td>John</td>	<td>Sherwood</td>

If the content of this view is useful to Notes users, you may want to create a second view that includes all columns, but not the HTML tags. You can hide the views with HTML from Notes clients using the **Design** tab of **Design Properties** for the view. Likewise, you can hide the views without HTML from Web clients.

Use the View Applet (with caution)

The View Applet is intended to provide a view experience similar to that which one gets with the Notes client. The view is displayed in a window on the form. There may be scrollbars. Columns can be sorted by clicking on column headings. Categories expand and collapse independently from one another. Some styling options are available that can improve the look.

To use the View Applet, add an embedded view control to a view template and set the **Display** option to **Using Java Applet**:

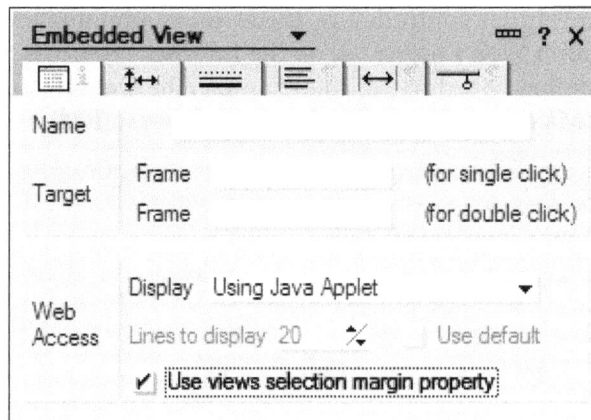

You set the size of the applet window and other attributes with **Embedded View Properties**. Some experimentation is likely to be required.

Using the View Applet, a view might render as follows:

Last Name	First Name	Age	City
ApeMan	Tarzan	48	TreeTown
Charming	Prince	22	Castleville
Lamb	Mary	18	Fleece
Little	John	29	Sherwood
Quinn	Jason	31	Glocca Morra

There are several issues with the View Applet, so it might not be the best choice to use. Issues include the following:

- If a JVM is not installed on the user's desktop, the applet will not load.
- The applet sometimes fails to initialize properly, requiring the page to be refreshed or the browser to be restarted.
- The applet can be slow to load.
- Clicking too fast on an applet scrollbar can hang a browser, especially in larger views.
- Styling options are limited.

The View Applet may be a good choice if you need something quick and short-term, if you are prototyping an application, or if it provides you with a desirable feature you cannot easily implement in another way. If you do use this option, let your users know about the performance and functional issues that can arise.

Creating Action buttons

View templates are forms that can accommodate buttons, fields, and computed text as needed to enhance your views. Most views include a few Action buttons, so this section offers suggestions about including buttons on view templates.

Provide view navigation buttons

Simple views intended to provide information (for example, a table of values) or links to a limited number of documents can stand alone quite nicely, embedded on a page or a view template. But if more than a handful of documents display in the view, you should provide users a way to move forward and backward through the view. If you use the View Applet, enable the scroll bars; otherwise add some navigational buttons to the view templates to enable users to move around in it.

Code next and previous navigation buttons

If you set the line count for a view, only that number of rows is sent to the browser. You need to add Action buttons or hotspots on the view template to enable users to advance the view to the next set of documents or to return to the previous set of documents—essentially paging backward and forward through the view.

Code a **Next** button with this formula:

```
@DbCommand("Domino"; "ViewNextPage")
```

Code a **Previous** button with this formula:

```
@DbCommand("Domino"; "ViewPreviousPage")
```

Code first and last buttons

Buttons can be included on the view template to page to the first and last documents in the view. Code an @Formula in a **First** button's Click event to compute and open a relative URL. The link reopens the current view and positions it at the first document:

```
@URLOpen("/"+@WebDbName+"/"+@Subset(@ViewTitle;-1) +
"?OpenView&Start=1")
```

For a **Last** button, add a Computed for Display field to the view template with this @Formula:

```
@Elements(@DbColumn(""):"NoCache"; "" ; @ViewTitle; 1))
```

The value for the field (vwRows in this example) is the current number of documents in the view. This information is used in the @Formula for the **Last** button's Click event:

```
url := "/" + @WebDbName + "/" + @Subset(@ViewTitle;-1) ;
@URLOpen(url + "?OpenView&Start=" + @Text(vwRows))
```

When **Last** is clicked, the view reopens, positioned at the last document.

Please note that for very large views, the @Formula for field vwRows may fail because of limitations in the amount of data that can be returned by @DbColumn.

Let users specify a line count

As computer monitors today come in a wide range of sizes and resolutions, it may be difficult to determine the right number of documents to display in a view to accommodate all users. On some monitors the view may seem too short, on others too long.

Here is a strategy you might adapt to your application, that enables users to specify how many lines to display. The solution relies on several components working together:

- Several Computed for display fields on the view template
- A button that sets the number of lines with JavaScript
- **Previous** and **Next** buttons that run JavaScript to page through the view

The technique uses the **Start** and **Count** parameters, which can be used when you open a view with a URL. The Start parameter, used in a previous example, specifies the row or document within a view that should display at the top of the view window on a page. The Count parameter specifies how many rows or documents should display on the page. The Count parameter overrides the line count setting that you may have set on an embedded view element.

Here are the Computed for display fields to be created on the view template. The Query_String_Decoded field (a CGI variable) must be named as such, but all the other field names in this list are arbitrary. Following each field name is the @Formula that computes its value:

- **Query_String_Decoded**:
  Query_String_Decoded
- **vwParms**:
  @Right(@LowerCase(Query_String_Decoded); "&")
- **vwStart**:
  @If(@Contains(vwParms; "start="); @Middle(vwParms; "start=";
  "&"); "1")
- **vwCount**:
  @If(@Contains(vwParms; "count="); @Middle(vwParms; "count=";
  "&"); "10")
- **vwURL**:
  "/" + @WebDbName + "/"+ @Subset(@ViewTitle;1) + "?OpenView"
- **vwRows**:
  @Elements(@DbColumn(""; "NoCache"; ""; @ViewTitle; 1))
- **countFlag**:
  "n"
- **newCount**:
  "1"

Add several buttons to the view template. Code JavaScript in each button's onClick event. You may want to code these scripts inline for testing, and then move them to a JavaScript library when you know they are working the way you want them to.

The **Set Rows** button's onClick event is coded with JavaScript that receives a line count from the user. If the user-entered line count is not good, then the current line count is retained. A flag is set indicating that the line count may have been changed:

```
var f = document.forms[0] ;
var rows = parseInt(f.vwRows.value) ;
var count = prompt("Number of Rows?","10") ;
if ( isNaN(count) | count < 1 | count >= rows ) {
  count = f.vwCount.value ;
  }
f.newCount.value = count ;
f.countFlag.value = "y" ;
```

The **Previous** button's onClick event is coded to page backward through the view using the user-entered line count:

```
var f = document.forms[0] ;
var URL = f.vwURL.value ;
var ctFlag = f.countFlag.value ;
var oCT = parseInt(f.vwCount.value) ;
var nCT = parseInt(f.newCount.value) ;
var oST = parseInt(f.vwStart.value) ;
var count ;
var start ;
if ( ctFlag == "n" ) {
  count = oCT ;
  start = oST - oCT ;
  }
else {
  count = nCT ;
  start = oST - nCT ;
  }
if (start < 1 ) { start = 1 ; }
location.href = URL + "&Start=" + start + "&Count=" + count ;
```

The **Next** button pages forward through the view using the user-entered line count:

```
var f = document.forms[0] ;
var URL = f.vwURL.value ;
var ctFlag = f.countFlag.value ;
var oCT = parseInt(f.vwCount.value) ;
var nCT = parseInt(f.newCount.value) ;
```

```
var start = parseInt(f.vwStart.value) + oCT ;
if ( ctFlag == "n" ) {
  location.href = URL + "&Start=" + start + "&Count=" + oCT ;
  }
else {
  location.href = URL + "&Start=" + start + "&Count=" + nCT ;
  }
```

Finally, if **First** and **Last** buttons are included with this scheme, they need to be re-coded as well to work with a user-specified line count.

The @formula in the **First** button's Click event now looks like this:

```
count := @If(@IsAvailable(vwCount); vwCount; "10") ;
parms := "?OpenView&Start=1&Count=" + count ;
@URLOpen("/" + @WebDbName + "/" + @Subset(@ViewTitle;-1) + parms) ;
```

The @formula in the **Last** button's Click event is also a little more complicated. Note that if the field vwRows is not available, then the Start value is set to 1,000. This is really more for debugging since the Start parameter should always be set to the value of vwRows:

```
start := @If(@IsAvailable(vwRows); @Text(vwRows); "1000") ;
count := @If(@IsAvailable(vwCount); vwCount; "10") ;
parms := "?OpenView&Start=" + start + "&Count=" + count ;
url := "/" + @WebDbName + "/" + @Subset(@ViewTitle;-1) ;
@URLOpen(url + parms) ;
```

Code expand and collapse buttons for categorized views

Two other navigational buttons should be included on the view template for categorized views or views that include document hierarchies. These buttons expand all categories and collapse all categories respectively:

- The **Expand All** button's Click event contains this @Command:

  ```
  @Command([ViewExpandAll])
  ```

- The **Collapse All** button's Click event contains this @Command:

  ```
  @Command([ViewCollapseAll])
  ```

Co-locate and define all Action buttons

Action Bar buttons can be added to a view template as well as to a view. If Action buttons appear on both design elements, then Domino places all the buttons together on the same top row. In the following image, the first button is from the view template, and the last three are from the view itself:

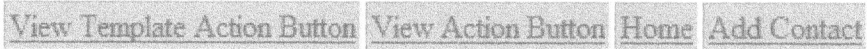

If it makes more sense for the buttons to be arranged in a different order, then take control of their placement by co-locating them all either on the view template or on the view.

Create your own Action buttons

As mentioned previously, Action Bar buttons are rendered in a table placed at the top of a form. But on typical Web pages, buttons and hotspots are located below a banner, or in a menu at the left or the right. Buttons along the top of a form look dated and may not comply with your organization's web development standards.

As discussed in *Chapter 3*, you can replace the view template and view Action buttons with hotspot buttons placed elsewhere on the view template:

- Create a series of hotspots or hotspot buttons on the view template, perhaps below a banner.
- Code @formulas for the hotspots that are equivalent to the Action Bar button formulas.
- Define a CSS class for those hotspots, and code appropriate CSS rules.
- Delete or hide from the Web all standard Action Bar buttons on the view template and on the view.

Adding style to views

Views within an application ought to be styled consistently. Inconsistent styling diminishes the user's experience and, to some extent, his productivity. If your views are similar, use the same style rules.

Style Domino default views

As previously noted, default views can be styled in Designer to some degree. With a little effort, column headings and data rows can be improved.

But compared with CSS styling options, styling with Designer alone is limited, indeed. Views can be improved dramatically with just a few CSS rules. Let us take a look at how this might be done. Here is the finished product:

Here are the steps to style default views with CSS:

Step 1: Add HTML <div> tags and JavaScript to the view template.

As in the following illustration, add HTML <div> tags marked as Pass-Thru HTML to the view template, along with some JavaScript at the bottom of the form. Division tags enclose the view title and the embedded view itself. This is the complete view template (not showing the Action buttons):

```
<div id="viewtitle">
Contacts
</div>
<div id="embeddedview">




View:




</div>

<script language="JavaScript" type="text/javascript">
{ styleActionBar() ; }
</script>
```

Step 2: Create and link to a page containing CSS rules.

Create a CSS page and link to it from the view template's HTML Head Content area, as described in *Chapter 5, Cascading Style Sheets*. Add these CSS rules to the CSS style sheet:

```
/* ViewTemplate.css */
#viewtitle {
  color: #7F0000;
  font-family: Arial;
  font-size: 18pt;
  font-weight: bold;
  margin-bottom: 10px;
  padding-left: 10px;
  }
#embeddedview table {
  border-collapse: collapse;
  border-top: solid 4px #EEE;
  border-right: solid 4px #555;
  border-bottom: solid 4px #555;
  border-left: solid 4px #BBB;
  font-family: Verdana;
  font-size: 10pt;
  }
#embeddedview th {
  background-color: #DDD;
  border: none;
  border-bottom: solid 2px #7F0000;
  color: Blue;
  width: 8em;
  }
#embeddedview a {
  color: Red;
  text-decoration: none;
  }
#embeddedview a:hover {
  background-color: Red;
  color: White;
  }
```

Step 3: Style the Action Bar buttons.

To style the Action Bar, link to the `ActionBar.css` page in the view template's HTML Head Content area, and insert the `ActionBar.js` JavaScript library into the JS Header. Details about Action Bar styling were presented in *Chapter 5*.

Style HTML views

HTML views can be styled with CSS rules as well. As the view template for an HTML view already contains a `<table>` tag, simply add an ID attribute, in this case `dataTable`:

```
<table id="dataTable">



View:




</table>
```

In the view itself, add some class attributes to one or more of the column titles or column value formulas. For the **Age** column, here is a modified title including the class attribute:

```
<th class="age">Age</th>
```

And here is the column value for the **Age** column, again with the class attribute:

```
"<td class='age'>" + CustAge + "</td>"
```

Code CSS rules on a CSS page and link to it in the view template's HTML Head Content area. Note that the `#dataTable` ID name is used to qualify the `<th>` and `<td>` rules. This assures that these rules are applied only to the view table and not to other HTML tables that might exist on the view template:

```
#dataTable   {
  border-collapse: collapse ;
  border: solid 2px black ;
  }
#dataTable th     {
  background-color: yellow ;
  color: blue ;
  font-weight: bold ;
  padding: 3px ;
  text-align: left ;
  text-style: italic ;
  }
```

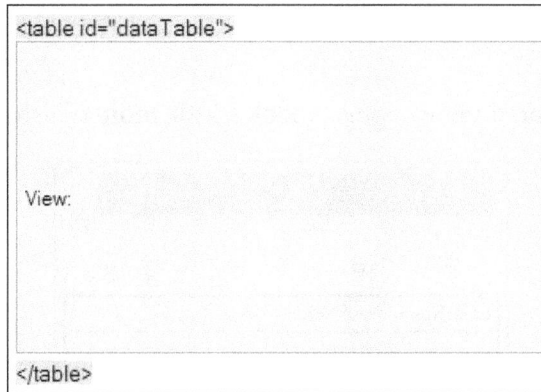

```
#dataTable td      {
  border: solid 1px black ;
  padding: 3px ;
  }
#dataTable th.age, td.age {
  text-align: center ;
  width: 4em;
  }
```

And finally, the rendered view begins to look a little more polished:

Home	Add Contact

Contacts

Last Name	First Name	Age	City
ApeMan	Tarzan	48	TreeTown
Lamb	Mary	18	Fleece
Charming	Prince	22	Castleville
Quinn	Jason	31	Glocca Morra
Little	John	29	Sherwood

Opening documents in a separate window

The main purpose of a view is to provide a list of documents that can be opened by clicking on entries in the view. By default, documents open in the same browser tab or window as the parent view. If you want documents to open in a new window or tab, here is how this can be done:

If a view is displayed using the `$$ViewBody` field on a view template, modify the formula that creates the document links by adding the `target` attribute to the `<a>` tag. Here, `target='_blank'` is added to the @formula for the Computed form field `docURLItem` as discussed in a previous topic:

```
db   := "/" + @WebDbName ;
vw   := "/" + @Subset(@ViewTitle;1) ;
doc  := "/" + @Text(@DocumentUniqueID) + "?OpenDocument" ;
link := db + vw + doc ;
"<li>" +
"<a href=\"" + link + "\" target='_blank'>" + ContactLast + "</a>" +
  ", " + ContactFirst +
"</li>"
```

If a view is displayed using an embedded view control, then specify **_blank** for the **Frame** attribute on the **Info** tab of **Embedded View Properties**:

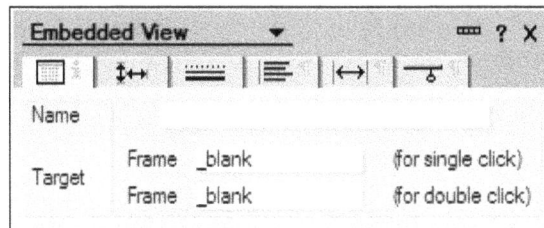

Adding view scrollbars dynamically

It is possible to add scrollbars to Domino views without using the View Applet. This technique might be appropriate for views whose line count will not exceed the **Maximum lines per view page** server setting discussed earlier. In other words, if the server setting is 1000 and a view never exceeds 1,000 rows, then adding a scrollbar as described here might work well.

Again, there are several pieces to this solution which must work together. (For the purpose of this illustration, I simply duplicated records to create a larger number of documents.). To begin, here's the finished product:

Here are the steps to add scrollbars to a view:

1. Add `<div>` tags to the view template:

    Add two HTML divisions to the view template. The `embeddedview` division encloses the embedded view control, and the `viewwrapper` division encloses the `embeddedview` division. The `viewwrapper` division is the container to which the scrollbars attach. Here is the complete view template with HTML marked as Pass-Thru HTML:

    ```
    <div id="viewtitle">
    Contacts with Scrollbars
    </div>

    <div id='viewwrapper'>
    <div id='embeddedview'>
    <table id='datatable'>



    View:




    </table>
    </div>
    </div>

    <script language="JavaScript" type="text/javascript">
    { styleActionBar() ; }
    </script>
    ```

2. Code a CSS rule for the `viewwrapper` division:

    Add this CSS rule to your CSS style sheet. The background color of the `viewwrapper` division is set to a light gray (so that you can see it). The **overflow** attribute turns on the scrollbars:

    ```
    div#viewwrapper {
      background-color: #EEE ;
      padding: 0 ;
      overflow: auto ;
      }
    ```

3. Set the line count for the embedded view:

   Set the line count for the embedded view on the **Info** tab of **Embedded View Properties**. Remember that this is the maximum number of rows that the view should ever contain, and it must be no larger than the number allowed by the server. In this example, the line count is set to **500**:

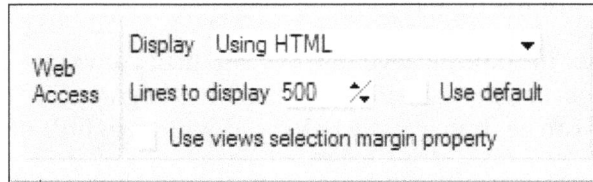

	Display Using HTML ▼
Web Access	Lines to display 500 ↕ Use default
	Use views selection margin property

4. Code a JavaScript function:

   Add this function to the JS Header or to a linked JavaScript library. When this function runs, it resets the height and width of the `viewwrapper` division to account for how the user may have adjusted the size and shape of his browser's window. Note that you may have to experiment a little with the values for height and width that are applied to the `viewwrapper` division by this function:

   ```
   function resizeView() {
     var ch = document.body.clientHeight ;
     var vw = document.getElementById("viewwrapper") ;
     vw.style.height = ch-200+"px" ;
     vw.style.width = "400px" ;
     }
   ```

5. Code a JavaScript function call in the view template's HTML Body Attributes area:

   The **onresize** event fires whenever the user resizes the browser window. In the view template's **HTML Body Attributes** area, code the following @formula:

   ```
   "onresize='resizeView()'"
   ```

6. Code a JavaScript function call in the onLoad form event:

   In the view template's onLoad event, add the following JavaScript function call. This sets the scrollbars in place when the view template first loads:

   ```
   resizeView()
   ```

Summary

Crafting views for the Web can be simple or time-consuming. As we have seen in this chapter, very little time is required to create basic, functional views. More time—and some knowledge of CSS and JavaScript—can produce substantially better looking views. There are many options to consider, and some experimentation is required to achieve just the right results.

Topics in this chapter introduced several ways in which views can be designed, rendered for the Web, and styled with properties in Designer or with CSS rules. Even older default views can be dramatically enhanced with very little effort.

8
Agents

Web applications rely on agents for server-based work. Think of an agent as a program that manipulates documents within and between applications. Agents can be simple actions specified with a wizard or they can consist of named lines of code written in Formula Language, LotusScript, or Java. These programs are stored in Domino applications and then run on-demand or automatically on a schedule. In all cases, they run within the context of an application, and from a web application point of view, they run on the server and not in the browser.

It has been said that you can do just about anything you can imagine with LotusScript, from large tasks such as accessing every application on a server to discrete tasks such as twiddling the bits in a design element's Properties. You should develop a familiarity with LotusScript regardless of your personal programming language preferences. Domino developers who came before you left a lot of this stuff lying around, and you will be called upon to fix and enhance it from time to time.

An existing application can contain dozens of agents accumulated over the years as the application design morphed and evolved. As you discover an application, pay attention to the agents. In truth, this can be the most daunting task you face. Not only do you need to learn the code, but this is where you see how those previous developers solved problems.

Topics in this chapter focus primarily on how agents written in LotusScript can provide functionality for web users, although some techniques are also appropriately coded for use with the Notes client. Most of the sample agents are written in LotusScript, and they illustrate various techniques and strategies. Experiment with them, and then adapt them for your own purposes as you see fit.

Topics in this chapter include these:

- General guidelines for LotusScript agents
- Setting appropriate agent attributes
- Trapping errors and writing messages
- Accessing documents with agents

General LotusScript agent guidelines

Before getting into the details of coding agents, here are a few suggestions that apply to all agents:

- Give agents meaningful names and aliases
- Structure and document agents appropriately
- Use agent subroutines and libraries
- Harvest ideas from Designer Help

Give agents meaningful names and aliases

By now, it should be second nature to name design elements, including agents, so that future developers can grasp the essential purpose of those elements right away. For instance, the general intention of an agent named `Repair Status Fields (Dev Tool)` is relatively easy to understand even without looking at the code.

Since an agent can be invoked with a URL, you may want to avoid problems with spaces (and special characters) either by giving an agent a name with no spaces or by adding an alias with no spaces:

```
Repair Status Fields (Dev Tool) | RepairStatusFields
```

If permitted in **Agent Properties**, the primary name of an agent displays in the Notes Actions menu.

You can use the alias to invoke the same agent from a web page. Here are two examples of how to launch an agent with @formulas attached to a web page button's `Click` event:

```
@Command([ToolsRunMacro]; "RepairStatusFields")

@URLOpen("/" + @WebDbName + "/RepairStatusFields?OpenAgent")
```

Structure and document agents

Most agents invoked from web pages are written in LotusScript, although Java and Formula Language can be used, if appropriate. When you look at an existing script, especially if it has been worked on by several developers over a period of years, you may find something that is hard to follow, full of commented-out code, and perhaps overly complicated. Take some time to clean it up.

- Version the agent so that you retain a copy of the old code for reference purposes
- Add a block of comments at the top of the agent and add good notes
- Co-locate all Dim statements below the comment block
- Remove unnecessary, commented-out lines of code
- Add a basic error trap, if the agent lacks one
- If a subroutine is very large, consider breaking it up into smaller subroutines

Use agent subroutines and LotusScript libraries

By default, a LotusScript agent starts with two subroutines, Initialize and Terminate. If the process is brief enough, then all the code can be placed in the Initialize subroutine. However, if the process turns out to be lengthy, you may want to break it up into multiple subroutines and use Initialize as an organizing process, calling the other subroutines in order. Variables can be passed by specifying them on Call statements or by declaring them in the module level Declarations area.

You may also find LotusScript subroutines and functions located in LotusScript libraries. Libraries should be used for subroutines and functions that are called by more than one agent. If you intend to add a new subroutine to a library, you will need to code at least a stub in the library before a calling agent will compile. Also, be sure to link to the library from the agent's module level Options area with a Use statement identifying the LotusScript library.

```
Option Public
Use "Common Subs"
```

The important design consideration here has to do with how many individual subroutines you create and where you put them. The more complicated you make the code, the more difficult it will be for the next developer to work on the application. Keep things as simple and as well-organized as possible. Place functions and subroutines that do similar things together. Keep the size of each module, subroutine, or function to a reasonable number of lines of code—not too many and not too few. If an agent calls a library subroutine or function, leave a comment in the agent identifying the library that contains the called code.

Harvest ideas from Designer Help

Don't be shy about harvesting ideas from **Designer Help**. As you know if you have written LotusScript agents before, code samples can be copied directly from **Help,** pasted into an agent, and then modified. **Designer Help** also indicates which techniques work on the Web and which do not. Short of calling an IBM support desk, **Help** is the definitive guide to how things (should) work.

Setting agent attributes

A number of attributes are set in **Agent Properties** that define important agent characteristics. Key properties are noted in this section.

Set who can view and run an agent

Who can view and run an agent is set on the **Security** tab of **Agent Properties**. By default, **All readers and above** can see and run an agent. If you require that running an agent be restricted to one or more entities listed in the application's ACL, then uncheck the default and check one or more servers, groups, roles, or people who are allowed to invoke the agent.

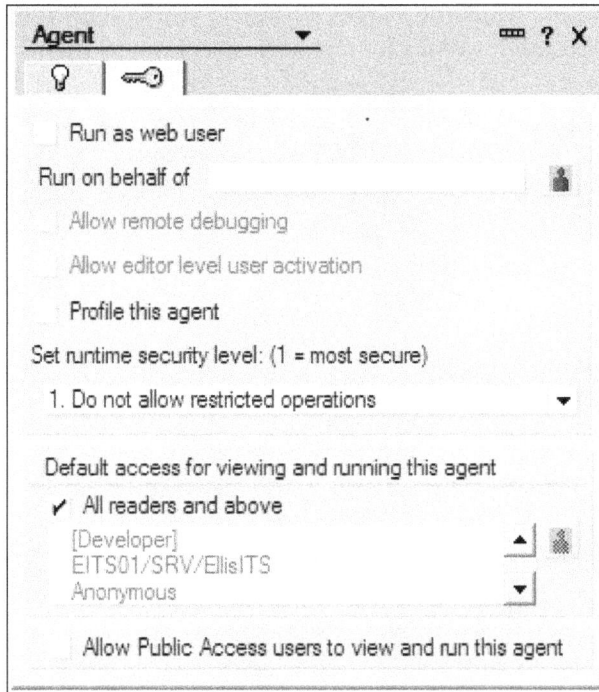

Set an agent's runtime context

Most agents invoked from a web page are set to trigger **On event**. Agents triggered **On schedule** run according to a schedule of times and days, which is also defined in **Agent Properties**. Both techniques can be used in web applications.

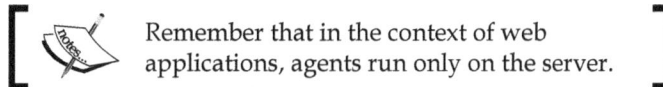

> Remember that in the context of web applications, agents run only on the server.

If you want an agent to display in the Notes Actions menu, then set the **Runtime Trigger** to **On event** on the **Basics** tab of **Agent Properties** and select **Action menu selection** as in the following image; otherwise, select **Action list selection**. Either attribute works for agents invoked on demand from the Web.

Also, take care to set the **Runtime Target** properly; you will most often set the **Target** to **None** and code the agent to select which documents to process.

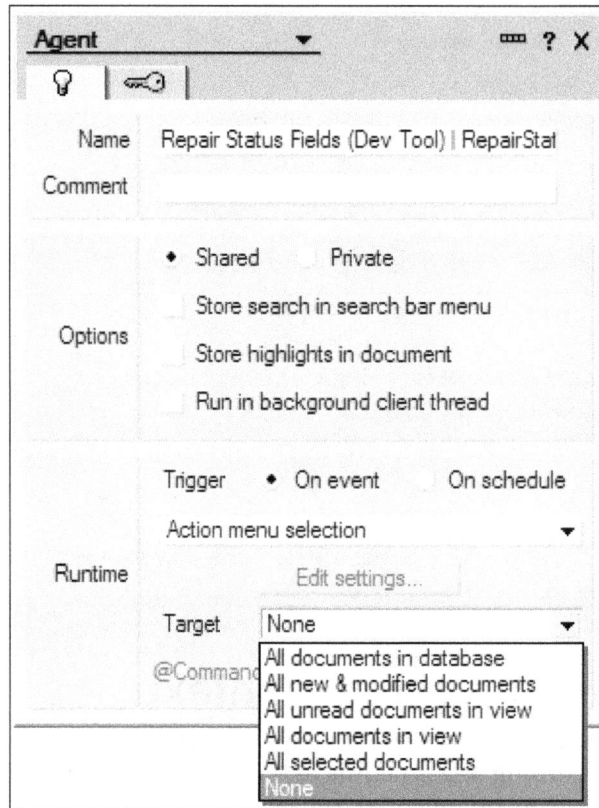

Note that if you select the **Runtime Trigger, On event** selection **Action list selection**, then the agent is considered (somewhat) hidden, and you must surround the name with parentheses when invoking it with a button or hotspot. Use either of these commands:

```
@Command([RunAgent]; "(SecretAgent)")

@Command([ToolsRunMacro]; "(SecretAgent)")
```

Set an agent's runtime privileges

Determining who can see and run an agent is not the same as determining what the agent is allowed to do. When the agent runs, it runs with the privileges of someone. You might think that an agent would run with the same privileges as the user who invoked it, but that does not have to be the case. An agent can run with the authority of the user who invoked it or with someone else's authority. There are three options:

- Run as the current web user
- Run as a specific person, group, or role
- Run as the person (Notes ID) who signed the agent

When you set the authority to **Run as web user**, then the agent runs with the application access and privileges of the user invoking the agent, as defined in the application's ACL.

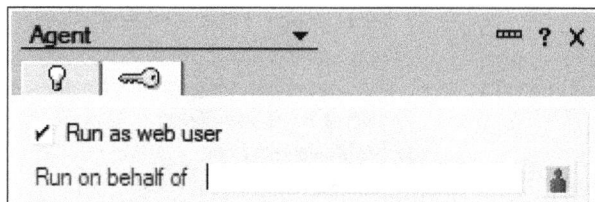

When you set the authority to **Run on behalf of** (and fill in the blank), then the agent runs with the application access and privileges of the specified group or person, also as defined in the application's ACL. This may be an appropriate setting if the agent does something requiring elevated privileges.

If you do not specify either of these options, then the agent runs with the privileges granted in the application's ACL to the signer of the agent (could be the developer or an authorized signing ID or a server). In this case, the signer (or a group of which he is a member) must be granted access to the application or else the agent fails. For example, if your application is signed by a specific authorized ID before being migrated to production, then that ID must be authorized to access the application in order for the agent to run.

Hide unused agents

Normally, you should delete unused design elements to keep the design as clean as possible. But you may want to hold onto agents more or less permanently, especially if they served to repair or update documents in an application. Someday you may be faced with the same or a similar problem, and being able to re-use or adapt an existing agent can save you considerable time.

You can hide an agent with **Design Document Properties**. Checking the option **Do not show this design element in menus of R4 or later clients** is a good choice, if you have some other way to launch the agent, such as clicking a button. But the options under **Hide design element from:** hide the agent from you as well, so you cannot run the agent once these options are selected.

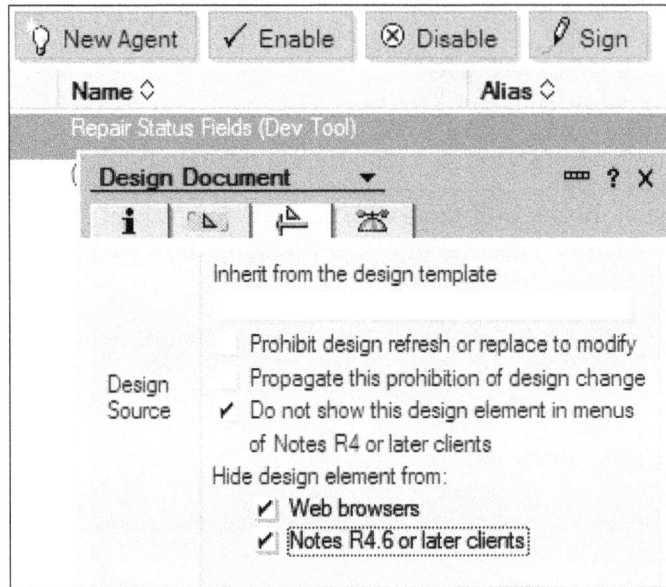

A slightly more involved strategy enables you to see and run the agent, but hides it from everyone who should not see it. First, define a special role in the application's ACL. In this example, the "Developer" role is defined. In the ACL, assign this role to whoever should be able to see the agent in the **Actions** menu and/or run it.

Next, adjust settings under the label **Default access for viewing and running this agent** on the **Security** tab of **Agent Properties**. This is an agent access list. Uncheck the default **All readers and above**, and select the special role (for example, **[Developer]**) whose assignees are allowed to see and run the agent.

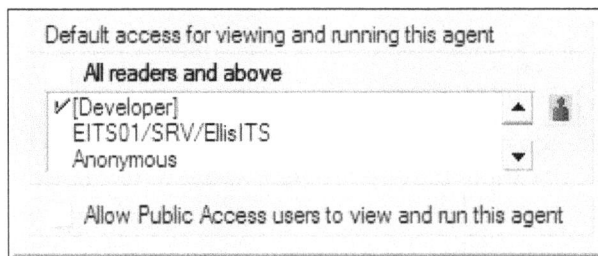

Now, the agent displays in the **Actions** menu in Notes for anyone assigned the Developer role and does not display for anyone else. On the Web, anyone logged in with the Developer role can run the agent, while anyone without the Developer role who tries to run the agent receives an HTTP error message:

HTTP Web Server: Couldn't find design note

In a similar manner, you can define a button to invoke the agent, and then secure the button with a hide-when formula.

Developing agents

As you look at existing scripts or begin to code your own, keep in mind the general suggestions highlighted in this section. These strategies apply to most agents. If an existing agent does not include a basic error trap, for instance, then you should consider putting one in when you work on the agent.

Use web safe @formulas and LotusScript

As you look to write a new agent or to web-enable an existing Notes application, keep in mind that certain LotusScript classes, properties, and methods do not work in server agents invoked from web applications. Check **Designer Help** for specifics.

For example, background agents written in LotusScript cannot use the UI classes, so an agent that tries to use such a class fails when invoked from the Web.

```
Dim workspace As New NotesUIWorkspace
Call workspace.OpenPage("Page2")
```

Rewrite such agents. Here is one way to achieve the same result:

```
Dim session As New NotesSession
Dim db As NotesDatabase
Set db = session.CurrentDatabase
url$ =  "[/"+db.Filepath+"/Page2?OpenPage]"
Print url$
```

Also, keep in mind that in existing Notes applications, you might find LotusScript coded in locations (for example, in a button's Click event) where it will not work in web applications. For example, if a button's Click event were coded with this LotusScript, the button would not display on the Web:

```
Sub Click(Source As Button)
  Msgbox("Hello!")
End Sub
```

Recode the function (if you can) to use web safe @formulas or JavaScript code.

Include a basic error trap

Any script can fail, so every script should contain code to handle errors gracefully. When an error occurs in a script, control passes to a few lines of code for exception processing. A simple error handler provides a useful error message and then quits. More sophisticated error handlers might attempt to repair the error and continue.

Since an agent invoked from the Web runs on a server, an error message must be sent somewhere. You have some choices:

- Write messages to the Domino Log
- Write messages to the browser as a web page
- Write messages to the browser as a JavaScript alert
- Write messages to an Agent Log

If you use the MessageBox statement or function, then the error message goes to the Domino Log, which is a system file to which Domino writes messages about events transpiring on the server. You must be authorized to access the Domino Log on the server in order to view the messages.

Here is a tiny agent with an error and a basic error handler. The error handler sends a message to the Domino Log. The message contains the names of the application, the agent, and the subroutine, as well as identifying the line of code that failed and some information about the error itself. There is no attempt to recover from the error. Every agent should include at least this kind of basic error trap.

```
Sub Initialize
  Dim msgPrefix As String
  msgPrefix = "Web Sandbox 08 / RepairStatusFields / Initialize "
  On Error Goto ErrorHandler

  Dim v As Variant
  Print v(0)
```

```
    Exit Sub

'**** E R R O R   H A N D L E R ****
ErrorHandler:
  Msgbox(msgPrefix & "**** E R R O R **** " _
  & Cstr(Err()) & " at line " & Cstr(Erl) & " : " & Error() )
End Sub
```

To demonstrate this error handler, attach the following @formula to a button on a web page, and then click the button. Remember to surround the name of the agent with parentheses (if you enabled **Action list selection** on the **Basics** tab of **Agent Properties**).

```
@Command([ToolsRunMacro];"RepairStatusFields")
```

When the agent runs, the error is detected and control transfers to the label `ErrorHandler:`. The code then writes a message to Domino Log.

Interrogate the log file to locate messages. There may be a delay before the message is written, depending upon how busy the server is.

The first of these next two messages comes from our agent, and it clearly indicates which line of code failed. The second message indicates that the failing agent did not attempt to recover from the error.

11/13/2010 09:56:32 AM HTTP Server: Agent message: Sandbox8 / RepairStatusFields / Initialize ** E R R O R **** 184 at line 8 : Variant does not contain a container**

11/13/2010 09:56:32 AM HTTP Server: Agent 'Repair Status Fields (Dev Tool) | RepairStatusFields' error: No RESUME

Write messages to the browser as a web page

Instead of writing error messages to the Domino Log, you may choose to write those messages out to the web browser as a page for immediate feedback. If you do this, provide sufficient instructions so that an end user knows exactly what to do should he encounter an error. Here is a modified error handler that sends messages to the browser. Note the inclusion of HTML tags in the `Print` statements.

```
'**** E R R O R   H A N D L E R ****
ErrorHandler:
  Print "<html><body>"
  Print "<h2>Attention !</h2><p> An error occurred.</p>"
  Print "<p>Please send what you were doing to the Administrator.</p>"
  Print "<p>Sandbox8 / RepairStatusFields / Initialize</p>"
```

```
Print "<p>Error at line " & Cstr(Erl) & " : " & Error() + "</p>"
Print "<p>Use the back button to return to the application.</p>"
Exit Sub
```

Here is the error message page displayed in a browser:

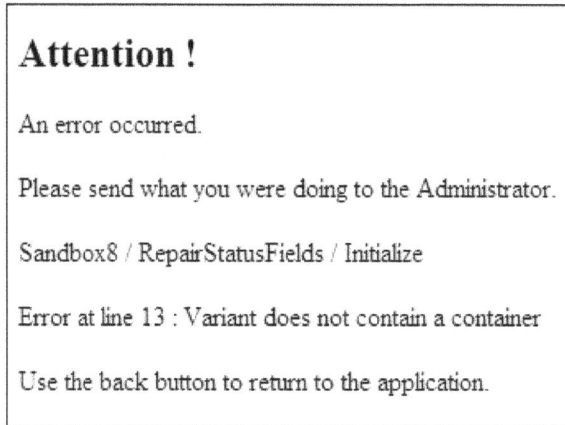

> **Attention !**
>
> An error occurred.
>
> Please send what you were doing to the Administrator.
>
> Sandbox8 / RepairStatusFields / Initialize
>
> Error at line 13 : Variant does not contain a container
>
> Use the back button to return to the application.

Instead of instructing the user to click the browser's back button, you might include a clickable link that redirects him to some known point in the application.

Write messages to the browser with a JavaScript alert

If you like, you can display error messages with the JavaScript `alert()` function. In this version of the error handler, LotusScript `Print` statements send some JavaScript to the browser. If an error occurs, then the alert displays, and when the user clicks the **OK** button, the previous page displays. This technique is similar to the previously discussed option, but it is a little trickier to code. Pay attention to the punctuation on the `Print` statements. The outer double quotation marks are required by the `Print` statements. The inner single quotation marks are required by the JavaScript code in order to concatenate several short strings into a long message.

```
'**** E R R O R   H A N D L E R ****
ErrorHandler:
  Print "<script type='text/javascript'>"
  Print "var errmsg = 'Attention!\n\nAn error occurred.' + "
  Print " ' \n\nPlease let the Administrator know what happened.' + "
  Print " ' \n\nSandbox8 / RepairStatusFields / Initialize' + "
  Print " ' \n\nError at line " & Cstr(Erl) & " : " & Error() + " ' +
"
```

```
Print " ' \n\nClick the OK button to return to the application.' ; "
Print "alert(errmsg) ; "
Print "history.go(-1) ; "
Print "</script>"
Exit Sub
```

The result is a bit more polished.

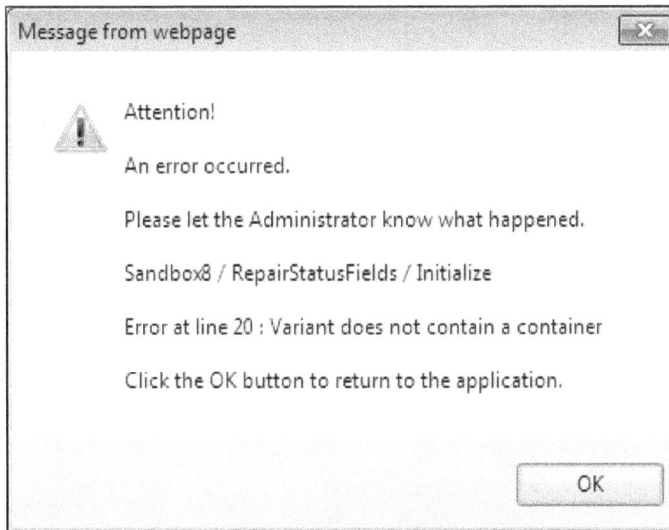

In addition to looking better, this JavaScript error handler can be a *huge* time saver. If you are used to writing error messages to the Domino Log and then waiting a few minutes to see what happened, try this JavaScript technique. Feedback about an error condition is immediate. Your development productivity should improve dramatically.

Write messages to an agent log file

Setting up an agent log file is a bit more complicated, but doing so is an elegant way of managing messages from your application. You can use an agent log only for error messages or for other messages, if you like.

Begin by creating a log file using the **Agent Log** advanced template.

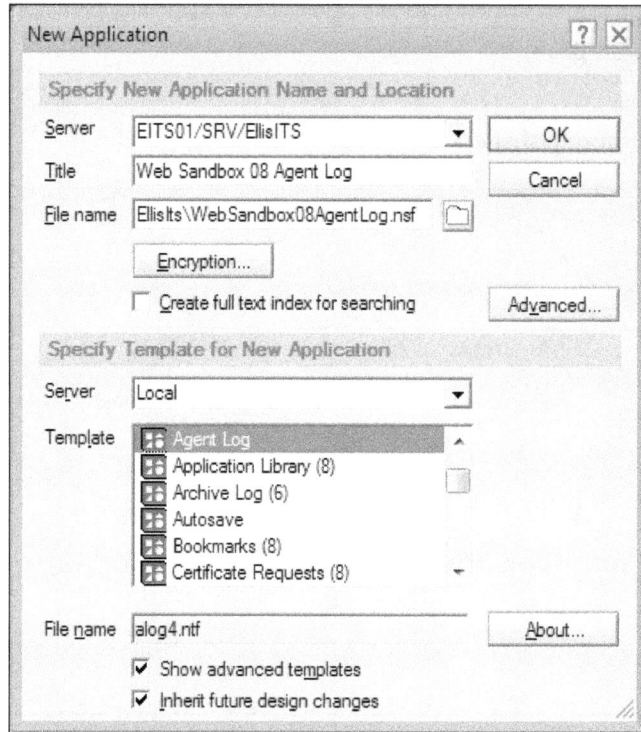

In your agents, code some lines to open the log file. Note that the `On Error` statement must come after the log initialization statements. Also, note that the format of the argument list for the `OpenNotesLog()` method as illustrated here is appropriate when an agent is invoked from the Web, but it may not be appropriate if the agent is invoked from the Notes client.

```
' Set up for agent log
Dim session As New NotesSession
Dim db As NotesDatabase
Dim agent As NotesAgent
Dim appLog As NotesLog
Dim e as Integer
Set agent = session.CurrentAgent
Set appLog = session.CreateLog(agent.Name)
Call appLog.OpenNotesLog( "", "EllisITS\WebSandbox08AgentLog.nsf" )
On Error Goto ErrorHandler
```

The error handler composes a message, writes it to the agent log, and then closes the agent log.

```
ErrorHandler:
  e = Err()
  errmsg = msgPrefix & "**** E R R O R **** " & _
  Cstr(Err()) & " at line " + Cstr(Erl) + " : " + Error()
  Call appLog.LogError( e, errmsg )
  Call appLog.Close
  Exit Sub
```

Opening the agent log reveals any logged messages.

Web Sandbox 08 Agent Log	Agent Name	Time	User	LogType	Message
Agent Activity	Write to Agent Log				
		02/05/2011 01:35:53 PM	Anonymous	✖	Web Sandbox 08
		02/05/2011 01:45:44 PM	Anonymous	✖	Web Sandbox 08

Note that the agent must have sufficient authority to write to the agent log. In this example, Anonymous is allowed Editor access to the agent log and the agent is running as the web user.

Of course, the agent log can be used to write normal messages as well at any time during processing using the `LogAction()` method. Be sure to close the agent log before exiting the agent.

```
Call appLog.LogAction( msgPrefix & "*** Start ***" )
.

.
Call appLog.LogAction( msgPrefix & "*** Close ***" )
Call appLog.Close
Exit Sub
```

Working with documents

Perhaps the majority of agents in an application are intended to manipulate one or more documents. On the Web, agents can be invoked by clicking buttons or hotspots on forms or pages. @Formulas coded to launch agents can take several forms, including these. The second example illustrates how to open an agent with a constructed URL.

```
@Command([ToolsRunMacro];"(TestAgent1)")

@URLOpen("/"+@WebDbName+"/TestAgent1?OpenAgent")
```

Agents are commonly run also as a result of loading or saving a document. Formulas in the WebQueryOpen and WebQuerySave form events determine which agents run at these points.

Topics in this section address issues related to creating agents to work with forms and documents on the Web.

Use WebQuerySave

After a web form is submitted, but before the document is actually saved into the database, an agent named in an @formula in the form's WebQuerySave event runs. If an agent is not invoked in this event, then no agent runs.

Code the WebQuerySave event as in this illustration. Note that the **Runtime, On event** selection **Action list selection** is selected, so that the agent's name, **SaveDocument**, must be surrounded by parentheses.

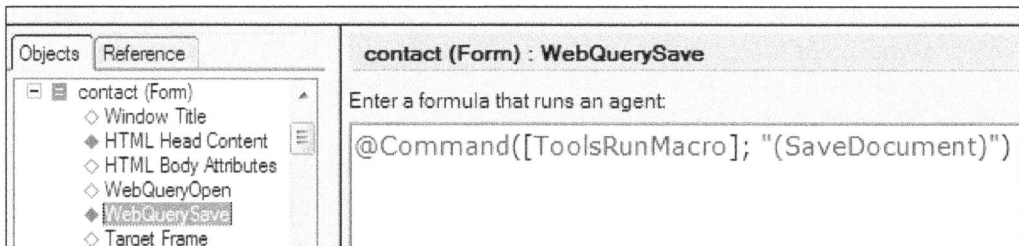

Objects	Reference		contact (Form) : WebQuerySave
⊟ 🗒 contact (Form)			Enter a formula that runs an agent:
◇ Window Title			
◆ HTML Head Content			@Command([ToolsRunMacro]; "(SaveDocument)")
◇ HTML Body Attributes			
◇ WebQueryOpen			
◆ WebQuerySave			
◇ Target Frame			

Whatever processing needs to be done before the document is saved into the application can be coded in the WebQuerySave agent. Processing might include such things as computing a sequence number for the document, issuing e-mail notifications, and writing messages to a log file.

There is no need to save the document in the WebQuerySave agent. The document is automatically saved after the agent finishes, unless the agent prevents the save.

Access a document from an agent

To retrieve field values from a document, an agent must gain access to or link to that document. In some circumstances, you can use the session document context to achieve the link. In other circumstances, you must access the document through its UNID.

Access a document open in the browser

To enable an agent to access a document currently opened for Read or Edit in a browser, invoke the agent with either of these commands:

```
@Command([ToolsRunMacro]; "agentname")

@Command([RunAgent]; "agentname")
```

The linkage from the agent to the document is arranged through the DocumentContext property of the NotesSession object.

[See **Designer Help** for more information about the DocumentContext property as used in web applications.]

This familiar code snippet shows how a NotesDocument object (doc) is initialized within an agent.

```
Dim session As NotesSession
Dim doc As NotesDocument
Set session = New NotesSession
Set doc = session.DocumentContext
```

Assuming that the **Generate HTML for all fields** option is enabled on the **Defaults** tab of **Form Properties**, then form values can be retrieved from a document open in Read mode as well as in Edit mode.

Access a document not open in the browser

If an agent needs to access a document already saved in a database, either to retrieve stored values or to manipulate the document as a whole, it can locate that document by its UNID. There are several ways a document's UNID can be made available to an agent.

If the document currently open in the browser contains a field that holds the UNID of the second document, then the agent can access that second document by retrieving its UNID from the open document through the session context as previously described.

Alternatively, the UNID of the second document can be coded as the value of a parameter in the query string of the URL used to invoke the agent. The agent retrieves the UNID from the query string and then uses the UNID to locate the document.

This technique can be used to access the backend or database copy of a document currently open in a browser. However, it cannot be used to access field values of the document as currently open in the browser. The agent cannot access unsaved changed values in the browser; it will only be able to access the document as currently stored in the database.

Here is one way to pass a document's UNID to an agent.

First, code a form button or hotspot whose `Click` event value is similar to the following @formula. Note that parameter DOCID is included on the URL.

```
@URLOpen("/" + @WebDbName + "/GetDocValuesURL?OpenAgent" +

"&DOCID=" + @Text(@DocumentUniqueID))
```

In this example, the value of the DOCID parameter is the UNID of the document currently displayed in the browser. The agent accesses the document as saved in the database (and not the browser version).

Next, code the agent. Include a way to extract the value of the UNID from the query string. In this example, the `For Next` loop parses out parameter-value pairs from the query string.

```
Sub Initialize
   Dim session As New NotesSession
   Dim db As NotesDatabase
   Dim doc As NotesDocument
   Dim argarray As Variant
   Dim argcount As Integer
   Dim argstring As String
   Dim aDOCID As String
   Dim errmsg As String
   Dim e As Integer, i As Integer

   argstring = session.DocumentContext.Query_String(0)
   argarray = Split(argstring,"&",-1)
   argcount = Ubound(argarray)

   For i = 1 To argcount
     parm = argarray(i)
     e = Instr(parm,"=")
     value = Mid$(parm,e+1)
     parm = Left$(parm,e-1)
     Select Case Ucase(parm)
     Case "DOCID"   : aDOCID = value
```

```
     Case Else        : errmsg = "Yes"
     End Select
   Next

   Set db = session.CurrentDatabase
   Set doc = db.GetDocumentByUNID( aDOCID )

End Sub
```

Detect the type of client invoking the agent

An agent may provide functionality that is identical for users accessing the application with the Notes client and with a browser. On the other hand, certain agent logic might pertain only to one type of client and not the other. An agent can detect which client is running using the following strategy.

First, add a hidden Computed for display field to a form. In this example, the name of the field is ClientType and its value is the following @formula:

```
@BrowserInfo("BrowserType")
```

The key is to test for a client type of "Notes". Remember that an agent accessing a document through the session context must be invoked with an @Command. Here is a skeleton agent:

```
Sub Initialize
   Dim session As NotesSession
   Dim doc As NotesDocument
   Dim aType As String
   Set session = New NotesSession
   Set doc = session.DocumentContext

   aType = doc.ClientType(0)

   If atype = "Notes" Then
     Msgbox("You are running the Notes client.")
   Else
     Print "<p>You are running a " + aType  + " browser."
   End If

End Sub
```

Detect whether a document is in Read or Edit mode

If for some reason an agent needs to know whether a document open in the browser is open in Read mode or in Edit mode, here is a strategy that can be used to detect the state of the document.

As in the previous topic, add a hidden Computed for display field to a form. In this example, the name of the field is EditMode and its value is the following @formula:

```
@If(@IsDocBeingEdited; "Edit"; "Read")
```

Now the agent can retrieve the value of the field and do whatever it needs to do.

```
aEditMode = doc.EditMode(0)
```

Prevent a document from being saved

To prevent a document from being saved — perhaps it did not pass validations or perhaps it was just a temporary document — add a hidden Computed field named SaveOptions to a form. In the WebQuerySave agent, code this line (assuming that doc refers to the document) to prevent the document from being saved:

```
doc.SaveOptions = "0"
```

If the document should never be saved, simply set the default value of the SaveOptions field to a text "0" on the form, and no documents composed with that form will ever be saved.

Redirect the browser to the next page

Once an agent completes processing, you may want it to redirect the browser to a new page rather than code the new location as the value of form field $$Return, which can also specify a URL. This is easily accomplished with a Print statement that sends the URL to the browser. As in this example, surround the URL with square brackets to indicate that the text should be treated as a URL:

```
Print "[http://www.google.com]"
```

There are many ways to compose a valid URL within an agent. Here are some samples:

To redirect to the database itself, try the following lines:

```
Dim dbpath As Variant
dbpath = Evaluate("@WebDbName")
Print "[/" + dbpath(0) + "]"
```

To redirect to the default view, or really to any view by name, try the following lines:

```
Dim session As NotesSession
Dim db As NotesDatabase
Dim dbpath As String
Dim tmp As Variant
Set session = New NotesSession
Set db = session.CurrentDatabase
dbpath = db.filepath
tmp = Split(dbpath,"\")
dbpath = Join(tmp,"/")
Print "[/" + dbpath + "/$defaultview?OpenView]"
```

In this case, backward slashes are converted to forward slashes programmatically, as opposed to using the Evaluate("@WebDbName") function as in the preceding example. Both transformations accomplish the same thing with regard to backward slashes.

To redirect back to the same document in the default view, try the following lines: (In this and the next example, the Dim statements for session, doc, and dbpath are omitted.)

```
Set session = New NotesSession
Set doc = session.DocumentContext
dbpath = Evaluate("@WebDbName")
Print "[/" + dbpath(0) + "/$defaultview/" + doc.UniversalID + _
"?OpenDocument]"
```

To redirect back to the document's parent view requires a couple of steps. First, define a Computed for display form field named ViewTitle with the following @formula:

```
@URLEncode("Domino";@Subset(@ViewTitle;1))
```

If the document already exists, the function @ViewTitle returns a value. If the document is new, then @ViewTitle returns nothing.

Here are the lines of code for the agent. Note that the value of the `ViewTitle` form field is tested; if it is blank, then the default view is selected.

```
Dim vwtitle As String
Set session = New NotesSession
Set doc = session.DocumentContext
dbpath = Evaluate("@WebDbName")
vwtitle = doc.ViewTitle(0)
If vwtitle = "" Then vwtitle = "$defaultview"
Print "[/" + dbpath(0) + "/" + vwtitle + "?Openview]"
```

Process selected documents in a view

It is sometimes convenient to enable users to process multiple documents at once. With the Notes client, you select a set of documents in a view and then invoke an agent (or some other action) to process all selected documents. You can include a similar feature in a web application, and there are a couple of ways to do this. Here is one way.

In this example, a document approval process is implemented.

Four design elements are required:

- A form used to create documents, which are to be modified
- A view, which displays the documents along with checkboxes
- A temporary form, which embeds the view and provides a way to invoke an agent
- An agent, which processes documents selected in the view

First, create a form with a field named `Status` or something similar whose default value is blank. Create some documents with the form.

Second, create a view which displays the documents. For **Web Access**, enable **Allow selection of documents** on the **Advanced** tab of **View Properties**.

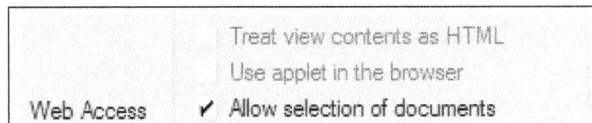

Third, create an approval form. This form is used to select documents for approval, but it is never saved. Remember to enable **Generate HTML for all fields** on the **Defaults** tab of **Form Properties**. Here is a sample form as it appears in Designer:

Surprisingly, there is a lot going on with this form. Each form element deserves a brief explanation.

- **timestamp field:** The `timestamp` field is a hidden Computed for display field, intended to minimize problems with caching the form. The value of the field is `@Now`.

- **SaveOptions field:** The `SaveOptions` field is a hidden Computed field intended to prevent the document from being saved. Its value is a text `"0"` as discussed in a previous topic.

- **$$SelectDoc field:** The `$$SelectDoc` field represents the checkboxes that Domino inserts to the left of the view entries when the view displays on the Approval form. When the form is submitted to the agent for processing, this field contains a list of document UNIDs corresponding to the documents selected on the form. The field is an Editable Text field. Enable **Allow multiple values** on the **Field Info** tab of **Field Properties**.

In addition, add an HTML type attribute on the **Field Extra HTML** tab of **Field Properties** as in the following image. *Do not hide the field using a hide-when formula.*

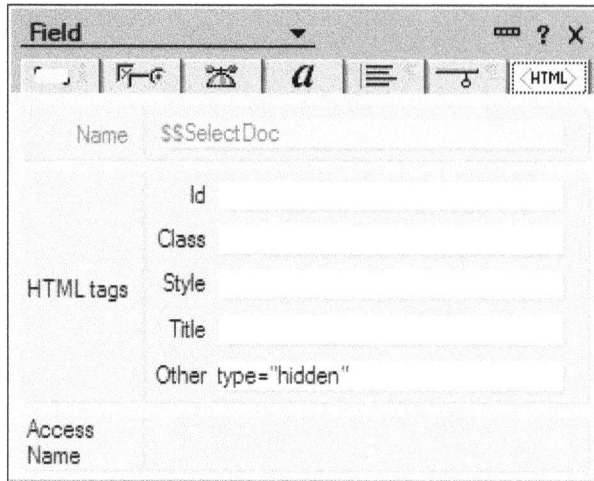

- **Approve button:** The **Approve** button's Click event contains the following formula, which submits the form:

```
@Command([FileSave]);
@Command([FileCloseWindow]);
```

- **Cancel button:** The **Cancel** button's Click event contains the following formula, which closes the Approval form and reopens the application:

```
@URLOpen("/" + @WebDbName)
```

- **$$ViewBody field:** The $$ViewBody field is the container that holds the view showing the documents we may want to approve. The default value of this field is the name of the view.

```
"Documents Pending Approval"
```

- **WebQuerySave event:** The form's WebQuerySave event contains the following formula, which invokes an agent to process the selected documents:

```
@Command([ToolsRunMacro];"(ApproveSelected)")
```

Fourth (remember, creating the Approval form was "third" in this list), code the agent invoked in the Approval form's WebQuerySave event. In this sample agent, the list of selected document UNIDs is retrieved into variable selUNIDList; the ContactStatus field of each selected document is updated; the document saved; and finally the browser is redirected back to the application's launch point.

```
Sub Initialize

    Dim session As NotesSession
    Dim db As NotesDatabase
    Dim doc As NotesDocument
    Dim selDoc As NotesDocument
    Dim selUNIDList As Variant
    Dim selUNID As String
    Dim i As Integer

    Set session = New NotesSession
    Set db = session.CurrentDatabase
    Set doc = session.DocumentContext
    selUNIDList = doc.GetItemValue( "$$SelectDoc" )
    i = 0
    Forall unid In selUNIDList
      If unid <> "" Then
        Set selDoc = db.GetDocumentByUNID(unid)
        If Not selDoc Is Nothing Then
          selDoc.ContactStatus = "Approved"
          Call selDoc.Save(False, False)
        End If
      End If
    End Forall

    Dim dbpath As Variant
    dbpath = Evaluate("@WebDbName")
    Print "[/" + dbpath(0) + "]"
    Exit Sub

End Sub
```

With all the design elements in place, add a button into your application to launch the Approval form. Here's the @formula:

```
@URLOpen("/" + @WebDbName + "/ApprovalForm?Open")
```

Finally, click the button to open the Approval form. Here is how the form looks before documents are selected and before the `Approve` button is clicked.

Approval Form

Select Contacts and then [Approve] [Cancel]

	Last Name	First Name	Age	City	Gender	Meal	Status
☐	ApeMan	Tarzan	48	TreeTown	Male	Breakfast	
☐	Charming	Prince	22	Castleville	Male	Lunch	
☐	Lamb	Mary	18	Fleece	Female	Breakfast	
☐	Little	John	29	Sherwood	Male	Snack	
☐	Quinn	Jason	31	Glocca Morra	Male	Dinner	

Writing special purpose agents

Undoubtedly, you will come across many, many agents as you discover applications and tackle maintenance chores. What do agents do? Anything you like. Here are two examples of processes you will likely encounter.

Send e-mail notifications

Applications can issue e-mail to notify users of events that transpire within the application. Perhaps a new task has been assigned or an old one completed, and the responsible parties are so informed. A notification might be triggered when someone changes a field on a document, such as a status field. Alternatively, a scheduled agent might run periodically and issue notices for overdue items, and so on.

Notification agents like this work pretty much the same way for Notes users or web users, with one notable difference: for the web user, the notification might include a clickable URL which opens the browser directly to the document requiring his attention. This kind of notification is particularly important for users who do not use Lotus Notes e-mail.

Here is an example of an agent that issues a notification including a URL. In the agent, the temporary memo `newMemo` receives its `SendTo` and `Subject` values from the document currently open in the browser; the `SendTo` value should be a proper Notes name, of course. The `Body` of the memo is constructed in the agent.

```
Sub Initialize

    Dim session As New NotesSession
    Dim db As NotesDatabase
    Dim doc As NotesDocument
    Set session = New NotesSession
    Set db = session.CurrentDatabase
    Set doc = session.DocumentContext

    Dim newMemo As NotesDocument
    Set newMemo = New NotesDocument( db )

    newMemo.Form = "Memo"
    newMemo.SendTo = doc.Actionee(0)
    newMemo.Subject = doc.Subject(0)

    Dim body As NotesRichTextItem
    Set body = New NotesRichTextItem( newMemo, "Body")
    Call body.AppendText("Greetings:")
    Call body.AddNewline(2)
    Call body.AppendText("You have been assigned an action item.")
    Call body.AddNewline(2)
    Call body.AppendText("Click this link to open the document.")
    Call body.AddNewline(2)
    Call body.AppendText(doc.HttpURL)

    Call newMemo.Send(False)

End Sub
```

The agent is invoked from a form with an @Command, which enables access to document fields through the session document context.

```
@Command([ToolsRunMacro];"(SendEmail)")
```

And here is a sample e-mail generated by the agent (viewed with the Notes client).

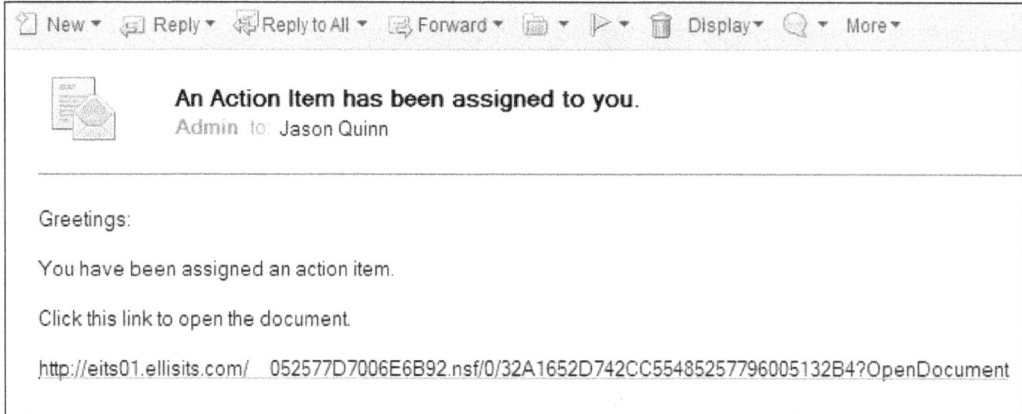

New ▼	Reply ▼	Reply to All ▼	Forward ▼	▼	▷ ▼	Display▼	▼	More ▼

An Action Item has been assigned to you.
Admin to Jason Quinn

Greetings:

You have been assigned an action item.

Click this link to open the document.

http://eits01.ellisits.com/ 052577D7006E6B92.nsf/0/32A1652D742CC554852577796005132B4?OpenDocument

Export data to a spreadsheet on the Web

Exporting data to a CSV file, which can then be imported into a spreadsheet, is quite straightforward with the Notes client. But many users of Domino web applications do not have access to the Notes client. If this is the situation in your organization, you should consider providing a way for users to extract data from web applications.

In older applications, you may find that a report is written to a web page as an HTML table; users then copy and paste that HTML table directly into a blank spreadsheet created with an application such as Microsoft Excel. If this is the technique provided by a previous developer, you can do better.

In this example, the full contents of a view are written to a spreadsheet in order to illustrate how this can be done. In many cases, an agent instead creates a document collection with documents that match certain criteria, and then provides a spreadsheet containing that more limited data.

For this example, simply embed a view on a form, and then add a button to the form to invoke the `WriteToSpreadsheet` agent. Here is the formula for the button:

```
@URLOpen("/" + @WebDbName + "/WriteToSpreadsheet?OpenAgent&viewname=" +
@Subset(@ViewTitle;1))
```

You can provide to the agent the name of the view to be exported in any way you choose; in this example, the name of the view is coded at the end of the query string of the URL that invokes the agent. The agent decodes the query string to extract the name of the view, and then writes rows of data from that view to the spreadsheet.

Here is an example of an agent that extracts data directly into a spreadsheet. Error handling is omitted, but a few comments are included to aid in reading the code.

```
Sub Initialize

    Dim session As New NotesSession
    Dim db As NotesDatabase
    Dim view As NotesView
    Dim doc As NotesDocument
    Dim colcounter As Integer, currentcol As Integer
    Dim columnHeadings As String
    Dim fileName As String
    Dim formula As String
    Dim queryString As String
    Dim row As String
    Dim viewColumnCount As Integer
    Dim viewColumns
    Dim viewName As String

    ' Get the name of the view from the query string
    Set doc = session.DocumentContext
    queryString = doc.Query_String_Decoded(0)
    viewName = Strright(queryString,"viewname=")

    Set db = session.CurrentDatabase
    Set view = db.GetView(viewName)

    ' Create a list of view columns to include in the export
    viewColumnCount = view.ColumnCount - 1
    Redim viewColumns(0 To viewColumnCount) As Integer
    colcounter = 0
    currentcol = 0
    columnHeadings = ""
    Forall c In view.Columns
      formula = c.Formula
      ' Ignore columns with icons and constants
      ' Use this form to keep Computed columns
      If Not c.isICon And  formula <> "1" And  formula <> """1""" Then
      ' Use this form to remove Computed columns
      'If Not c.isICon And  Not c.IsFormula Then
        viewColumns(colcounter) = currentcol
        columnHeadings = columnHeadings + "<th>" + c.Title + "</th>"
        colcounter = colcounter + 1
      End If
```

```
      currentcol = currentcol + 1
   End Forall

   Redim Preserve viewColumns(0 To colcounter-1) As Integer

   ' Open MS Excel and write out the column headings
   filename = db.Title + "-" + viewName + ".xls"
   Print |Content-Type:application/vnd.ms-excel|
   Print |Content-Disposition: Attachment; filename="| + fileName + |"|
   Print "<table border=0>"
   Print "<tr>"+columnHeadings+"</tr>"

   ' Write out the rows from the view to the spreadsheet
   Set doc = view.GetFirstDocument
   While Not (doc Is Nothing)
      row = "<tr>"
      Forall c In viewColumns
         row = row + "<td>" + Cstr(doc.ColumnValues(c)) + "</td>"
      End Forall
      Print row + "</tr>"
      Set doc = view.GetNextDocument(doc)
   Wend
   Print "</table>"
End Sub
```

When the spreadsheet is created, its gridlines are turned off by default. Turning gridlines on results in a very usable file.

	A	B	C	D	E
1	Last Name	First Name	Age	City	Gender
2	ApeMan	Tarzan	48	TreeTown	Male
3	Charming	Prince	22	Castleville	Male
4	Lamb	Mary	18	Fleece	Female
5	Little	John	29	Sherwood	Male
6	Quinn	Jason	31	Glocca Morra	Male

Summary

Domino applications rely on agents to perform many tasks, both on-demand and on-schedule. Most often agents are written in LotusScript, but they can also be coded with Formula Language or Java. Topics in this chapter have introduced and explored key techniques for coding agents and integrating them with other design elements in Domino web applications.

Security and Performance

9

Domino provides many standard security features, most of which can be used in web-enabled applications. Domino security is multilayered with controls to protect the server, the application, application design elements, documents, and fields on documents. You should develop a reasonably good understanding of these features, how they are implemented, and how they can influence the design of an application.

If you are discovering an existing application, learn about how security is implemented in the design, especially how groups, roles, and readers and authors fields are used. Map out how workflow and document state changes relate to the security features. Understanding these relationships provides considerable insight into how the application works and what you have to do to make changes.

If you are developing a new application, design it with security in mind. It is more difficult to bolt on security later than to implement it during initial development. Even if your requirements do not include such concerns, press your customer to consider the matter early in the project.

Be mindful of how the application performs when it goes into production. While it is true that applications generally run faster on fast hardware and over a fast network, poor response time today can be the result of application issues rather than infrastructure issues.

Application performance problems may not present themselves immediately. Testing an application under normal and heavy load conditions may be difficult until after it has migrated to production and accumulated a fair number of documents. So, "tuning" an application during development is often more a matter of implementing sensible design and following recommended best practices.

Many topics in this chapter are relevant to applications developed for the Notes client as well as for the Web, since most of the concerns are the same. Special emphasis is placed on security aspects that are relevant only to web-enabled applications. This chapter focuses on these topics:

- Planning security
- Managing Lotus groups and application ACLs
- Using the security features of design elements
- Measuring application responsiveness
- Improving application performance

Security

In most applications, security controls are implemented fundamentally to protect data stored in documents against unauthorized access and against unauthorized change or deletion. As the developer, you will need to know who accesses your application, what they are allowed to see, and what they are allowed to do and when they are allowed to do it.

Two key concepts can guide application security deliberations.

Layered security, also referred to as **defense in depth**, refers to the implementation of several barriers that must be penetrated before a user is allowed to access specific data. Depending upon organizational and application requirements, these are the kinds of controls that can be implemented:

- A user must have a Notes account and password to access the Domino environment.
- A user must be authorized to access the server hosting the application.
- A user must be authorized to access the application.
- A user must be authorized to use certain design elements, such as views and forms.
- A user must be authorized to access a specific document.
- A user must be authorized to edit a specific document.
- A user must be authorized to access specific fields on a document.
- A user must have access to encryption keys that decrypt data in encrypted fields.
- A user must be authorized to update data in fields.
- A user must be allowed to save changed data.

As a developer, some of these decisions are made for you by the organization and the Domino administrators. For example, you will likely not be involved directly in establishing server-level security, unless your application is the only application running on a server.

Note that for web applications, data stored in fields is typically not encrypted, since encryption keys are stored in Notes ID files, and web users do not have access to those keys. However, if requirements call for some level of encryption, web traffic between browsers and the application can be encrypted using technologies such as **SSL (Secured Sockets Layer)**.

The **principle of least privilege** governs the design by specifying that a user sees only what he is allowed to see to perform his job, and nothing more. Security rules, similar and related to the business rules that govern workflow, define in a general way who gets to do what. Knowing what security rules are implemented in a design is extremely important to understanding how an application works.

General guidelines

Like other aspects of application design and development, working out the security rules or profile for an application is often iterative, since some issues tend to emerge only as development proceeds. In existing designs, if the security rules are undocumented, it might be useful to write them down as you figure them out.

Here are a few suggestions to keep in mind as you work on the security aspects of a design.

Plan your security

As much as possible, work with your customer to understand and define the security rules. Create a taxonomy of classes for real or potential users—Readers, Authors, Analysts, Editors, Reviewers, Approvers, Administrators—whatever maps to the way people intend to use the application. Consider the role Anonymous users may play.

Consider what sets of privileges should be enabled for different user classes. Strive for detail. To guide the discussion with your customer, formulate questions such as these:

- In general, should access to the application and its data be limited to a specific group of users?
- Should a class of users be able to read only a subset of documents?
- Should a class of users be able to read but not edit all documents?

- Who can create documents?
- Who can edit all documents?
- Who can assign actions to handle issues represented by documents?
- Who can edit documents, and at what stage in the workflow?
- What fields should be editable and by whom?
- Who can approve or reject documents?
- Who can complete, archive, or delete documents?
- Who is allowed to see which Action buttons and under what conditions?

Domino groups are created in the Domino Directory and then added to an application's ACL to enable access to the application. Groups are granted certain privileges in the ACL, and when a user is added to a group in the Directory, he gains access to the application with the privileges assigned to the group. An individual's Domino name can be added directly to an application's ACL to authorize application access, but this is generally not recommended.

Roles can be defined in an ACL to refine the privileges granted to Domino groups. The name given to a role is arbitrary, but it should reflect the kind of work and responsibilities expected of that role within the application. Role names like Admin, NewsEditor, Advisor, and Approver convey meaning.

Access to an application is granted in the application's ACL. Privileges within the application are instantiated using various features of design elements. Access lists and hide-when formulas control who can see and use elements such as buttons, views, and agents. Access to documents can be controlled with document Readers and Authors fields. Very complex security rules can be implemented using these standard Notes features.

Manage Domino groups

Domino groups are most often created by Domino administrators. But maintaining those groups—adding and deleting members—can be delegated. Find out what your organization's policy is with regard to who maintains the Domino groups. Several options exist including these:

- Groups are managed by the Domino administrator.
- Groups are managed by the Help Desk.
- Groups are managed by the application developer.
- Groups are managed by the application administrator or owner.

Whoever manages the Domino groups is the primary gatekeeper for who accesses the application, and therefore he or she should be both trustworthy and reliable. If the policy is not hard-and-fast, you might consider assigning this responsibility to the application administrator or owner or another knowledgeable and interested application user. If such a user understands that he is responsible for administering an important component of the application's security, then he will likely pay more attention to the matter, and this can help surface issues earlier in the development process.

If a user maintains the Domino groups for his application, you may want to provide him with written documentation about how to do this, from both the Notes client and web browser perspectives. Modifying group membership may be an infrequent task, and it is easy for users to forget how to do this.

Specify anonymous access

Anonymous access is unauthenticated access—a Notes ID file and password are not required. There may be occasions when this kind of access is appropriate, but in a business setting, this would be somewhat unusual. For an application that collects anonymous surveys or suggestions from the public, anonymous access makes sense, but normally this should not be acceptable.

If your application truly requires anonymous access, then it must be enabled in the server document controlled by the Domino administrator. The application's ACL must also include an entry for Anonymous, with sufficient privileges.

Check the status of anonymous access to the server in the Domino Directory. Look at the server document, **Ports** tab / **Internet Ports** tab / **Web** tab. Find the **Web** section and check the Authentication option for Anonymous. It should look something like this:

Web	Directory	Mail	DIIOP	Remote

Web (HTTP/HTTPS)	
TCP/IP port number:	80
TCP/IP port status:	Enabled
Enforce server access settings:	Yes
Authentication options:	
Name & password:	Yes
Anonymous:	Yes

If anonymous access is allowed to the server, then your application's ACL must grant sufficient access privileges to either the Anonymous or Default entries. In this example, Editor access is granted, but the access level might be set to Author, Reader, Depositor, or No Access as required by the application.

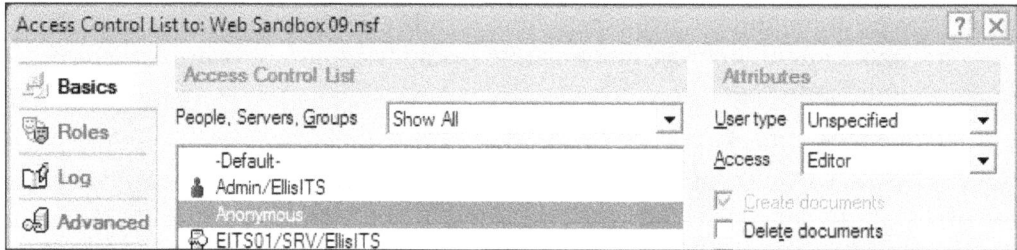

Note that if there is no entry for Anonymous in the ACL, then unauthenticated users receive the privileges granted to the Default entry. For web applications, set ACL privileges for both entries.

If anonymous access is not required, add an entry for Anonymous anyway with no access rights to the application. Guard against unauthorized access to the application.

If you need to allow everyone in the organization to access an application , but you do not want to create and maintain a huge Domino group, then add a wildcard to the ACL with an appropriate access level. Here is a wildcard that implements pseudo-anonymous access for all authenticated users within an organization.

```
*/EllisITS
```

Set the maximum Internet access level

On the ACL's **Advanced** tab, assure a proper setting for **Maximum Internet name and password** as shown at the bottom of the following screenshot:

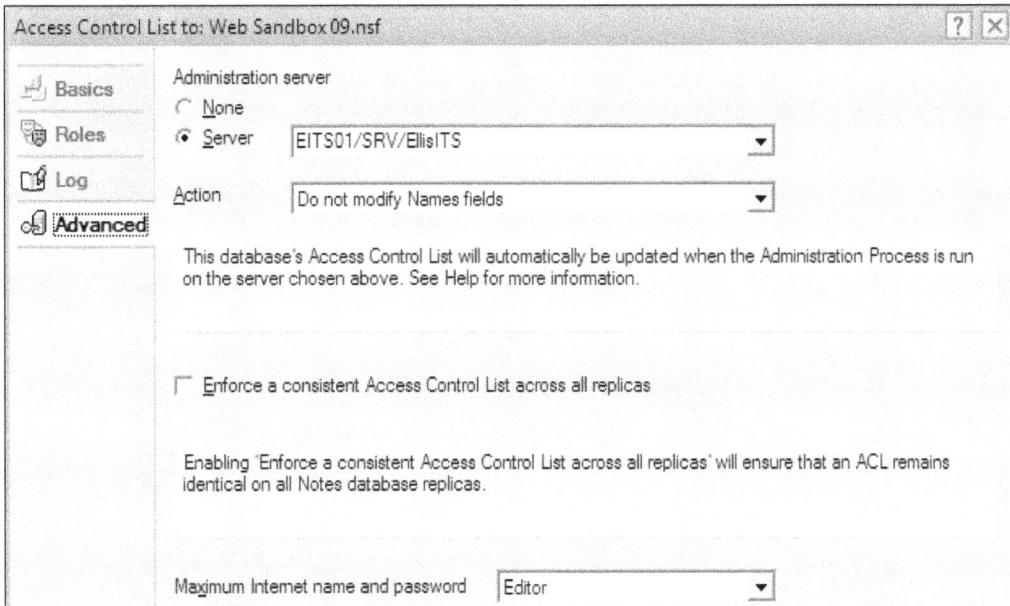

This setting may reduce a group's access level as granted in the ACL, but it cannot increase it.

If the **Maximum Internet name and password** setting is lower than that required by a group, users receive an unexpected login screen when they attempt to do something that requires the higher level of access. Worse, there may be no way to satisfy the login. For example, if the maximum Internet access level were set to Reader, then composing a new document or editing an existing one becomes problematic. In most cases, Editor access should work, and there may be little practical reason to set this value to a higher level.

Manage the application ACL

Adhering to the principle of separation of authority, you as the developer may not have Manager access to a production database, and therefore you may not be able to change the application's ACL at will. Find out who has that authority and what is the procedure required to make changes.

ACLs for the development, staging, and production instances of an application should be synchronized. If it is not possible to keep settings identical, keep them as close to each other as possible, especially the staging and production instances. Inconsistent application behavior can result from inconsistent security; if security in the staging environment is different from that in production, testing may not reveal certain kinds of problems.

Consider carefully whether or not it is a good idea for you as the developer to have special privileges in the production application. On the one hand, with some "super authority," you may be able to diagnose and fix problems more readily. On the other hand, your extra privileges may give you a view of the application that is quite different from that seen by users. A good compromise might be to request special privileges when you need them, and otherwise to retain the same privileges as an application administrator. One way to do this would be to add a troubleshooting group with special privileges to the ACL. When you need extra privileges, add yourself to that group.

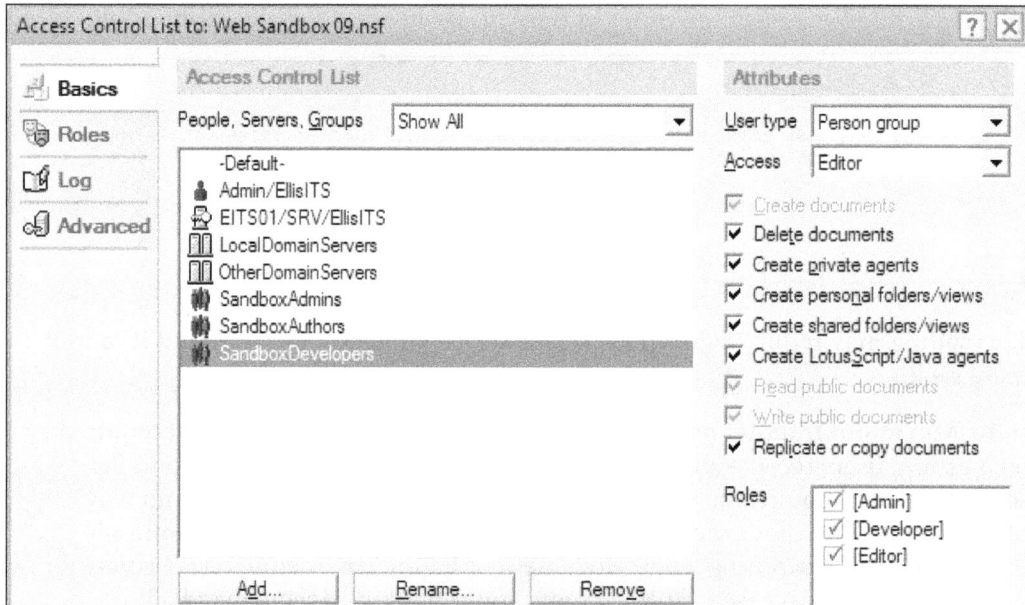

Enable SSL

As mentioned previously, if network packets between browsers and the server must be encrypted, then Secure Sockets Layer can be enabled. SSL requires the Domino administrator to install an SSL certificate on the server. Once that is installed, the developer can require SSL encrypted communications by checking the **Require SSL connection** option on the **Database Basics** tab of **Database Properties**.

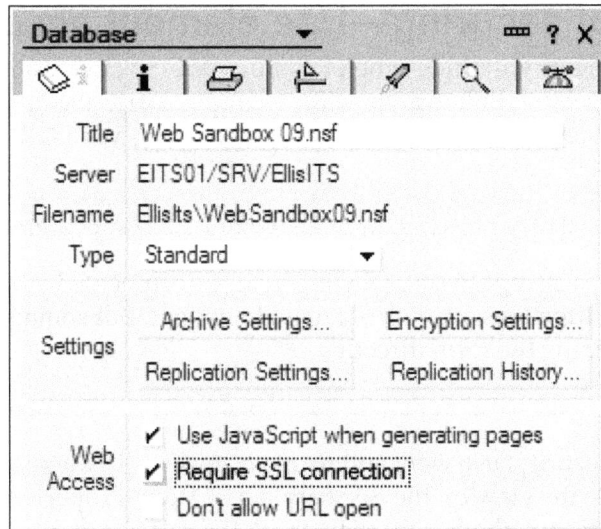

Prevent opening an application in a browser

If for some reason you need to deny access to an application from the Web, an easy way to do so is to enable the **Don't allow URL open** property on the **Database Basics** tab of **Database Properties**. Enabling this attribute effectively prevents the application from being opened in a browser, regardless of all other settings.

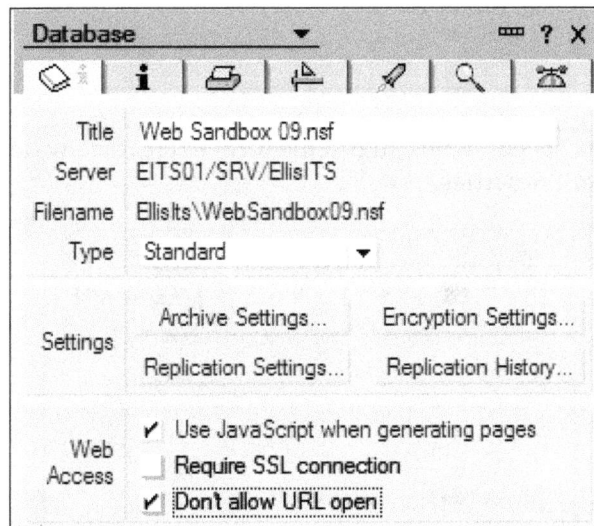

Hiding is not securing—Use element access lists

Hiding design elements with hide-when formulas does not necessarily provide security. Hiding a hotspot link to a view, for example, keeps the link from displaying on a page. But the view may still be opened by specifying a full URL in the browser address bar.

```
http://192.168.1.210/ellisits/WebSandbox09.nsf/AppCands?OpenView
```

A design might also attempt to control who creates documents by hiding from ineligible users a button that composes a new document. But someone can still create a document by opening the form directly.

```
http://192.168.1.210/ellisits/WebSandbox09.nsf/Customer?Open
```

To provide better security, use view and form access lists. In the case of a view, specify who can use the view on the **Security** tab of **View Properties**. Uncheck the property **All readers and above,** and then check the roles or groups allowed access to the view.

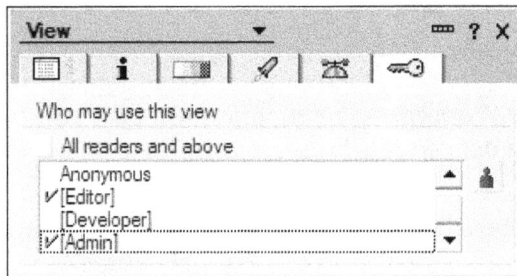

In the case of a form, specify who can use the form to create new documents on the **Security** tab of **Form Properties**.

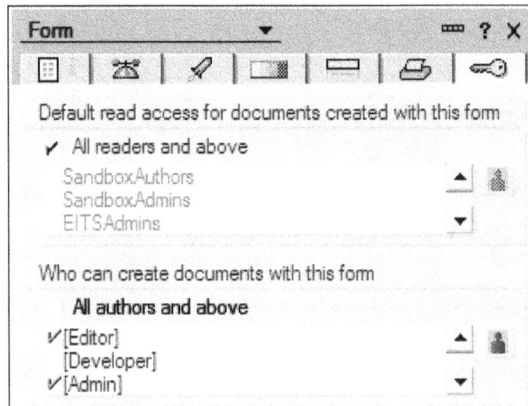

Even more important is controlling Edit mode access to existing documents. You may come across a design that hides an **Edit** button from anyone who is not allowed to edit an existing document. This seems like a reasonable strategy, but the "unscrupulous" user still may be able to open the document in the Edit mode.

When a document opens in the Read mode, its full URL may appear in the browser address bar. In this example, the UNIDs of the view and the document are clearly displayed.

```
http://192.168.1.210/ellisits/WebSandbox09.nsf/500e5c3691e04217852577
df0006029d/4d998ff18f40d57085257796005132a3?OpenDocument
```

If the view and document UNIDs do not display in the address bar, they generally can be copied from the page source and then appended to the application's URL. In either case, by changing the right-most component from ?OpenDocument to ?EditDocument, the document opens in Edit mode.

```
http://192.168.1.210/ellisits/WebSandbox09.nsf/500e5c3691e04217852577
df0006029d/4d998ff18f40d57085257796005132a3?EditDocument
```

The best way to control access to existing documents is to use Readers and Authors fields, a topic touched upon later in the chapter.

Understand application backup and restore procedures

Occasionally an application becomes corrupted. If this happens, the Domino administrator can run Domino utilities like Fixup and Updall, which may correct the problem. However, there are occasions when a database is not repairable and must be restored from a backup copy — for example, a user may have inadvertently deleted some documents.

The main point here is that you, as the developer and as a support agent for the application, should be aware of how and when the database is backed up, who can do a restore, how a restore is requested, and how long the restore is likely to take. Most likely the Domino administrator will know the procedures to follow, but you as the developer should understand them as well. If you do not do the restore yourself, you will likely have to explain the process to your users and reassure them.

Obviously, if the application is not being backed up, there is a significant risk to the data stored in the database. Take steps to correct this oversight.

It is also a good idea to practice the restoration process occasionally, if day-to-day events or business continuity drills do not provide you with that opportunity.

Add security to forms and documents

Forms provide the visible structure for displaying and entering data stored in documents. Topics in this section highlight a few security issues related to working with forms and documents on the Web.

Understand the "Generate HTML for all fields" attribute

As discussed in Chapter 3, it is generally the case that JavaScript code running in the browser should be able to access any field on a form, those that display as well as those that are hidden. Check the **Generate HTML for all fields** attribute on the **Defaults** tab of **Form Properties** to instruct Domino to send all form fields to the browser.

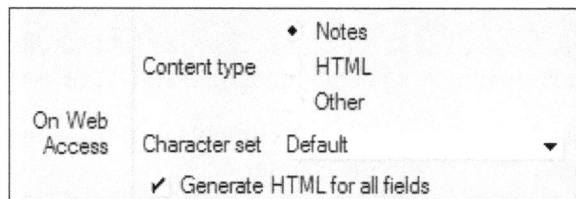

```
                              • Notes
          Content type       HTML
                             Other
On Web
 Access  Character set  Default                    ▼

          ✓ Generate HTML for all fields
```

Be mindful, however, that a minimally savvy user can see hidden fields by viewing the page source. With only a little effort, values of both hidden and displayed fields can be viewed. In this example, the document is open in Read mode:

```
<input name="HideFields" type="hidden" value="Y">
<input name="Return" type="hidden"
value="[/EllisIts/Sandbox9.nsf/PostEdit?OpenPage]">
<input name="HasBeenSaved" type="hidden" value="Y">
<input name="ViewTitle" type="hidden" value="Customers">
<input name="ClientType" type="hidden" value="Microsoft">
<input name="EditMode" type="hidden" value="Read">
<input name="SaveOptions" type="hidden" value="1">
<input name="Server_Name" type="hidden" value="192.168.1.210">
<input name="WhoCanEdit" type="hidden" value="[Admin]">
<input name="Gender" type="hidden" value="Male">
<input name="SelectedMeals" type="hidden" value="Breakfast, Lunch">
<input name="Actionee" type="hidden" value="Jason Quinn/users/
EllisITS">
<input name="Subject" type="hidden" value="An Action Item has been
assigned to you.">
<input name="CustLast" type="hidden" value="ApeMan">
<input name="CustFirst" type="hidden" value="Tarzan">
```

```
<input name="CustAge" type="hidden" value="52">
<input name="CustCity" type="hidden" value="JungleTown">
<input name="CustStatus" type="hidden" value="Active">
<input name="CustStatusDisplay" type="hidden" value="Active">
<input name="CustEmployer" type="hidden" value="State of Texas">
<input name="Status" type="hidden" value="">
<input name="CustIncome" type="hidden" value="50,000"></form>
```

Clearly, hiding fields provides no real confidentiality.

Prevent users from reading existing documents

If a user has at least Read access to an application, the assumption may be that he can read all documents within it. But if application requirements dictate that certain users, groups, or roles should *not* be allowed to view selected documents, then those documents can be protected by including one or more Readers field on them. Readers fields govern who is allowed to view documents.

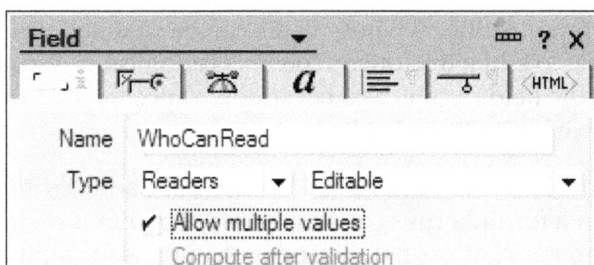

A Readers field is defined as a (usually hidden), multi-valued Editable or Computed field of type "Readers" whose value can be static or changed programmatically. If a user should be able to read a document, then his canonical name, his group, or a role assigned to him is added to the list of values in the field. A backdoor role should be included in the list, or in a different Readers field altogether, to assure that someone can always read the document. In this example, the field WhoCanRead is defined with its default value computed as a list of roles.

```
"[Admin]" : "[Editor]"
```

Anyone assigned either the **[Admin]** role or the **[Editor]** role can read documents created with this form. Anyone whose name is programmatically added to the field can also read the document.

```
@SetField("WhoCanRead";"[Admin]":"[Editor]":
@Name([Canonicalize];"Jason Quinn/users/EllisITS"))
```

If a document contains no Readers fields, or if all Readers fields are blank, then anyone with Reader access or higher to the application can view the document.

> It is important to add the default server group "LocalDomainServers" or another server group to a Readers field especially if documents replicate between servers. Servers, like regular users, are unable to read documents protected by Readers fields unless they are specifically allowed to do so.

Prevent users from editing existing documents

As mentioned previously, a savvy user can toggle a document from Read mode into Edit mode simply by changing the right-most component in the URL from ?OpenDocument to ?EditDocument. A standard way to prevent users from editing existing documents is to use an Authors field on the document in combination with assigning users the Author access level in the application's ACL.

An Authors field is defined as a (usually hidden), multi-valued Editable or Computed field of type "Authors" whose value can be changed programmatically. If a user should be able to edit a document, then his canonical user name is added to the list of values in the field. Again, as a backdoor, a specific role can also be included in the list or in a separate Authors field.

In this example, the Authors field is named WhoCanEdit and **[Editor]** is set as its default value. When a formula runs (perhaps when the item is assigned to user Jason Quinn for handling), the Authors field is updated, and Jason can then toggle the document into Edit mode.

```
@SetField("WhoCanEdit";"[Editor]":
@Name([Canonicalize];"Jason Quinn/users/EllisITS"))
```

At some later point in the workflow, perhaps after Jason marks the document as complete, his name is removed from the Authors field.

```
@SetField("WhoCanEdit";"[Editor]")
```

Jason can no longer toggle the document into Edit mode. If he attempts to do so, a login prompt displays indicating that he should log in with more privileged credentials.

Readers and Authors fields can also be updated by LotusScript agents. LotusScript treats these fields as if they were arrays.

Prevent users from editing selected fields using a Controlled Access Section

In classic applications, enabling a user to edit some fields on a form while preventing him from editing other fields is cumbersome. Two strategies can be used.

The first strategy involves using one or more Controlled Access Sections. Fields with the same read-only or edit characteristics are placed within a Controlled Access Section. A Computed access formula for the section defines who may edit fields in the section.

To implement this strategy, define a hidden, multi-valued Editable or Computed Text field on the form. In this example, the field is named `SectionEditors`, and its default value is set to **[Editor]**. As in the previous discussion of Authors fields, the value of the `SectionEditors` field can be changed programmatically in response to changes in the state of the document. To enable Jason Quinn to edit fields in the Controlled Access Section, his name is added to the `SectionEditors` field.

```
@SetField("SectionEditors";"[Editor]":
@Name([Canonicalize];"Jason Quinn/users/EllisITS"))
```

When he is no longer allowed to edit the fields in the Controlled Access Section, his name is removed from the `SectionEditors` field.

```
@SetField("SectionEditors";"[Editor]")
```

What makes this work is the section's Access Formula, which is coded in the **Formula** tab of **Section Properties**. This formula must resolve to a list of the roles, groups, or user names allowed to edit fields in the section.

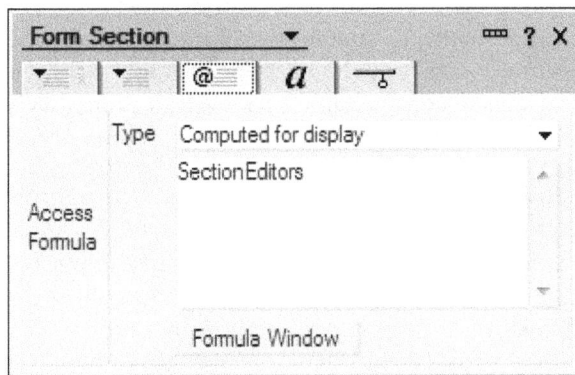

In this example, since the `SectionEditors` field already contains a list, a role and optionally a user name, the required Access Formula consists only of the name of the field.

Prevent users from editing selected fields using hide-when formulas

A second technique, used to enable a user to edit some but not all fields on a form, consists of creating pairs of fields. The primary field is an Editable field that displays if the user is allowed to edit it. The companion field is a Computed for display field that takes its value from the primary field and displays if the user is not allowed to edit the primary field.

The primary field never displays in Read mode, while the companion field always displays in Read mode. Hide-when formulas govern which field displays in Edit mode. Such formulas can be quite complex depending upon the security rules defined for the fields.

The primary advantage of using paired fields in this manner is that restricted fields need not be co-located as they must be when using a Controlled Access Section as discussed in the previous topic. The primary disadvantage to this technique lies in the potential complexity and number of hide-when formulas that have to be written.

Do not use field encryption

As mentioned before in this chapter, field encryption typically should not be used in web applications, since encryption keys are stored in Notes ID files and web users do not have access to those keys. See the previous topic on using SSL if encryption is required.

Track document changes

For audit purposes, it may be important to record events that occur in the handling of specific documents. For example, management may want to know when documents were submitted, who approved them, and when they were completed. Applications sometimes use a combination of a document history field and various hidden date fields that record when certain workflow events occur.

Messages appended to a history field on each document can provide a clear understanding of when certain workflow events occurred. When a document is created, a message initializes the field. At each step in the workflow, another message is appended to the field. Messages should be time-and-date stamped and should include the name of the person performing the function. Typically a history field displays in Read mode and is hidden in Edit mode to preclude tampering.

There is no real magic about a document history field. Here is an @formula attached to a button that (among other things) appends a message to a document's `History` field.

```
@SetField("History"; History + @NewLine + @NewLine +
@Text( @Now ) + " : " + @Name([CN];@UserName) +
" assigned this document to " + @Name([CN];Actionee) + "."
```

Although a simple history field like this contains an easy-to-read summary of events, the date-and-time stamps are fairly useless for performing any calculations (for example, how long a task lingered between steps in the workflow). To provide this kind of data for analysis, create some hidden date fields that are updated whenever workflow events occur. A simple formula stores the date:

```
@SetField("DateAssigned"; @Now);
```

The time difference between the date fields provides the necessary information about the workflow.

Make a form available to anonymous users

If your application requires anonymous users to complete and submit a form, but otherwise to have no access to the application, use this strategy.

Design a form with whatever features are appropriate. At minimum, the form should have these elements.:

- A Computed when Composed field named `$PublicAccess` whose value is set to a text `"1"`

- A button to save the document (either with an @formula or by invoking an agent)

- A navigational redirection (either with a `$$Return` field or through the saving agent)

In addition, enable the attribute **Available to Public Access users** on the **Security** tab of **Form Properties**.

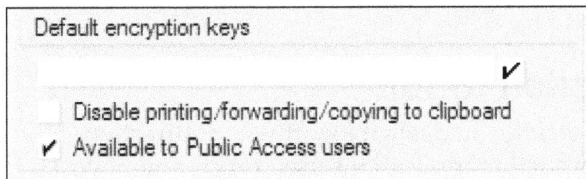

In the application's ACL, enable Anonymous to read and write public documents.

Provide a link from some other location (for example, a web page) that composes the public access form.

```
http://192.168.1.210/ellisits/WebSandbox09.nsf/PublicDoc?Open
```

In general, it may be best to limit the functionality of an application with anonymous requirements to those features required to collect the data. For additional processing, consider moving the anonymously submitted documents to a more full-featured application to which anonymous users have no access.

Control navigation options

Limiting the views and other features made available to users is generally a matter of using hide-when formulas to control what displays on the screen. If links to views do not display, then most users will not spend the effort trying to figure out how to take a look at things they are not supposed to see. Hiding features is also called obfuscation. Keep in mind that hiding hotspots and other features is not true security.

Code an explicit logoff

An application can include an explicit logoff with redirection. This may be particularly appropriate for applications used on common workstations or in public settings.

An @formula, attached to a hotspot, logs out from the application, and then presents the default design element, perhaps the application's Welcome page.

```
"/" + @WebDbName + "?Logout&RedirectTo=/" + @WebDbName
```

Manage agent security

Agents can make changes to documents, and therefore it is important to control who can invoke them and what they are allowed to do. See Chapter 8 for a discussion of agent run-time context and privileges.

Performance

From a user's perspective, a web application performs well if it does what it is supposed to do quickly and in a manner that requires a minimum of effort on his part.

Responsiveness has to do with how quickly results appear after a button or hotspot is clicked. Good design contributes to how easy it is to use and maintain the application. Responsiveness and good design both contribute to good performance.

The responsiveness of an application running over the web can be erratic and sometimes downright poor due to conditions on the network or on the host server. Packets of information travel back and forth between the server and the browser, and packets related to your application compete for time with all other applications currently using the common digital pathways. If network traffic is high or network bandwidth is low, users may perceive your application as responding slowly, even though it is working as designed and the host server has ample capacity. If the host server is bogged down with too many applications running simultaneously, that too can negatively impact the responsiveness of your application. You have little influence over network and server constraints. On the other hand, if network traffic is low and the server has ample capacity and your application still responds sluggishly, then you have work to do.

The design of an application can be intuitive and easy to use or not. Designs requiring unnecessary effort negatively impact user productivity, and that is not a good thing. You as the developer do have considerable control over design issues.

Topics in this section highlight a few ways in which applications can be made more efficient both from a processing standpoint and from a usability point of view. Some of these suggestions pertain to the application, whether or not it is accessed from the web. Other suggestions are more web-specific. In the interest of space, only a few suggestions are included here.

General guidelines

Domino provides many, many design features and options, each useful in certain circumstances. Some features consume processor and storage resources if included or left active, so if a feature is not required for an application, then it should be turned off or eliminated. Address the heavy hitters as a matter of course, but don't forget about other opportunities to squeeze performance out of a system.

In many situations, spending a lot of time trying to fine-tune your application's responsiveness may not be worth the effort. If network bandwidth is satisfactory and the server has adequate capacity, spending hours and hours trying to save a small fraction of second in response time is not worth it. On the other hand, if your application is a high-volume or mission-critical utility, or if the infrastructure is constrained, you may want to go well beyond the recommendations in this chapter.

This author's particular bias is toward applications that are as lean as they can be, and at the same time easy to use and easy to maintain. It's all a matter of balance.

Listen to your users

Some users put up with poor performance and functionality for any number of reasons. Others complain about anything and everything at the drop of a hat. One of your jobs as a developer is to listen to what your users say about the application and to correct the flaws that they report.

When a user calls to complain about a web application's performance, a number of questions should come to mind:

- Is network access to non-Domino resources also sluggish?
- Are other applications on the same server delivering poor response time?
- Are many people affected or only this one user?
- Is this an ongoing problem or a one-time occurrence?
- Is the application responding when accessed with the Notes client?
- Is the entire application slow or just particular features?
- Is the user complaining about how the application is put together rather than about how it responds?

Asking these kinds of questions can help to narrow down the kind and scope of a performance problem.

If it does indeed appear that there is an issue with the application, see for yourself. Log into the application as a user and try to reproduce what your customer was doing. Often you will notice symptoms he does not see. If at all possible, visit with the user and watch him while he works. Ask questions and take notes. At all times listen attentively to what he says.

Design for ease of use

Chapter 2 discussed a number of issues related to application usability. Think about how users interact with your application. If possible, sit with them and discuss which features are easier and which are more difficult to use. A classic user complaint is that programmers don't spend enough time asking them what works best.

Ask questions such as these:

- Does the application launch to the most useful page or view? Is it slow to initialize?

- How readable are the onscreen fonts? Too small or too large? Good colors?

- Are headings, labels, and messages clear and understandable?

- Are hotspots and buttons located, labeled, and styled consistently throughout the application?

- Does the typical user scroll up or down, or left or right, to view important design elements?

- Are there too few or too many rows displayed in the views?

- Are form fields organized in a sensible manner? Lined up? Similar information co-located?

- Are required fields clearly marked?

- Is there a good balance of white space and design elements?

- Are there unnecessary confirmation messages?

- Is there sufficient onscreen guidance?

Simple improvements, such as clearly identifying required fields or eliminating unnecessary confirmation dialogs, will improve user productivity and satisfaction.

Archive or delete old documents

Work with the application owner to understand the potential for archiving documents. Applications with large numbers of documents require more disk storage and processing time. Functions that take longer with more documents include these:

- Opening views
- Searching for documents
- Running agents to process all documents in the application
- Copying, backing up, and restoring the application

If unnecessary documents can be deleted or moved to an archive, then the primary application should perform better. And don't forget to look at a related agent log.

Remove obsolete code and design elements

There may be little noticeable performance impact in keeping previous versions of design elements in the template or in retaining features in the design that are not needed or used. But unnecessary design elements do make a template more cumbersome to work with and they contribute to application clutter. Version the templates as a whole so that old design elements remain available to you, but then remove unnecessary elements from the production design. At the very least, this should make you more productive.

Clean up and optimize code

Especially when writing agents, developers focus on perfecting functionality first and foremost. Making an agent run faster is usually not a priority. Developers know that things like re-initializing a constant within a loop are not good, but in the interest of completing the agent quickly, such minor flaws are left uncorrected.

It is unlikely that practicing programmers will have the time or skills required to evaluate specific coding practices in depth, but on the Web you can find results of studies where knowledgeable people have done just that. Spend some time reviewing articles with specific coding and other performance-related recommendations. For example, you can find results such as these, which pertain to LotusScript:

- Using nested If statements can be 40 percent faster than using a single complex If statement.
- For/Next loops can run 60 percent faster than Do loops.

- The performance of nested loops can be improved by several hundred percent by making the outer loop the one with the smaller bounds.

Other performance assertions relate to non-coding practices:

- Pages load up to 10 times slower when using SSL.
- WebQueryOpen agents slow the opening of forms.
- Retrieving data from a view is 10 percent faster than retrieving it from a document.

It is reasonable to consider whether it is worth the effort to recode an agent or to implement another performance recommendation when the application is running well as-is. Certainly this is a judgment call; you may be able to estimate how much time is required to make changes, but quantifying improvements in efficiency and responsiveness may be difficult. In general, optimized code will deliver better performance and consume fewer server and network resources. As time permits, clean up the code.

Use tools to assess response time

If you are investigating a reported response time problem, you should take a look at the Domino Log on the server. The log provides some information about application processing and failures. If you can narrow down the timeframe of a reported problem, the Log may provide additional clues and insight, especially about what else was going on at the same time.

If web traffic logging is enabled on your server, you may find some useful information in those logs as well. To see if such logging is available, check the server document in the Domino Directory. Look for this section on the **Internet Protocols** tab / **HTTP** tab.

Enable Logging To:	
Log files:	Disabled
Domlog.nsf:	Enabled

In this example, web traffic is being logged in the `Domlog.nsf` database, a system file on the server. The number of records in such a database can be very large, so what is recorded may be limited by the Domino administrator. Errors and request processing times are recorded, and this information provides some insight regarding how well the server and application agents are working.

You may have or be able to acquire performance monitoring tools for your environment. Ask other developers or the Domino administrator about this. If such tools are not installed locally, do some web research to see what is currently available that may be of service to you.

Here is an example of output from a Firefox add-on called Tamper Data (or tamperdata) that provides some insight about how long it takes for HTTP requests to return pages to the browser. In contrast to the information in `Domlog.nsf`, this information may be more representative of how the end-user sees response time.

Time	Duration	Total Duration	Size	Method	Status	URL
12:40:10.791	49 ms	1293 ms	-1	GET	304	http://192.168.1.210/ellisits/sandbox9.nsf
12:40:12.042	17 ms	17 ms	10362	GET	200	http://192.168.1.210/ellisits/sandbox9.nsf/allcustomers?OpenView
12:40:12.061	2 ms	2 ms	-1	GET	304	http://192.168.1.210/ellisits/sandbox9.nsf/sandbox1.css
12:40:12.087	0 ms	0 ms	unknown	GET	pending	http://192.168.1.210/favicon.ico

(Tamper Data - Ongoing requests. Start Tamper Stop Tamper Clear. Filter)

Improve forms

Over time, as a form passes through the hands of several developers, a certain amount of debris collects in it. Everything in the form is processed in one way or another, and some elements may be sent to the browser unnecessarily. For example, if the JS Header contains a thousand lines of JavaScript, then all that code is transmitted to the browser every time a document using that form is opened. A better design would move the JavaScript to a library from which the code would be retrieved only when needed and then cached for future use.

In general, eliminate everything from a form that does not need to be on that form.

Limit the use of images

Forms and pages that include images take longer to load than comparable forms and pages that do not include images, and larger images take longer to load than smaller images. Eliminating images, or reducing their size, can improve application responsiveness. See Chapter 2 for additional comments.

Use Ajax calls to retrieve data

One of the more dramatic improvements that can be made to forms is to use Ajax calls to retrieve options into checkbox, radio button, or keyword list fields. Adding this functionality to classic applications takes some effort, but it is well-worth the investment of time. Chapter 6 reviewed this technique in detail.

Use simpler hide-when formulas

Complex hide-when formulas take more time to process, so limit the complexity as well as the number of such formulas. It may be appropriate to compute a hide-when value in a hidden field and then refer to that field in the hide-when formulas themselves. Maintenance of such formulas is simpler since a change need be made in only one place.

Validate fields with JavaScript

If a form validates fields in a WebQuerySave agent, consider moving that validation into JavaScript running in the browser. Validation then avoids a server round trip and will seem instantaneous to users. See Chapter 6 for a fuller discussion of this topic.

Improve views

Views present data to users in structured, predefined ways. In most Domino applications views are indispensible since they are the primary means by which documents are located and opened. Here are some general suggestions about views that can influence application responsiveness and ease of use.

Remove unused or redundant views from the design

Views are re-indexed whenever an included document is saved or changed. Re-indexing takes time and reduces the overall performance of an application. Unused or redundant views provide no value, but they do continue to consume resources. If there is a chance you might want to re-use a view or reference it at a later date, go ahead and save it in an archived template, but remove it from the production template.

Some views may no longer be required, or their usefulness (or lack thereof) becomes apparent only after the application is in production for a while. Check with the application owner to see if some views may be eliminated.

If two views are similar, evaluate whether they might be combined into a single view without adding too many additional columns.

Limit the data displayed in views

The more columns of data included in a view, the longer it takes the server to process it, the longer it takes the network to transmit it, and the longer it takes the browser to render the result to the screen. Performance can be improved by limiting the data included in views.

Consider these options:

- Include columns only for required information; avoid throwing in extra columns that "might be of interest". Remove columns that add no value for users.
- Limit the amount of data included in a column; for example, display only the first 25 characters of a title or subject field.
- Use the View Selection Formula to further limit the number of documents included in the view.

Remove unnecessary view column sorting

View columns can be enabled for dynamic sorting, ascending or descending or both. Such dynamic sorting is an alternative to presenting information in different orders in separate views.

Enabling columns for sorting increases the time required to re-index a view, so keep the number of sort-able columns to a minimum. Check with your users to see which sorts are really needed and which were just thrown in for good measure.

Minimize the use of view column formulas

The contents of a column can be computed from values on the associated documents. Column formulas take time to run, and each time a view is re-indexed, those formulas run again.

Minimize the use of column formulas. Instead, add hidden Computed fields to forms, and compute any derived values that are needed. When documents are saved, those fields are computed once. Display values from the Computed fields in views.

This approach is especially useful if requirements can be anticipated before documents are created. Adding or modifying such a view to an existing application presents an obvious problem. Older documents do not include the new Computed fields. All existing documents may have to be updated for satisfactory results.

Avoid time-based view column formulas

Column formulas can include references to the current time and date. Time-based column formulas can cause a view to be re-indexed every time it is accessed, whether or not documents are changed. For frequently accessed views, this can result in a serious performance degradation.

Avoid using @formula functions such as @Now.

Create views as an alternative to common searches

If users always search for documents, rather than using views to locate them, the issue may be that the right views are not available. Searches are time-consuming and therefore impact user productivity. Discuss this issue with your users and provide more relevant views.

Modify database properties

A number of database attributes can affect performance in general. Many of these options are enabled on the **Advanced** tab of **Database Properties**. Here is an example of this tab. Note that more current versions of Domino offer additional options.

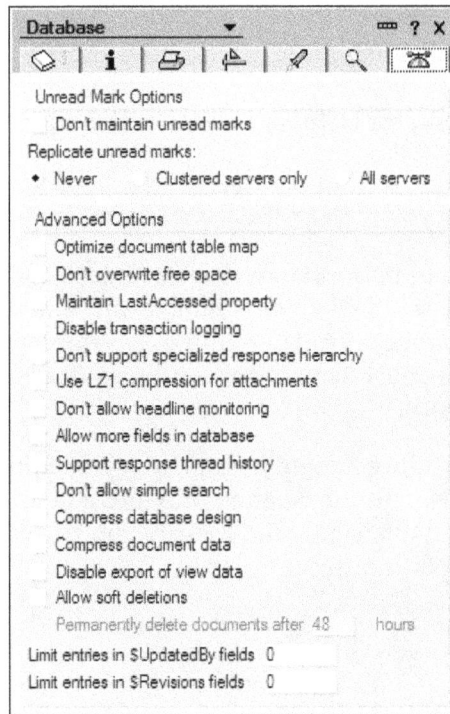

If performance is a significant concern for your application and you have already addressed issues discussed earlier in this chapter, investigate these advanced application options in Designer Help to see which ones might be relevant or helpful.

Investigate Domino server options

Keep in mind that the Domino server also can be tuned to some degree to improve application performance. Work with your Domino administrator to review and possibly alter server configuration settings. Look first at settings that specifically address caching and agents on the **HTTP** and **Domino Web Engine** tabs located on the **Internet Protocols** tab.

Consult Domino Administrator Help for assistance in understanding the options.

Summary

Addressing the security and performance aspects of designs is perhaps not as interesting as perfecting a set of views or styling forms with CSS or writing clever agents. But these issues can be critical to fulfilling development requirements and delivering a secure product that enhances user productivity. These are also challenging issues to be sure.

Topics in this chapter introduced a number of key considerations applicable to most Domino applications. This information provides a good foundation for understanding and actively managing the security and performance requirements of web-enabled Domino applications.

10
Testing and Debugging

Testing applications and debugging them go hand in hand. Of course, developers test during development, or they would not know if their codes work. But when the development phase of a project is winding down, a more formal quality assurance (QA) phase should be winding up. How thoroughly an application should be tested depends in part upon how many features are changed or added. Obviously, more extensive change requires more extensive testing.

If you are a less experienced Domino developer, you may be assigned the task of testing applications written by other programmers. If so, you are one of the most important people on the project; it is your job to assure that the application is as issue-free as possible. The more bugs you find during testing, the fewer bugs your customers will find after the application goes into production. Ask if your organization provides any guidance on application testing. Study such guidance thoroughly. Strive to develop good testing and documentation skills.

Things can go wrong with a Domino web application during development as well as after the application migrates to production. Troubleshooting problems gets easier the more problems you solve, the more knowledgeable you are about the technology, and the more debugging tricks you have up your sleeve. Several troubleshooting suggestions were made in previous chapters. Additional options that may be of use are offered here. Many of these strategies are appropriate to all Notes development, and others pertain particularly to web applications.

In this chapter, we cover a number of topics including the following:

- Test environments
- Engaging other people for testing
- Test plans
- Testing strategies
- Tracking defects

- Debugging strategies
- Diagnostic views and repair agents
- Documenting problems and getting back to users

Testing

Application testing should ferret out code failures, features that do not work correctly, navigational dead ends, usability issues, problems with data, security holes, performance problems, and any issues concerning assumptions made earlier in the project. Some organizations are more rigorous than others when it comes to testing practices and documentation, and naturally you will work within such guidelines, if they exist. In situations where you are left to your own devices, do as much testing as is possible within the time and resource constraints of the project.

As a developer, you work on a series of projects over time, and every project requires testing. Many aspects of QA are the same for every project. So setting up a rich testing environment and a consistent testing protocol that can be used repeatedly will save time over the long haul and will contribute to more uniform testing results.

Topics in this section cover some general strategies which you should consider. Follow up these discussions by browsing some of the numerous resources on the Web.

Test with different browsers

Applications can behave differently in different web browsers, and Domino web applications are not immune to browser idiosyncrasies. So start by identifying which browsers your users use to access your web-enabled applications. This may be more or less difficult to determine. In the simplest case, your application is accessed only through an intranet, and organizational standards dictate the specific browser installed on every desktop. If this is your situation, then focus on which versions of that browser are currently installed, and find out when the next version will be deployed.

On the other hand, if there are no standards or if your applications are used by the public via the Internet, then your testing environment can be considerably more complex. Make a list of the most likely browsers and browser versions. Check the IBM Lotus website for a list of browsers supported for the version(s) of Domino running in your installation.

For each supported and likely browser, set up a test bed of some sort, either on a discrete desktop or in a virtual machine. It is reasonable for a single desktop (or desktop image) to host one version of Internet Explorer, one version of Firefox, and perhaps a version of Chrome, Opera, or Safari. Another desktop can host a second set of versions, and so on. If your community includes Macintosh or Linux desktops, then test machines should be set up to mimic those environments as well. If your applications are accessed by mobile devices, secure appropriate hardware.

Obviously, the more testing platforms there are, the more time-consuming will be the actual testing. But don't short change this side of the development cycle. An application feature may work perfectly well in all versions of IE but fail inexplicably in some version of Firefox, or vice versa.

Test with different user privileges

It is important to use multiple Notes accounts for testing. As an application grows more complex, it likely relies on ACL roles to grant certain privileges to some users and not to others. Or perhaps the application implements a workflow where one person creates documents and another approves them. Using a single Notes account to "play both roles" will not assure that all your hide-when formulas and other security measures work the way they are supposed to.

A good strategy is to use one test account for each unique role defined in the application's ACL, plus one for the developer. That way, the developer can maintain Manager privileges over the ACL, while assigning lesser privileges to other test accounts.

Of course, some organizations are restrictive about how many accounts employees are allowed to have or to share, and you may work for an organization that is pretty tight about this sort of thing. Take this book to your manager and security people, and tell them that you absolutely cannot do your job to the best of your ability, if you do not have two or more testing accounts with which to work.

Craft the staging environment to resemble the production environment

The staging and production environments should resemble each other closely. Applications should reside in the same file path, for example.

If you hold a test account, then that account and your users' accounts should have the same privileges in staging as they do in production. If you do not have a test account, your developer account should have no more privileges in staging than do your users. You must be able to see and interact with the application exactly as they do. Elevated privileges can hide the very anomalies you seek to discover.

Most likely, you will want to create some Domino test groups for your application that include only users who agree to participate in testing. Using production groups increases the possibility that users not involved with testing will receive erroneous notifications from application agents.

Self-contained applications are easier to test than applications that access external data, but if your application requires co-requisite applications, then those co-requisite applications should reside in staging as well, so that your application refers to the staging versions and not the production versions. If your application accesses an external relational database, then a staging version of that database should exist such that your application does not access or update the production database. You may need help in setting up such external resources.

Engage other people for testing

When you develop code, you test it from your perspective and with your knowledge of how it works internally. Your white box testing can give you insights about what may fail under what conditions, and you can test for those conditions. At the same time, you tend to interact with an application consistently because you know how it is supposed to work — you may not interact with it the way other people would.

Especially with complex applications, where it is difficult or impossible for one person to test exhaustively every option or every logical path, it is important to engage other people to assist. Ideally, people who will use the application in production will agree to give some time to the testing effort.

If a quality assurance testing department exists within your organization, ask for their services at the appropriate time. Alternatively, it may be possible to engage an outside QA tester or testing service, especially if the project has high visibility or is of critical importance.

These black box testers, who know nothing about how the application works from a programming point of view, can provide insights about features, usability, and style that can help you polish the application. Implementing testers' suggestions will influence in a positive way user acceptance of and satisfaction with the product.

Test every feature if possible

Testing should focus primarily on new and changed features. These are the parts of the application that are most likely to fail—after all, the rest of the application may have been working in production for some time. But you should always perform **regression testing** to assure that errors or other unintentional changes have not been introduced elsewhere into the application. Time constraints may limit the scope and depth of regression testing, but review at least the basic functionality of all the major parts. Pursue any intuitions or hunches which occur to you as well.

Pay special attention to the security requirements of an application. Work with your testers to create scenarios or test cases so that security controls are exercised. If Readers and Authors fields are used, make sure that eligible users can access appropriate documents and that ineligible users cannot. Assure that features which require elevated privileges can be used by testers with elevated privileges and not by others. Don't assume that security works—demonstrate it.

It is very helpful to provide testers with a clear understanding of how an application behaves, before and after it is changed. If a good user manual or help system is available, descriptions and images in those references can provide a baseline of expectations. In addition, it can be very helpful to enable side-by-side comparisons of the current production design and the updated design. Provide this by creating two instances of the application on the staging server, one with the old design and one with the new. If at all possible, keep the same documents in both instances.

Ideally, every feature and every function is thoroughly tested with every client option. Realistically, that's not likely to happen with most Domino applications due to the time it would take. If in-depth testing is a project requirement, however, take extra care to develop a detailed test plan, estimate the time it will take to run through the test plan once, and then multiply that time by the number of clients (Notes and browsers) for which testing is required. Share this information with the project sponsor and with your manager so that they understand the resources and time involved.

Test responsiveness

As discussed in the previous chapter, web application responsiveness can be heavily impacted by constraints in the network or on the server. An ideal testing environment consists of network and server components that are identical to those used in production. It also enables introducing and eliminating competing workloads so that applications can be assessed under various server and network load conditions. Such an environment provides a better understanding of how applications should respond when they move to production.

Practically speaking, there are limits to how well an application's performance can be tested. The following two factors are likely to hide issues related to load:

- Fewer realistic documents in the test database
- Fewer simultaneous users

Your organization may allow you to copy the entire production database to the staging server. If so, this is an excellent strategy for resolving the issue of too few realistic documents. However, there may be security or privacy concerns which prevent you from doing this. As an alternative, consider writing an agent to automatically create a large number of documents in your test instance.

Stressing the application with a sufficient number of simultaneous users may also be problematic, since it is unlikely that you will be able to enlist enough testers to work on this project at the same time. After all, they have their own jobs to do.

If load testing is important, you might consider looking into automated testing tools. Commercial and open source options exist that may work in your environment. Do your homework here and perhaps seek expert advice from performance analysts familiar with Domino. Start with an open source option, such as Apache JMeter, to get your feet wet. Implementing automated testing tools takes time and possibly money, and you want to be sure that the results you get are worth it.

Create a written test plan

Written test plans guide testers in a more formal way. They identify what is to be tested and, by omission, what is not tested. Write up a test plan that specifically targets the original requirements as provided to you, but which also generally tests the application to assure that you have not unknowingly regressed any functions. If the application has been reworked extensively, then develop a more comprehensive plan.

Test plans can be lengthy and formal, or short and informal. In any case, they should be written down and saved for future reference. Begin building the test plan during the design and development phases.

For a more comprehensive test plan, start with an outline consisting of the application's major features. For example:

- Initial page or frameset
- Navigation
- Views
- Forms

- Reports
- Workflow
- Notifications
- Security
- Integrated help
- Dynamic configuration options

Build out the outline until you have a good list of all the elements that should be checked. Then for each element, write out specific objectives. Identify which roles can perform restricted operations. Write each objective as a task to be performed.

- Create and save a new Order document
- Edit an existing Order document
- Submit an Order document for processing
- Approve an Order ([Approver] role only)
- Archive an Order document ([Admin] role only)

If there are specific actions or issues to be checked, add more detail including expected results.

- Enter an invalid number in the `Quantity` field (error message should display)
- Select a weekend for the `DateRequired` field (error message should display)
- Submit an Order without entering quantity (error message should display)

You may also want to organize testing in phases, with each phase probing progressively deeper into the application. For example, during phase one, you might focus just on basics. Test to assure that:

- The application launches correctly
- Navigational links work
- Required features work (for example, views open, new documents are created)
- Element layouts and style are acceptable
- Spelling and punctuation are correct
- About and Using documents are complete

During phase two, testers assess key features in more detail. Assure that:

- Form fields validate
- Documents can be saved and edited
- Error messages are appropriate
- Search features work

During phase three, testers assess workflow, scheduled agents, and security. Assure that:

- Workflows are fully exercised with two or more actors
- Scheduled agents run and produce desired results
- Users with different roles can access only what they are privileged to access

Go over the test plan with the application owner and with your testers. Seek additional suggestions and incorporate any that will enhance the testing effort. Encourage testers to evaluate anything not included in the test script. Make assignments if appropriate and set some deadlines for getting back to you with results.

Keep in mind that the more tests run and observations made, the higher will be the owner's and your confidence that bugs have been found. The more you polish the application, the higher the user satisfaction. On the other hand, be mindful of how much time you have for testing and resolving any new issues, and pace yourself accordingly.

Track defects

It is very important to establish a method for capturing and tracking issues during testing. An **issues log** can be kept in a spreadsheet or project plan, in a Domino Document Library or Wiki, or in a special application designed to track bugs. Browse the Web for some options. Before you step gingerly into an external product, check the requirements. Many of these products, even the free ones, require the installation of a database, a web server, and one or more scripting languages.

Any and every problem or suggestion related to the project should be noted in the issues log. Assign an identifier to each item and capture summary information.

- Identifier
- Version tested
- Title or subject
- Status
- Date submitted

- Description and evidence / steps to reproduce
- Submitter's name
- Assignee name
- Action taken
- Date resolved
- Version resolved in
- Comments

The issues log becomes your to-do list as user testing continues. If changes are made, roll the fixed application design to staging for additional testing. Continue this process until you and the application owner are satisfied that all known issues are resolved.

Create detailed user documentation while testing

User-oriented documentation may be thin or non-existent for an application. A period of thorough testing offers an excellent opportunity to create a user guide. Good documentation requires real focus and attention to detail, the same effort required during testing. Inconsistencies and usability issues should pop out very quickly.

If possible, engage a tester who is also a good technical writer for this task. Have the application owner or a power user review the resulting documentation for clarifications. As the project winds down, provide the owner with a copy of the finished product, and store the master copy in the design template or in an approved document repository.

Require user sign-off

If you are new to an organization, you may find that previous developers did not require user acceptance testing for any number of reasons. If so, it's time for a change. The application owner or his delegate should accept responsibility for all aspects of the application and actively participate in the planning and testing of it. When the owner is satisfied that the application works as it should, require him to sign-off formally or via e-mail prior to migrating the design to production.

Monitor the application after Go Live

After the design rolls to production, monitor the application closely for a few days. There are always a few post-production tasks to complete.

- Monitor the Domino Log on the server hosting the application and look for messages associated with the application
- Monitor the application's agent log, if one exists
- Register your application in whatever organizational registries may be required
- Check with the application owner; don't assume he will contact you
- Complete all project-related documentation
- Create a list of suggested improvements that can be used as a starting point for the next release

Debugging

It is possible to write some code which runs perfectly the first time and does exactly what it is supposed to do. It happened to me once, and I was quite surprised. Without doubt, developers spend a good deal of time debugging and troubleshooting. This aspect of development can be extraordinarily frustrating, especially if you are under deadline or not very good at it. But successfully "shooting a bug" can also be quite satisfying.

Troubleshooting skill is partly technique, partly knowledge, and partly intuition born of experience. I suspect most developers would be hard-pressed to tell you how they do what they do. But you should get better at it the more often you do it.

General guidelines

Like a detective, troubleshooting a problem is first about gathering evidence or clues, and then it's about putting those clues together to point to the source of the problem. When presented with an issue, gather information from log messages, screen shots, output files—if you've been a developer for any length of time, you know basically what to do.

Reproduce the problem

A user can be a poor witness. Have him write down exactly what he was doing when the problem occurred. Ask for screenshots. Ask what made the problem happen, when it first appeared, if it happens to everyone or just to him. Ask questions until you have a clear picture of what it is that went wrong and how you can reproduce it.

Then reproduce the problem for yourself. For non-random problems, this should not be too difficult. If you cannot reproduce it, troubleshooting becomes a lot harder, and assuring that you fixed a problem is nearly impossible.

Follow the steps outlined by your user. If his report is incomplete, go to his location and ask him to show you the problem and the steps to reproduce it. Observe everything. Gather details about his operating system, browser settings, and his JVM. Most likely, you will see clues that your user does not see.

Use the production system to gather symptoms, but do not experiment with the production design. Reproduce the problem on your development system. Recreating the exact conditions of the failure in a separate database may require some work. If the problem exists with a limited number of documents, it may be possible to copy those documents into a development database. Also, you may need to copy a number of configuration or keyword documents. So much depends on the nature of an application's design that prescribing how to reproduce a problem without knowing the application is not possible.

Isolate the failure

If you are fortunate to have access to more sophisticated debugging tools, then use them. But if you are on your own, you can still find the root cause of most problems using simple and commonsense strategies.

Focus on isolating the problem to a specific component, sequence of actions, or set of circumstances. Alter the conditions of your interaction with the application to gather additional information. If you can identify the specific design element (for example, a form or agent), then you are half-way to the solution, and in many cases this will be readily apparent.

With the major design element identified, save a full copy of it and then start modifying that element in order to determine which parts of it are working and which parts are not. Exactly how you modify the design element depends upon what kind of an element it is and what you suspect might be wrong with it. For example, with a LotusScript agent, strategically place `MsgBox` functions into one or more subroutines, run the agent, and then check the Domino Log or an Agent Log configured for your application to see what comes out (see *Chapter 8, Agents,* for a discussion of agent logs). In a similar manner, insert `alert` functions into JavaScript code. Move the messages around until you isolate the small segment of code that fails.

For a form which refuses to open on the Web, the problem could be with any formula in any location. Look at your most recent modifications, but if that doesn't help, start stripping out pieces of the form until it does display.

Keep narrowing your focus until the specific problematic features or logic become obvious. A brute force, divide and conquer strategy is not very elegant, but it usually gets the job done.

Code a $$ReturnGeneralError form

As discussed in *Chapter 4, Navigation,* include a $$ReturnGeneralError form in your application. If this form exists, Domino displays it for many detected errors. You can code a single general-purpose form and then include it in each of your applications. See the previous chapter for more details.

Check the Domino Log

The Domino Log on the server is a general repository for messages from Domino tasks and application agents. It is also often a good source for clues about what is going wrong with your application. Open the Log on your development server and make a bookmark. When an unexpected result occurs during testing, immediately check the time you experienced the problem. Then open the Log, Miscellaneous Events. Select the bottom-most entry and double-click to open the latest document.

As mentioned previously, insert `Msgbox` functions at strategic locations in your LotusScript agents and libraries, run the agents and then check the logs. Make sure that all your agents include error traps with appropriate messages as discussed in *Chapter 8, Agents.*

Depending upon how busy your server is, messages generated by your error or debugging code may not be written to the Domino Log immediately. If the latest time stamp in the Log is not later than your event, close the log document for a minute or so and then try again.

Use the Web

With a specific error message or some precise keywords that describe the problem, search the Web for additional insights. Don't "go it alone" for long. Use the collective insight of fellow developers to help clarify what might be wrong. You may find a write-up that immediately provides a solution, or you may read about similar problems that spark some ideas of your own.

If you are actively engaged in an IBM Forum or another active developer's blog or website, you can post your problem and ask for suggestions. Do this only after diligently searching for an existing write-up. Post clearly and succinctly, with sample code if appropriate. But don't wait for someone else to solve your problem; help may never come.

Use Design Synopsis

Especially, if you are working with an unfamiliar problematic application for the first time, try using Design Synopsis to locate references to specific text. In most current versions of Designer, locate this tool in the left-hand **Design Pane**.

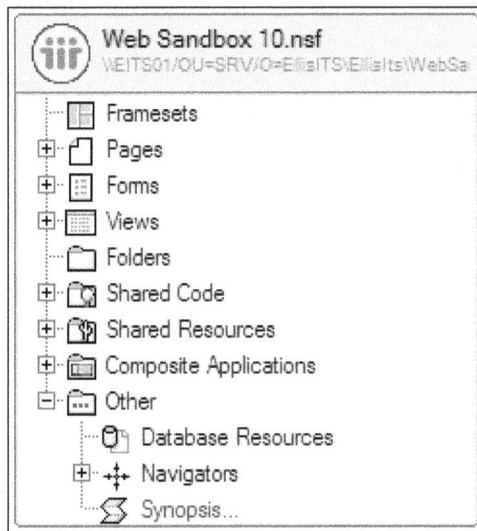

Open **Design Synopsis**, select design elements of interest, refine the output as you see fit, and click the **OK** button.

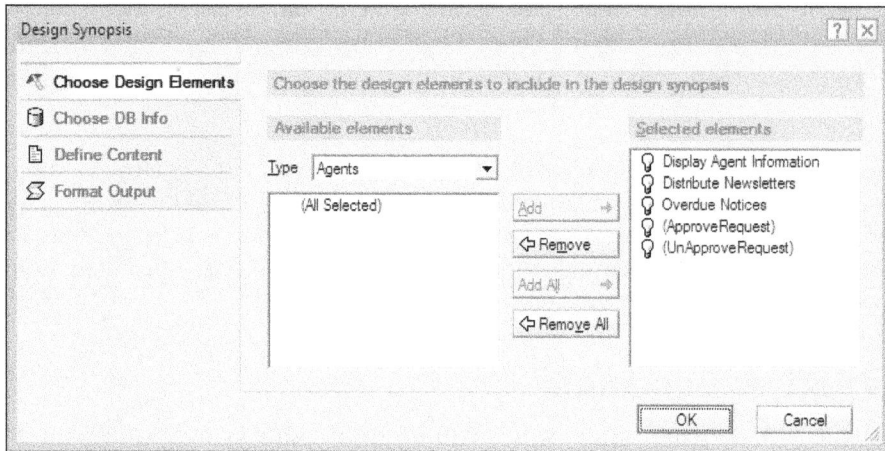

Results are written to a temporary document. Scroll through it or search for specific text. In larger applications, be prepared for a lengthy document.

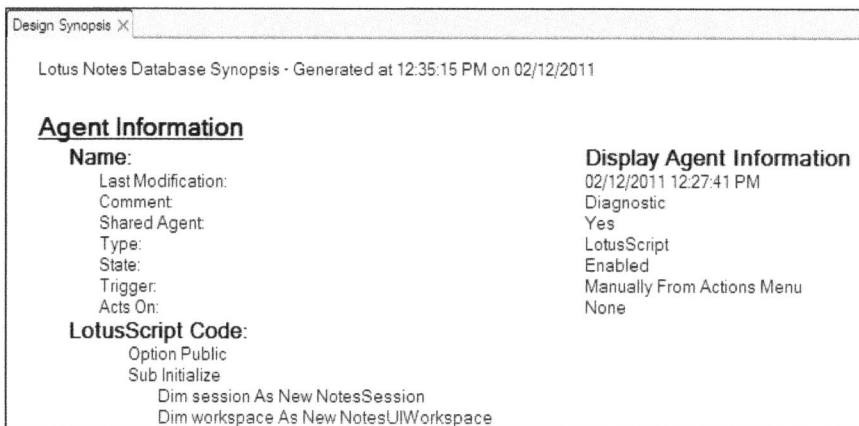

Troubleshoot forms

Faulty forms may just not open on the Web, resulting in less than helpful **Page Not Found** errors. These can be a bit tricky to troubleshoot. A common cause of this error is a faulty @formula.

Forms can contain many @formulas, any one of which, if incorrect, can prevent the form from displaying on the Web. Use REM statements to comment out potentially faulty @formulas until you find the one causing the problem.

```
@Command([ToolsRunMacro];"(ApproveRequest)");
REM { @URLOpen("/"+@WebDbName) };
```

Even if a form displays, @formula values may be incorrect and difficult to reason out. This is especially true with a complicated hide-when formula or a complex $$Return formula. To see how a formula evaluates, insert some computed text on the form whose value is the problematic formula.

If a button does not display, check the code in the Click and onClick events. If no code exists in either of these events, then the button will not display on the Web. Code the value of @True (@formula) in the Click event or true (JavaScript) in the onClick event.

If a button displays but does nothing when clicked, assure that you are using @formula functions compatible with the Web or that the library containing JavaScript functions is properly linked to the form in the form's JS Header.

Dynamically display hidden fields on the Web

If your form is enabled to **Generate HTML for all fields** on the **Defaults** tab of **Form Properties**, then you can view the page source to see the values of hidden fields. Here is somewhat more convenient way to check these values.

First, place hidden fields and labels in a table. Do not format the table, labels, or fields with Designer. Do *not* hide these fields or labels with hide-when formulas. Assign an ID to the table in **Table Properties**.

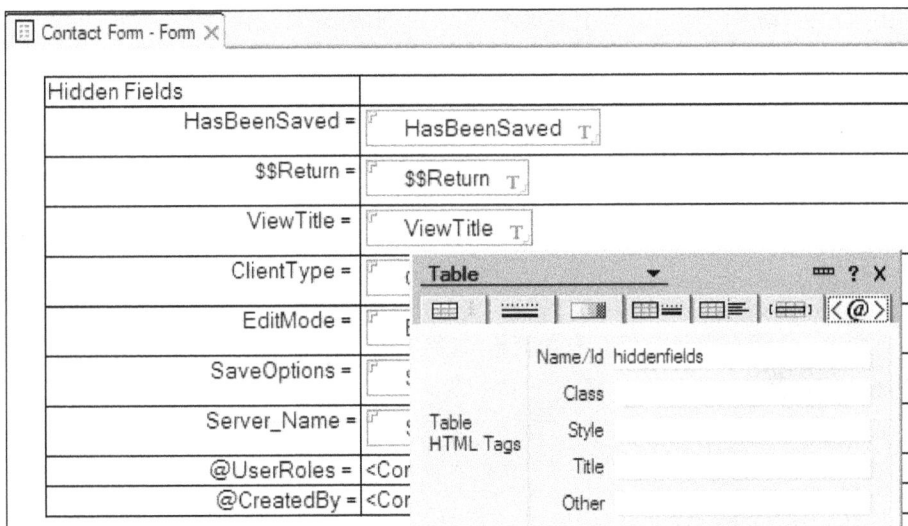

Add CSS rules for the table and the table cells. The rule for the table simply hides the table when the form is first loaded. The rule for the cells adds some style—your preference.

```
table#hiddenfields {
  display: none;
  }
table#hiddenfields td {
  color: #FF0000;
  font-family: Verdana;
  font-size: 8pt;
  }
```

Add a button to the form with this JavaScript coded in the button's `onClick` event:

```
if (document.getElementById("hiddenfields").style.display != "block")
    document.getElementById("hiddenfields").style.display = "block";
else document.getElementById("hiddenfields").style.display = "none";
```

Also, you should probably code a hide-when formula on the button to hide it, if the user is not assigned a special role.

```
@IsNotMember("[Developer]";@UserRoles)
```

Now when the form displays, the hidden fields do not display initially. But when the button is clicked, the fields display. Clicking the button again hides the fields.

Hidden Fields	
HasBeenSaved =	Y
$$Return =	[/ellisits/websandbox10.nsf/All%20Contacts?OpenView]
ViewTitle =	All%20Contacts
ClientType =	Microsoft
EditMode =	Read
SaveOptions =	1
Server_Name =	192.168.1.210
@UserRoles =	$$WebClient, [Developer], [Admin], [Editor]
@CreatedBy =	Admin/EllisITS Anonymous Admin/EllisITS Anonymous Admin/EllisITS

Debug

Expire the cache

If stale data reappears in fields when a recently saved document is reopened in Read mode, the problem may be cached data. One relatively effective strategy for handling this problem involves the use of one or more `<meta>` tags coded into the form's HTML Head Content area. Here is what the @formula might look like:

```
@NewLine+
"<META HTTP-EQUIV='expires' CONTENT='0'>"+
@NewLine+
```

Debug CSS

As noted in *Chapter 5, Cascading Style Sheets*, CSS rules can be added to a form in many ways. Here, assume that you have co-located all your CSS rules onto one or more page elements within the application.

A CSS problem is likely to result from one of these causes:

- The form or page does not link to the CSS rules page properly
- The content type of the CSS rules page is incorrect
- A CSS rule is not attached to a design element properly
- A CSS rule conflicts with HTML formatting
- One CSS rule is superseded by another CSS rule
- A CSS rule is incorrect

If none of your CSS rules is working, check the syntax of the link to the CSS page. For example, check the @formula in a form's HTML Head Content area.

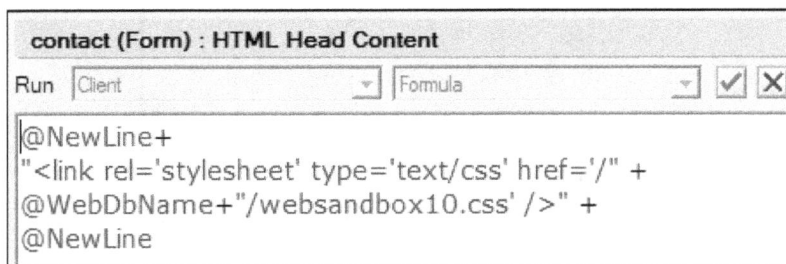

contact (Form) : HTML Head Content			
Run	Client ▾	Formula ▾	✓ ✕

```
@NewLine+
"<link rel='stylesheet' type='text/css' href='/" +
@WebDbName+"/websandbox10.css' />" +
@NewLine
```

The purpose of the formula is to construct a valid HTML `<link>` tag with correct attributes. The punctuation can be tricky. View the page source in your browser for clues to any errors.

If the link to the CSS rules page is correct, check the content type of the page itself on the **Page Info** tab of **Page Properties**.

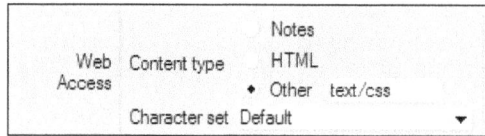

If some CSS rules are working, but a specific CSS rule is not, check to see that the CSS rule is properly attached to its design element. In this example, a button is not styled correctly according to the rules we defined for the button class. We view the source, but there is no class= attribute as expected.

```
<input type="button" value="Approve" id="Approve" style="button"
onclick="return
_doClick('85257811000A3799.ebbede74e813965e852577f80009ab44/$Body/0.
D2E',
this, null)">
```

The **Button Extra HTML** tab in **Button Properties** reveals that we did not enter the class name properly. In this example, the button class is incorrectly entered as a **Style** attribute rather than a **Class** attribute.

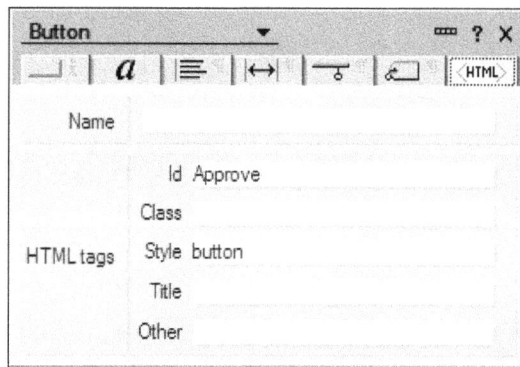

A problem like this could result also from a simple misspelling.

If you apply style and format with Designer, then those attributes may be translated into HTML formatting tags and transmitted to the browser where the HTML tags can override the CSS rules. In this example, the text Welcome Everybody! was formatted in Designer as dark blue and bold. The HTML tags are marked as Pass-thru HTML.

Note the extra HTML tags in the page source as seen in the browser.

```
<span class="welcome"><b><font color="#000080">Welcome
Everybody!</font></b></span>
```

Removing the Designer-applied style from the text (reverting to the defaults) results in cleaner HTML and proper styling with CSS.

```
<span class="welcome">Welcome Everybody!</span>
```

As noted in *Chapter 5, Cascading Style Sheets,* multiple CSS rules can be applied to the same design element. Inline rules supersede internal rules coded at the top of a page; internal rules in turn supersede external rules in linked external files. In this example, the inline rule supersedes the same value as defined in the class. Avoid this kind of issue by co-locating ALL your CSS rules on the same page.

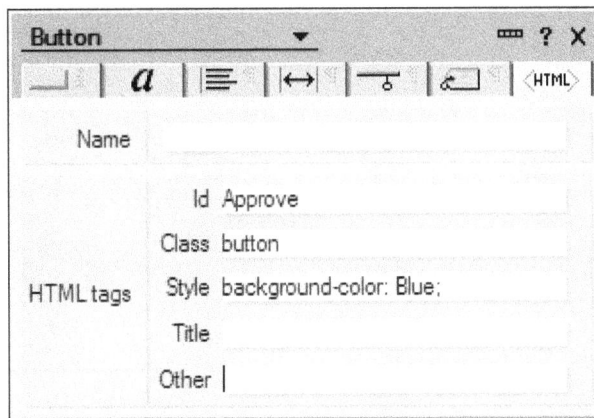

Incorrect CSS gives incorrect style. There are no error messages or any other indication of failure. CSS simply works or it doesn't. If you eliminate all the possibilities discussed in this topic, then study your CSS rules. Look for spelling and punctuation errors. Make sure you have used acceptable attributes. If you do not have a CSS style guide handy, access one of numerous resources on the Web.

Use browser-based debugging tools

As your web applications become more complex, you should consider learning to use web-oriented debugging tools that can give you insights into CSS, JavaScript, the DOM, and so on. **Firebug** is a popular Firefox add-on, available at the following location:

```
http://getfirebug.com/
```

If your organization mandates the use of Internet Explorer, you may still find value in working with tools like Firebug, or you may find some alternatives (for example, Firebug Lite) which work directly with Internet Explorer.

Keep in mind that browsers interpret some CSS and JavaScript in subtly different ways, so if you debug in Firefox, those results may not translate exactly to IE.

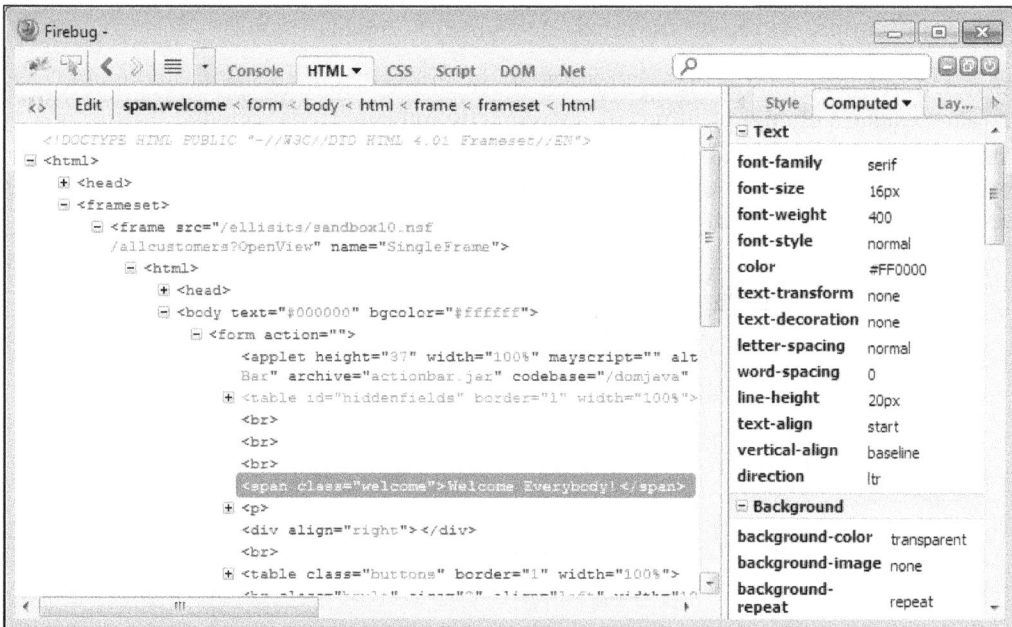

Troubleshoot agents

Debugging agents used in web-enabled applications is not dissimilar to debugging agents for Notes applications. Some debugging strategies, such as inserting MsgBox functions, work differently—messages are written to the Domino Log rather than to the Client. And some options, like @Prompt, do not work at all since they are not implemented on the Web.

In the case of simple messages, you can improve the immediacy of feedback when a LotusScript agent runs by replacing a MsgBox statement with a few LotusScript Print statements that send JavaScript to the browser.

```
Print "<script type='text/javascript'>"
Print "alert('ApproveRequest Agent Started')"
Print "history.go(-1) ;"
Print "</script>"
```

When the agent runs, an alert is displayed:

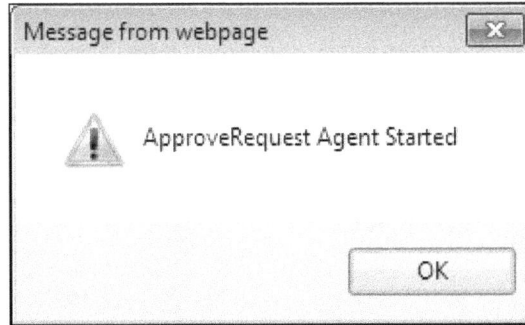

If multiple alerts are included in the script, include the `history.go(-1)` statement in only that last alert or else all alerts will not display.

Incorporate dynamic debugging messages

Messages intended to assist with debugging agents should not continue to be issued after the application design is migrated to production. At the same time, it would be useful to be able to turn on those messages in production to investigate a reported anomaly. Here is a technique which can be used to accomplish these contradictory objectives.

First, add a field or two to a configuration or application profile document, which is indexed in a view. In this example, the `Debugging` field is defined with the options of `Yes` or `No` and is hidden if the user is not assigned the [Developer] role in the application's ACL.

In an agent, retrieve the value of the `Debugging` field with code similar to the following:

```
Dim session As New NotesSession
Dim db As NotesDatabase
Dim configDoc As NotesDocument
```

```
Dim configView As NotesView
Dim debugFlag As Variant

' Get the Debugging value from the Configuration document.

Set db = session.CurrentDatabase
Set configView = db.GetView("SysConfig")
Set configDoc = configView.GetFirstDocument
If configDoc.Debugging(0) = "Yes" Then
  debugFlag = True
Else
  debugFlag = False
End If
```

Now, add one or more debugging messages to an agent with logic dependent upon the value of the Debugging field in the configuration document.

```
If debugFlag Then
  Msgbox("ApproveRequest **** S T A R T ****")
End If
```

Open the configuration document in Notes and toggle on the debugging flag. When the agent runs, messages are written to the Domino Log. Toggle the flag off, and messages are not written to the Log. This simple scheme can be elaborated to provide different levels of debugging messages, if necessary.

Create troubleshooting tools—display scheduled agent information

It can be useful to create standalone troubleshooting tools that can be popped into applications as appropriate. Restrict access to these tools to the application administrators or developers with whatever security measures are appropriate.

In this example, an agent gathers information about scheduled agents and then writes that information to a temporary form. This agent might be useful if the developer cannot easily determine which scheduled agents are enabled in production.

The form contains only a few fields. Here is what it looks like in Designer:

Agent Information - Form ✕

SaveOptions ᴛ

Agent Information - DisplayDate 🗓 Comment ᴛ

Scheduled Agents

Name	Status	Comment/Last Run/Server/Target
SchedAgentNames ᴛ	SchedAgentStatuses ᴛ	SchedAgentComments ᴛ

Here is the agent, minus error handling, debugging messages, and some other niceties.

```
Sub Initialize
    Dim session As New NotesSession
    Dim workspace As New NotesUIWorkspace
    Dim db As NotesDatabase
    Dim uidoc As NotesUIDocument
    Dim agentCount As Integer, i As Integer, k As Integer
    Dim  msgNames As String, msgStatuses As String
    Dim msgComments As String
    Dim newLine As String, newLine3 As String
    Dim server As String, target As String

    Set db = session.CurrentDatabase
    agentCount = Ubound(db.Agents)
    Redim agentsArray(agentCount) As NotesAgent

    i = 0
    Forall a In db.Agents
      Set agentsArray(i) = a
      i = i + 1
    End Forall

    msgNames = ""
    msgStatuses = ""
    msgComments = ""
    newLine = Chr(10)
    newLine3 = Chr(10) + Chr(10) + Chr(10)

    i = -1
```

```
    For k = 0 To agentCount
      Set agent = agentsArray(k)
      If  agent.Trigger = 1 Then ' Scheduled agent
        i = i + 1
        If i  > 0 Then
          msgNames = msgNames + newline
          msgStatuses = msgStatuses + newline
          msgComments = msgComments + newLine
        End If
        msgNames = msgNames + agent.Name + newLine3
        If agent.IsEnabled Then
          msgStatuses = msgStatuses + "Enabled" + newLine3
        Else
          msgStatuses = msgStatuses + "Disabled" + newLine3
        End If
        If agent.ServerName = "*" Then
          server = "-Any Server-"
        Else
          server = agent.ServerName
        End If
        Select Case agent.Target
        Case 0 : target = "None"
        Case 1 : target = "All documents in database"
        Case 2 : target = "Unknown"
        Case 3 : target = "All new & modified documents"
        Case 4 : target = "All selected documents"
        Case 5 : target = "All documents in view"
        Case 6 : target = "All unread documents in view"
        Case 7 : target = "Unknown"
        Case 8 : target =  "None"
        End Select
        msgComments = msgComments + _
        "C: " + Left$(agent.Comment,40) + _
        newLine + "L: " + Cstr(agent.LastRun) + _
        newLine + "S: " + server + _
        newLine + "T: " + target
      End If
    Next

    Set uidoc = workspace.ComposeDocument("","","Agent Information")
    Call uidoc.GotoField("SchedAgentNames" )
    Call uidoc.InsertText(msgNames)
    Call uidoc.GotoField("SchedAgentStatuses")
    Call uidoc.InsertText(msgStatuses)
```

```
Call uidoc.GotoField("SchedAgentComments" )
Call uidoc.InsertText(msgComments)
Call uidoc.GotoField("Comment")

End Sub
```

The agent is invoked from the Actions menu within Notes. Here's how it might display with two scheduled agents.

Agent Information – 02/12/2011 01:10 PM |

Scheduled Agents

Name	Status	Comment/Last Run/Server/Target
Distribute Newsletters	Enabled	C: Should run several times a day. L: 2/12/2011 12:28:03 PM S: CN=EITS01/OU=SRV/O=EllisITS T: All documents in database
Overdue Notices	Disabled	C: Disabled until further notice. L: 2/12/2011 12:28:15 PM S: CN=EITS01/OU=SRV/O=EllisITS T: None

Troubleshoot problems with data

Flaws in designs often result in incorrect data in documents. Even if the data is correct, understanding that data can provide useful insights into how an application functions and what it produces. Looking at the data as displayed in forms on the Web does not always tell the whole story, especially if documents contain hidden fields. Here are two suggestions for getting to know the data.

View field values in Document Properties

One of the reasons to use `Readers` and `Authors` fields, of course, is to truly prevent unauthorized users from viewing the data. Otherwise, they can find the values in documents with the **Fields** tab of **Document Properties**.

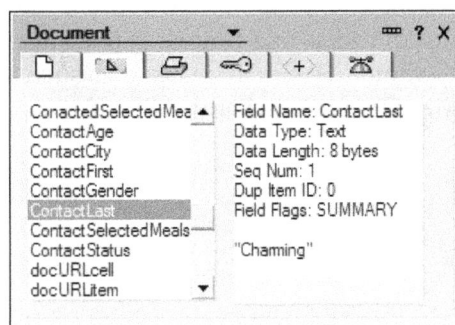

```
Document                          ▼         ▭ ? X
 ┌───┬───┬───┬───┬───┬───┐
 │ D │ ◰ │ 🖨 │ ☞ │ + │ ✂ │
 └───┴───┴───┴───┴───┴───┘
 ConactedSelectedMea ▲    Field Name: ContactLast
 ContactAge               Data Type: Text
 ContactCity              Data Length: 8 bytes
 ContactFirst             Seq Num: 1
 ContactGender            Dup Item ID: 0
 ContactLast              Field Flags: SUMMARY
 ContactSelectedMeals
 ContactStatus            "Charming"
 docURLcell
 docURLitem          ▼
```

Seeing the content of a field is very useful. Checking the field name and type also can be helpful.

Create diagnostic views

While you are enhancing an application, anticipate that someday you will want to look at any or all documents in the database in order to resolve a problem. Views designed for normal application functionality may just not be suitable for troubleshooting or discovering anomalies.

Create some simple diagnostic views that are unrelated to other features. Do not use them for lookups or other purposes. Someday you may want to change what displays in these views, and you do not want to concern yourself with impacting other features of the design by doing so.

One view should list all documents by creation date and time. Another view should show all documents categorized by form name. Other useful views may occur to you. Don't go overboard here; remember that re-indexing views does take server resources. But do build yourself these troubleshooting aids. Give them names which clearly and succinctly indicate the purpose for which they exist.

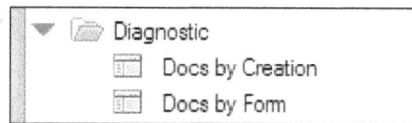

See *Chapter 7, Views*, for additional suggestions.

Write document repair agents

Not infrequently fields in documents must be changed, perhaps due to a flaw in the design, which introduced incorrect values, or due to a change in customer requirements. Or perhaps new fields need to be added to old documents as part of an upgrade.

Repair agents are often introduced as one-time or private agents. If they truly are one-time agents, then they should be clearly marked as such and hidden or deleted from the design after they are no longer useful.

If an agent is written to repair data, then it is possible that that agent will be needed again. Consider invoking such an agent from an action button included in a special administrator's document repair view. Hide the view and/or the button from less privileged users so as not to tempt them to "find out what this does." Over time, add additional repair utilities into the same view. And document these little gems.

Document problems and solutions

Troubleshooting can be very time consuming, and this time is lost time. Whenever you resolve a nasty bug, make notes about it—what the symptoms were, how you found the flaw, how you solved the problem.

If appropriate, update the Help Desk ticket promptly. Notify any interested parties that the issue is resolved. Consider whether this problem is likely to occur in other applications, and if so, alert fellow developers. Add notes to the application's test plan for future reference.

Keep a personal problem solving journal

Where you keep your notes may not be as important as is the act of writing them— which helps to solidify your understanding of the problem and the solution. If you are browsing the Web and come across some really good ideas, add those ideas to your collection.

Personally, I favor capturing such notes in a simple Domino database, which is searchable and transportable. A Domino Document Library is a good repository for notes, documents, and hyperlinks.

Report back to the user

Most users appreciate a response from you about problems they report. Make a telephone call, send e-mail, or better yet, stop over and make a short report. Your explanation should provide some detail in language suited to your audience. Don't try to impress with techno-babble; be succinct and gracious. Thank them for their help; encourage them to contact you if they have any questions. Reaching out in this manner is good customer service. It will be noticed and it will enhance your standing in your organization.

Summary

While it may be tempting to rush an upgrade into production, it is by far the better course of action to set aside adequate time to test features and functionality before doing so. Engaging users in the testing cycle can be extremely important in discovering bugs and usability issues, and getting customer signoff is also very important.

Both during the testing phase and after the application migrates to production, developers are called upon to troubleshoot and debug a wide range of problems. Troubleshooting skills develop over time with practice and with increased knowledge of the technologies in use.

Suggestions and examples in this chapter provide both a foundation for establishing a testing discipline and an introduction to debugging strategies appropriate to all Domino applications.

Index

diagnostic views, creating 196, 197
view templates, using 199

H

hacks 137
help
  another application, opening in separate
      window 122
  customized help pages, adding 122
  documents, using 121
  guidance text, adding 120
  link, adding to About 121
  meaningful labels, adding 120
  options 120
  titles, adding to design elements 121
Help Menu page 114
hidden Computed fields
  @DbColumn formulas, improving 89
  @DbLookup formulas, improving 89
  adding, for key document attributes access
      88
  CGI variables, accessing 88
  using 88
Hotspots
  Action Hotspot 108
  Button Hotspot 108
  Link Hotspot 108
HTML
  converting, to Notes Format 91
  special fields, using 90, 91
  using, for adding form value 89, 90
  using, for adding page value 89, 90
human factor issues
  accessibility, designing for 49
  clean design, creating 47
  display characteristics, designing for 48
  flexible designs, creating 47
  image resources, using 51
  image use, optimizing 50
  titles, adding to framesets 50

I

Infobox 52
Initbeforeunload() function 181
Insert Resource dialog 130
issues log 292

J

JavaScript
  about 155
  Ajax calls, using 183-191
  CGI variables, accessing 173
  fields, validating 173-175
  locating, in applications 161
  running, on load 171, 172
  user warning, giving 178-183
  using, in web applications 155, 156
JavaScript, locating in applications
  adding, in JS header 163
  adding, to web events 163, 164
  co-locating 169
  consolidating 169
  functions, placing in libraries 161, 163
  locations 161
  page element, using 165-168
JavaScript, using in web applications
  about 155
  behavior consistency, maintaining 157, 158
  browser detection, using 160
  browser object detection, using 158
  comments, posting 156
  JavaScript, disabling 157
Java View applet 79

K

key concepts, security
  defense in depth 258
  layered security 258
key properties
  content type (MIME) property 62

L

layered security 258
Link Hotspot 108
liquid designs 48
LogAction() method 241
Lorem Ipsum
  using 147

M

media attribute 152

Thank you for buying
IBM Lotus Domino: Classic Web Application
Development Techniques

About Packt Publishing

Packt, pronounced 'packed', published its first book "Mastering phpMyAdmin for Effective MySQL Management" in April 2004 and subsequently continued to specialize in publishing highly focused books on specific technologies and solutions.

Our books and publications share the experiences of your fellow IT professionals in adapting and customizing today's systems, applications, and frameworks. Our solution based books give you the knowledge and power to customize the software and technologies you're using to get the job done. Packt books are more specific and less general than the IT books you have seen in the past. Our unique business model allows us to bring you more focused information, giving you more of what you need to know, and less of what you don't.

Packt is a modern, yet unique publishing company, which focuses on producing quality, cutting-edge books for communities of developers, administrators, and newbies alike. For more information, please visit our website: www.packtpub.com.

About Packt Enterprise

In 2010, Packt launched two new brands, Packt Enterprise and Packt Open Source, in order to continue its focus on specialization. This book is part of the Packt Enterprise brand, home to books published on enterprise software – software created by major vendors, including (but not limited to) IBM, Microsoft and Oracle, often for use in other corporations. Its titles will offer information relevant to a range of users of this software, including administrators, developers, architects, and end users.

Writing for Packt

We welcome all inquiries from people who are interested in authoring. Book proposals should be sent to author@packtpub.com. If your book idea is still at an early stage and you would like to discuss it first before writing a formal book proposal, contact us; one of our commissioning editors will get in touch with you.

We're not just looking for published authors; if you have strong technical skills but no writing experience, our experienced editors can help you develop a writing career, or simply get some additional reward for your expertise.

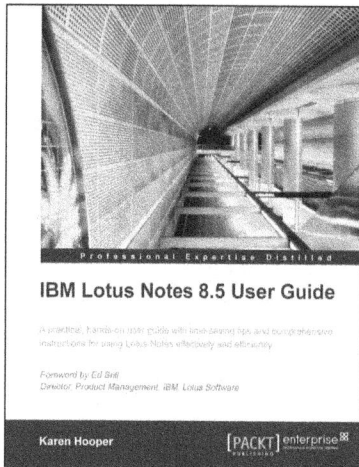

IBM Lotus Notes 8.5 User Guide

ISBN: 978-1-849680-20-2   Paperback: 296 pages

A practical hands-on user guide with time saving tips and comprehensive instructions for using Lotus Notes effectively and efficiently

1. Understand and master the features of Lotus Notes and put them to work in your business quickly

2. Contains comprehensive coverage of new Lotus Notes 8.5 features

3. Includes easy-to-follow real-world examples with plenty of screenshots to clearly demonstrate how to get the most out of Lotus Notes

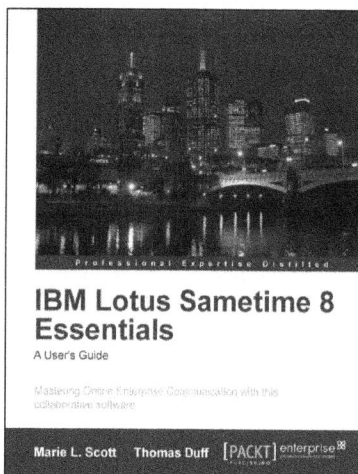

IBM Lotus Sametime 8 Essentials: A User's Guide

ISBN: 978-1-849680-60-8   Paperback: 284 pages

Mastering Online Enterprise Communication with this collaborative software

1. Collaborate securely with your colleagues and teammates both inside and outside your organization by using Sametime features such as instant messaging and online meetings

2. Make your instant messaging communication more interesting with the inclusion of graphics, images, and emoticons to convey more information in fewer words

Please check **www.PacktPub.com** for information on our titles

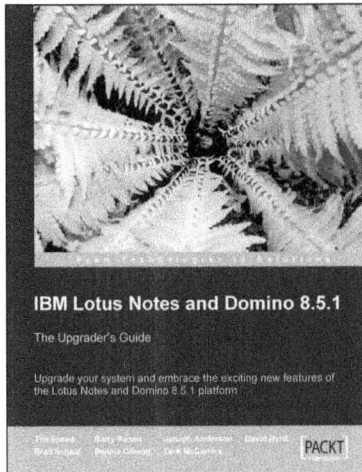

IBM Lotus Notes and Domino 8.5.1

ISBN: 978-1-847199-28-7   Paperback: 336 pages

Upgrade your system and embrace the exciting new features of the Lotus Notes and Domino 8.5.1 platform

1. Upgrade to the latest version of Lotus Notes and Domino

2. Understand the new features and put them to work in your business

3. Thoroughly covers Domino Attachment Object Service (DAOS), Domino Configuration Tuner (DCT), and iNotes

4. Explore other useful Lotus products, such as Lotus Sametime, Lotus Quickr, Lotus Connections, and IBM WebSphere Portal

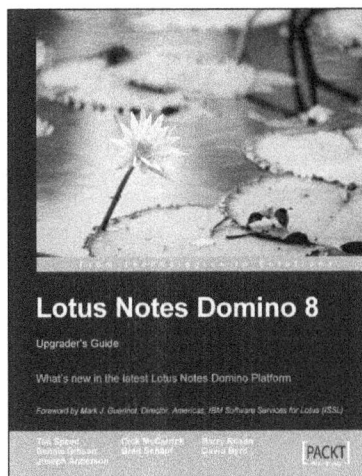

Lotus Notes Domino 8: Upgrader's Guide

ISBN: 978-1-847192-74-5   Paperback: 276 pages

What's new in the latest Lotus Notes Domino Platform

1. Upgrade to the latest version of Lotus Notes and Domino.

2. Understand the new features and put them to work in your business

3. Appreciate the implications of changes and new features

Please check **www.PacktPub.com** for information on our titles

www.ingramcontent.com/pod-product-compliance
Lightning Source LLC
Chambersburg PA
CBHW080915220326
41598CB00034B/5581